SETTING COURSE

A CONGRESSIONAL MANAGEMENT GUIDE

EDITION FOR THE **112th** CONGRESS

CONGRESSIONAL MANAGEMENT FOUNDATION

— *has been made possible by grants from* —

   **GENERAL DYNAMICS**

Deborah Szekely

©Copyright 1992, 1994, 1996, 2000, 2002, 2004, 2006, 2008, 2010 Congressional Management Foundation
©Copyright 1984, 1986, 1988 The American University

All Rights Reserved.
No part of this book may be reproduced in any manner, except for brief quotations used in critical articles or reviews, without written permission from the Congressional Management Foundation.

Congressional Management Foundation
513 Capitol Court NE, Suite 300
Washington, DC 20002
202-546-0100
www.cmfweb.org

Printed in the United States of America

ISBN: 978-1-930473-14-0

Table of Contents

TABLE OF FIGURES v

PREFACE vii

ACKNOWLEDGMENTS ix

INTRODUCTION xiii

PART I: TRANSITIONING TO CONGRESS AND SETTING UP YOUR OFFICE

CHAPTER ONE:
Navigating The First 60 Days: November and December 3
    Importance of Setting Priorities 4
    The Critical Transition Tasks 6
    Guiding Principles for the Transition 10
    Orientation and Organizational Meetings 13
    Conclusion 14
    Chapter Summary 16

CHAPTER TWO:
Selecting Committee Assignments 17
    Importance of Committee Assignments 18
    How the Committee Assignment Process Works 18
    Advice for Choosing and Pursuing Committee Assignments 23
    Conclusion 25
    Chapter Summary 26

CHAPTER THREE:
Creating a First-Year Budget 27
    Congressional Budget Primers 28
    The Member's Role in Budgeting 32
    Developing a First-Year Budget 33
    Veteran Office Advice on Developing a First-Year Budget 42
    Conclusion 44
    Chapter Summary 45

CHAPTER FOUR:
**Creating a Management Structure and a System for
Communicating with the Member** 47
    Selecting a Management Structure 48
    Designing a System for Member–Staff Communications 55

Communication Objectives 57
Conducting Effective Meetings 59
Conclusion 60
Chapter Summary 61

CHAPTER FIVE:
Hiring Your Core Staff 63
Importance of Hiring Only a Core Staff in November and December 64
Which Functions To Hire as Part of Your Core Staff 66
Fitting Core Staff to Your Mission and Goals 70
Hiring the Rest of Your Staff 71
Recruiting the Best Candidates 72
A Process for Hiring the Right Staff Candidates 73
Conclusion 79
Chapter Summary 80

CHAPTER SIX:
Selecting and Utilizing Technology 81
The Basic Congressional System 82
Glossary of Technology-Related Offices and Staff 83
Determining When to Upgrade 85
Critical Questions 87
Key Considerations 88
Six Steps to Making Wise Technology Purchases 90
CMF Technology Resources 91
Keeping Your System Running Smoothly 94
Conclusion 97
Chapter Summary 99

CHAPTER SEVEN:
Establishing District and State Offices 101
Importance of Decisions Concerning District/State Offices 102
Selecting the Number of District/State Offices 103
Office Location and Space Considerations 106
The Option of Senators Sharing Offices 110
Which Office To Open First 110
Furniture and Office Equipment 111
Conclusion 113
Chapter Summary 114

PART II: DEFINING YOUR ROLE IN CONGRESS AND YOUR OFFICE

CHAPTER EIGHT:
Understanding the Culture of Congress: An Insider's Guide 117
Constants in Congress 118

Table of Contents

    Three Congressional Trends: Close Party Ratios, Influx of New
        Members and Increased Partisanship 120
    Conclusion 124
    Chapter Summary 125

CHAPTER NINE:
Defining Your Role In Congress 127
    The Importance of Defining Your Role 128
    A Discussion of the Five Roles 129
    Balancing Major and Minor Roles 135
    Selecting Your Role 136
    Conclusion 139
    Chapter Summary 140

CHAPTER TEN:
The Member's Role as Leader of the Office 141
    The Member as Leader 142
    Organizational Culture 143
    Assessing and Understanding Your Leadership Style 149
    How to Address the Two Common Leadership Problems 152
    Conclusion 155
    Chapter Summary 156

PART III: MANAGING YOUR CONGRESSIONAL OFFICE

CHAPTER ELEVEN:
Strategic Planning In Your Office 159
    The Value of Planning 160
    The Planning Process 162
    Conducting an Effective Planning Session 164
    Conclusion 177
    Chapter Summary 178

CHAPTER TWELVE:
Budgeting and Financial Management 179
    The Strategic Importance of Budgeting 180
    Budgeting Toward Your Goals, Year After Year 183
    Establishing Financial Procedures for Your Office 187
    Tips for House and Senate Offices 191
    Conclusion 194
    Chapter Summary 195

CHAPTER THIRTEEN:
A Process for Managing Staff 197
    Rationale for a Performance Management System 198

    Implementing a Performance Management System 199
    How to Run Successful Staff Performance Meetings 206
    Handling Staff with Different Needs 208
    Evaluating Your System 212
    Conclusion 213
    Chapter Summary *214*

CHAPTER FOURTEEN:
Managing Constituent Communications 215
    The Growth of Constituent Communications 216
    Assessing the Priority of Mail in Your Office 218
    Establishing Mail Policies 220
    CMF Model Mail System 221
    Improving the Processing of E-Mail 232
    Proactive Outreach Mail 235
    Conclusion 237
    Chapter Summary *238*

CHAPTER FIFTEEN:
Strategic Scheduling 239
    Strategic Scheduling Defined 240
    Six Steps to Developing and Implementing a Strategic Schedule 241
    District/State Trips 246
    The Weeks in Washington 250
    Addressing Common Problems 255
    Scheduling Issues Faced by Members 260
    Conclusion 263
    Chapter Summary *266*

CHAPTER SIXTEEN:
Managing Ethics 267
    The Changed Ethics Environment 268
    Coping with the Changed Environment 270
    Guidelines for Managing Ethics in Congressional Offices 271
    The Top Four Areas of Ethical Risk 273
    A Nine-Step Process for Conducting Political/Ethical Analyses 275
    Conclusion 278
    Chapter Summary *279*

INDEX 283

AUTHORS 297

ABOUT CMF 301

Table of Figures

CHAPTER ONE: Navigating The First 60 Days: November and December
Figure 1-1: Urgency and Importance Matrix 5
Figure 1-2: Matrixing Typical Office Activities 6

CHAPTER TWO: Selecting Committee Assignments
Figure 2-1: House Committee Categories 21
Figure 2-2: Senate Committee Categories 22

CHAPTER THREE: Creating a First-Year Budget
Figure 3-1: Average Spending by Freshman House Offices in 2009..............34
Figure 3-2: Average Salaries of Congressional Staff 36
Figure 3-3: House Budget Worksheet 39
Figure 3-4: Senate Budget Worksheet 40

CHAPTER FOUR: Creating a Management Structure and a System for Communicating with the Member
Figure 4-1: Model 1: Centralized Structure 50
Figure 4-2: Model 2: Washington–District/State Parity Structure.................51
Figure 4-3: Model 3: Functional Structure 52
Figure 4-4: Pros and Cons of Management Structures 54

CHAPTER FIVE: Hiring Your Core Staff
Figure 5-1: Sample House Core Staff 68
Figure 5-2: Sample Senate Core Staff 69

CHAPTER SEVEN: Establishing District and State Offices
Figure 7-1: District/State Offices Maintained by Members 104

CHAPTER NINE: Defining Your Role in Congress
Figure 9-1: Congressional Role Selection Chart 138

CHAPTER ELEVEN: Strategic Planning in Your Office
Figure 11-1: Impact Achievability Grid..168
Figure 11-2: Scorecard for Goal Evaluation 169
Figure 11-3: Sample Goal-Oriented Action Plan..171

CHAPTER THIRTEEN: A Process for Managing Staff
Figure 13-1: Five Steps of Performance Management 199
Figure 13-2: Sample Staff Self-Evaluation Form 204

CHAPTER FOURTEEN: Managing Constituent Communications
Figure 14-1: CMF Mail System Flow Chart...227
Figure 14-2: Responding to E-mail With E-mail...234

CHAPTER FIFTEEN: Strategic Scheduling
 Figure 15-1: Model Speech/Event Evaluation Form 251
 Figure 15-2: Sample Event Scheduling Form..258
 Figure 15-3: How Often Members Go Home 262
 Figure 15-4: Sample Event Preparation Request Form 265

Preface

While running for Congress in 1982, Deborah Szekely learned that no manual existed to help freshmen set up their offices. Although she lost the election, in commissioning this book, she discovered a valuable way to serve the Congress. Without her enthusiasm and foresight, *Setting Course* simply would not exist. In the first edition in 1984, we predicted that Members of Congress would be in Deborah's debt for years to come. Twenty-six years later, that prediction has become fact. Many people have good ideas, but few have the ability to implement them. Fortunately, Deborah excels in transforming her ideas into projects, and her projects into successes. CMF remains indebted to Deborah for conceiving and funding the original edition of *Setting Course* and for her continued commitment to this book.

The 12th edition of *Setting Course* follows Deborah's vision of providing timely, proven guidance on the fundamentals of setting up and managing a congressional office. It offers ideas, models, and advice to guide Members of Congress — whether in their first, fourth, or tenth term. It combines the wisdom of previous editions with new insights and updated information for the 112th Congress.

CMF's mission is "good government through good management." Though it may seem idealistic to some, our experience has proven that greater effectiveness is both realistic and achievable. We believe that if Members of Congress implement the management and planning advice in this book, they can increase their own productivity and efficiency, thereby improving the effectiveness of Congress as an institution.

We are honored that **Deborah Szekely** and the following organizations support this mission and enable us to continue providing the critical guidance contained in *Setting Course* through their generous financial contributions. Without their support, this edition would not have been possible. We sincerely thank:

Society for Human Resource Management

American Institute of Certified Public Accountants

General Dynamics

As the world's largest professional association devoted to human resource management, the **Society for Human Resource Management (SHRM)** is dedicated to promoting effective management and leadership all over the globe. We are proud to partner with them to offer management advice and techniques to individual House and Senate offices through *Setting Course* and a variety of professional development programs. SHRM also was the exclusive sponsor for *Keeping It Local: A Guide for Managing Congressional District and State Offices.*

The **American Institute of Certified Public Accountants' (AICPA)** mission is to supply its members with the resources, information, and leadership they need to provide professional services that benefit the public, as well as their clients. Consequently, AICPA appreciates and values a book that offers critical information and management guidance to Members of Congress and their staff so they may better serve the citizens of our nation.

General Dynamics' commitment to excellence and continual improvement mirrors CMF's own dedication to our Capitol Hill audiences. The company promotes a culture of ethical behavior in all its dealings with shareholders, employees, customers, partners and the communities in which it operates all around the world. Their high standards for management and conduct make General Dynamics a natural partner for sponsoring this publication.

CMF is fortunate to produce *Setting Course* with such forward thinking organizations and supporters of the Congress who understand the powerful link between effective management and professional success — whether the goal is building a thriving business and meeting customer needs or formulating forward-looking public policy to address constituent concerns more effectively.

Thank you.

Bradford Fitch
President & CEO
Congressional Management Foundation

Acknowledgments

The Congressional Management Foundation (CMF) is indebted to a great many people for their help in producing *Setting Course*. We warmly thank all who contributed to its success.

Current Congressional Staff

Lynden Armstrong, Chief Clerk, Senate Committee on Rules and Administration
Brian Bean, Placement Office Administrator, Senate Sergeant at Arms
Gail Bergstad, State Representative, Sens. Kent Conrad and Byron Dorgan
Winfield Boerckel, Chief of Staff/Policy Director, Rep. Gwen Moore
Jeff Brinkley, Customer Support Analyst, Office Support Services, Senate Sergeant at Arms
Dave Cape, Director, Office Support Services, Senate Sergeant at Arms
Tamara Chrisler, Executive Director, Office of Compliance
Bernadette Connell, Customer Support Analyst, Office Support Services, Senate Sergeant at Arms
Nancy Davis, Supervisor/Project Coordinator, Office Support Services, Senate Sergeant at Arms
Chris Doby, Financial Clerk, Senate Disbursing Office
Michelle Donches, Budget Manager, Rep. Bart Gordon
Teresa Ervin, Deputy Chief of Staff, Sen. Saxby Chambliss
Margaret Fibel, Deputy for IT and Strategic Planning, Senate Disbursing Office
Russell Gore, Senior Associate Counsel, Office of House Employment Counsel
George Hadijski, Director, Office of Member Services, Committee on House Administration, Republican Staff
Tina Hanonu, Director of Technology Support, Office of the Chief Administrative Officer
Christopher Hoven, Administrative Assistant, Rep. Adam Schiff
Cathy Hurwit, Chief of Staff, Rep. Jan Schakowsky
Mary Suit Jones, Republican Staff Director, Senate Committee on Rules and Administration
Gloria Lett, Counsel, Office of House Employment Counsel
Chris McCannell, Chief of Staff, Rep. Michael McMahon
Ellen McCarthy, Professional Staff Member, Committee on House Administration, Majority Staff
Michael Modica, Customer Support Manager, Office of the Chief Administrative Officer

Susan Olson, Counsel, House Committee on Standards of Official Conduct
Robert Paxton, Chief of Staff, Secretary of the Senate
Mark Perkins, Professional Staff Member, Rep. Alcee Hastings
David Pike, Deputy Chief of Staff, Sen. Jeff Bingaman
Alan Salazar, Senior Political and Policy Advisor, Sen. Mark Udall
Sgt. Kimberly Schneider, Public Information Officer, Office of the Chief, U.S. Capitol Police
Judy Schneider, Specialist on the Congress, Congressional Research Service
Joe Shoemaker, Communications Director, Senate Majority Whip Dick Durbin
Gene Smith, District Director/Press Secretary, Rep. Howard Berman
Jeanne Tessieri, State Office Liaison, Office Support Services, Senate Sergeant at Arms
Connie Veillette, Professional Staff Member, Senate Committee on Foreign Relations, Republican Staff
Kathi Wise, Scheduler/Executive Assistant, Sen. John Barrasso
Todd Womack, Chief of Staff, Sen. Bob Corker

Former Congressional Staff

Jackie Aamot, Director, Financial Counseling, House Finance Office
Melissa Bennett, Scheduler, Rep. Rob Portman
Bob Bean, Minority Staff Director, Committee on House Administration
Steven Bosacker, Chief of Staff, Rep. Tim Penny
Wanda Chaney, House Information Resources, Office of the Chief Administrative Officer
Chris Chwastyk, Chief of Staff, Rep. Chet Edwards
Chick Ciccolella, Director of Information and Technology, Senate Committee on Rules and Administration
Debi Deimling, Executive Assistant, Rep. Mike Oxley
Paula Effertz, Office Manager, Sen. Jay Rockefeller
John Enright, Chief of Staff, Rep. Don Sherwood
Lani Gerst, Senior Professional Staff Member, Senate Committee on Rules and Administration, Majority Staff
Todd Gillenwater, Legislative Director, Rep. David Dreier
Bill Grady, District Director, Rep. Linda Sanchez
Joel Hinzman, Professional Staff Member, Committee on House Administration, Majority Staff
Krister Holladay, Chief of Staff, Sen. Saxby Chambliss
John Lapp, Chief of Staff, Rep. Ken Lucas
Diane Liesman, Chief of Staff, Rep. Ray LaHood
Cathy Marder, Office Manager, Sen. John Ensign
Dan Muroff, Chief of Staff, Rep. Michael Capuano
Jenny Ogle, Casework Manager, Sens. Mike DeWine and George Voinovich

Mary Paxson, State Scheduler/Field Representative, Sen. Craig Thomas
Margo Rushing, Administrative Director, Sen. Conrad Burns
Reynold Schweikhardt, Deputy Staff Director, Committee on House Administration, Majority Staff
Mark Strand, Chief of Staff, Sen. James Talent
Steve Sutton, Chief of Staff, Rep. John Kline
Cole Thomas, Operations Director, Sens. Mike DeWine and George Voinovich
Stacy Trumbo, Administrative Director, Sen. Craig Thomas
Jason Van Eaton, Deputy Chief of Staff, Sen. Kit Bond
Rob von Gogh, Special Projects, Office of the Chief Administrative Officer
Mary Watts, House Information Resources, Office of the Chief Administrative Officer
Marie Wheat, Chief of Staff, Rep. Jim DeMint
Tim Wineman, Financial Clerk, Senate Disbursing Office
Rowdy Yeates, Chief of Staff, Rep. Jim Kolbe

Former CMF Staff and Others

Beverly Bell, former CMF Executive Director and House Chief of Staff
Ira Chaleff, President, Executive Coaching and Consulting Associates; CMF Management Consultant and former Executive Director
Christopher Deering, Professor of political science, The George Washington University
Betsy Wright Hawkings, Chief of Staff, Rep. Michael Turner and former Rep. Christopher Shays; and former CMF Deputy Director
Meredith Persily Lamel, CMF Management Consultant and former Director of Training and Consulting Services
Steve Loy, Hewlett-Packard
Michael Patruznick, former CMF Director of Research
Chet Rogers, Professor Emeritus of political science, Western Michigan University; and former House AA
Craig Schultz, former CMF Director of Research
Laura D. Scott, CMF Management Consultant and former Deputy Director
Gary Serota, President, Affinity Marketing Services Corporation; and former CMF Executive Director
Rick Shapiro, CMF Management Consultant and former Executive Director
Patty Sheetz, Chief of Staff, Rep. Jeff Fortenberry; and former CMF Management Consultant
David Twenhafel, former CMF Director of Research
Doug van Norden, formerly of EDS/Hewlett-Packard
Don Wolfensberger, Director, The Congress Project, Woodrow Wilson International Center for Scholars; and former Chief of Staff for the House Rules Committee

Revising a publication of this scope and magnitude is a significant undertaking and could not have been completed without the dedication and hard work of CMF staff. I especially thank Brad Fitch, President & CEO, and Tim Hysom, Director of Communications & Technology Services, for their expertise in updating chapters to reflect current best practices and the environment on Capitol Hill. Thanks also go to Collin Burden and interns Van Van, Hyunkoo Jo, and Theodosia Tenia for their research and production assistance. Thanks also to Rich Pottern Design for the continual improvements in the design and layout of the book.

We must also acknowledge our predecessors. The first three editions of *Setting Course* were the joint product of The American University's Center for Congressional and Presidential Studies (CCPS) and CMF. We are proud to follow in the footsteps of the outstanding staff who collaborated on these editions: Burdett A. Loomis, Paul Light, James A. Thurber, Gary Serota, and Ira Chaleff.

CMF has worked diligently on these last nine editions of *Setting Course* to keep the guidance accurate and relevant. Readers and users who have corrections or suggestions for the next edition should contact us. We care deeply about improving our products and welcome all feedback.

Nicole Folk Cooper
Director of Marketing and Publications
Congressional Management Foundation
Editor, Setting Course (12th Edition for the 112th Congress)

Introduction

In the classic 1972 film, *The Candidate,* Robert Redford portrays an idealistic young man running for the Senate against an entrenched incumbent. The final weeks of the campaign are a frantic whirl of events, and no one — not the candidate, nor the campaign team — has time for a single thought beyond election day. Redford wins, of course — this is the movies — but on the way to deliver his victory speech in the famous final scene, he pulls his campaign manager aside and asks in a daze, "What do we do now?"

Where *The Candidate* ends, *Setting Course* begins.

Successful careers in Congress don't just happen; they are the result of careful planning and management. We believe that good management and planning techniques can be applied to congressional offices. More specifically, well-managed offices are more likely to achieve their political and legislative objectives. We also believe that improving the performance of individual offices enhances the overall effectiveness of the Congress and strengthens the public trust.

The need to apply management principles to a congressional office is especially true for freshmen, given the extraordinary challenges they face. Members-elect have two months from election day until swearing-in day before they are expected to be up and running — an insufficient time to finish the massive array of tasks they must complete to becoming a fully functioning House or Senate office. To employ the nautical metaphor of this book, coping with this shortage of time leaves freshman Members with the daunting initial challenge of trying to sail their boats in the ocean at the same time that they are building them. It is a demanding and dangerous task that requires significant management skills and courage to succeed.

Effectively setting and implementing priorities is also a discipline veteran offices must continually practice if they are to avoid the common congressional hazard of working very hard but accomplishing very little. This book is intended to help freshman and veteran Members better serve their constituents and to better serve their country. It is based on decades of CMF research into the best practices used by House and Senate personal offices.

We've divided *Setting Course* into three distinct sections to better serve the needs of our different audiences. New Members and their key transition staff can use Part I to better understand the critical transition decisions they face in November and December and to receive guidance for making these decisions. Part II is designed to help freshman and veteran Members understand the culture of Congress, choose a path to success within the institution, and become effective leaders of their offices. Part III provides guidance to freshman and veteran Members and their staff, on managing many of the critical functions of a congressional office: planning, budgeting, managing staff, constituent communications, scheduling and ethics.

This book has changed markedly in content and structure since the first edition in 1984, but the core guidance and wisdom of this book have remained relatively unchanged. Twenty-six years ago, *Setting Course* was an interesting experiment addressing the untested question: Would Members of Congress and staff read and apply sound management guidance from a written manual? Today, this book has become required reading for Members-elect and a valuable desktop reference for virtually every Chief of Staff and many veteran Members. We hope it is as helpful to you in setting your course for your career in Congress. Enjoy the journey.

Part I:
Transitioning to Congress and Setting Up Your Office

Chapter One:	Navigating the First 60 Days: November and December	3
Chapter Two:	Selecting Committee Assignments	17
Chapter Three:	Creating a First-Year Budget	27
Chapter Four:	Creating a Management Structure and a System for Communicating with the Member	47
Chapter Five:	Hiring Your Core Staff	63
Chapter Six:	Selecting and Utilizing Technology	81
Chapter Seven:	Establishing District and State Offices	101

Icons Used in Setting Course

 Notes a series of questions. Your unique answers can help you make decisions about managing an office and a career.

 Alerts you to a situation which Hill offices have found to be problematic. Proceed with caution and pay close attention.

 Notes a concept or recommendation that CMF has determined, through its research with congressional offices, to be helpful.

 Identifies an office or organization which you may wish to contact for further information on the topic.

 Notes a process or steps you can use in the operations of your office.

CHAPTER ONE

Navigating the First 60 Days: November and December

This Chapter Includes...

☆ A process for setting priorities during the transition

☆ Those key activities which should be your focus in November and December

☆ Guiding principles to help you make more informed decisions and maintain your focus during the transition

Not long ago, freshman Members of Congress could use most of the two months between Election Day and swearing-in day for a well-deserved vacation. Times have changed. Increasingly, what you do and don't do during the transition may well govern the success of your first term, if not your career.

You probably can (and should) find a few days to relax with friends and family. But only a few. Freshmen who get a late start and make rushed, uninformed decisions about their office operations are often not able to rebound and show accomplishments in their first terms.

It is equally important to recognize that you cannot do *everything* during the transition, nor should you. You simply don't have the time, resources or information. Rather, you should identify and concentrate on the essential tasks which will set the stage for a successful first term. Other, non-critical decisions should be deferred.

Part I of this book is designed to help you make these decisions and navigate your transition to Congress.

Importance of Setting Priorities

All Members, from the newly elected to the most senior, share a common problem. There is much more to do than can possibly be done. This is especially true for freshmen during November and December, when it seems you are trying to build and sail your office ship simultaneously.

You don't have much time or many resources (money, staff, office space) at your disposal. You probably don't have all the information you need to make knowledgeable decisions, or even perhaps a sense of what data would be most helpful. Yet your responsibilities are enormous, every decision appears critical and pressing, and the possibilities of what you could be working on are almost limitless.

There is hope, and it begins when you accept that you and your limited staff cannot and should not try to accomplish everything in the first 60 days. Some tasks are essential to your first-term success. Countless, tempting others will have little impact on your effectiveness, or can be safely delayed. It is far better to identify the critical activities and devote your energy to getting them done well than to overreach, spread your resources too thin and get a lot done poorly or just adequately.

> *"It is far better to identify the critical activities and devote your energy to getting them done well than to overreach, spread your resources too thin and get a lot done poorly or just adequately."*

Your first duty, therefore, is to set priorities and distinguish between critical and non-critical tasks for the first 60 days. To do so, you need to look at how each potential task will or will not contribute to your effectiveness as a Member.

Dr. Stephen Covey in *The Seven Habits of Highly Effective People* defined effectiveness in terms of bringing about "the maximum long-term beneficial results possible." Thus, in order to be effective, you need to know what results you are attempting to achieve. It is possible to be very efficient at getting a lot of things done without being effective. This applies to both you and your office.

For example, you could spend much of November and December drafting personal responses to all the mail you receive. You could work very productively on this task, but not very effectively, because it would do very little to help you achieve "long-term beneficial results." A much more effective approach would be for you to hire a Chief of Staff, who could then help you assemble staff, computers and supplies by January to answer current and future mail.

Dr. Covey uses two criteria, urgency and importance, to develop a matrix that can help you to determine where your time, energy, and resources need to be focused (see Figure 1-1).

Urgent tasks are those that need to be done right now, such as answering a ringing telephone. Important tasks are those that contribute to the achievement of goals and objectives. For example, selecting a good Chief of Staff is very important to your effectiveness as a Member.

Figure 1-1

Urgency and Importance Matrix

	Urgent	Not Urgent
Important	QUADRANT I Dealing with crises or handling projects with deadlines	QUADRANT II Planning, building relations and preventing crises
Not Important	QUADRANT III Interruptions; some calls, mail and meetings	QUADRANT IV Busy work; some calls and mail

Covey argues that the most crucial quadrant for long-term effectiveness is Quadrant II. By planning, building relations, and seeking to prevent crises, it is possible to achieve goals and objectives. The more time spent with Quadrant I activities — those that are urgent and important — the more you are responding to outside pressures rather than shaping your own activities. Time spent in Quadrants III and IV do little to contribute to long-term effectiveness.

Covey's model can help focus new Member activity during the transition. Figure 1-2 (on the following page) lists some of the activities in which new Members could be engaged during the transition, and their locations in the Covey quadrants.

By virtue of being a new Member of Congress, and representing a constituency, you are likely to have a higher percentage of activities placed in the urgent category, but one of the secrets to success is finding ways to reduce the kind of crisis management involved in constantly dealing with urgent issues. Investing time in Quadrant II activities reduces the need for crisis management. For instance, hiring a core staff can become a crisis if you don't get around to it until a week before the opening of Congress, and you don't have a clear idea of the type of staff you need. By spending time planning, budgeting and developing a management structure — all Quadrant II activities — you can develop a better sense of your staffing needs. Hiring a core staff may still be urgent, but with proper preparation it no longer has to be a crisis.

Figure 1-2

Matrixing Typical Office Activities

	Urgent	Not Urgent
Important	QUADRANT I • Hiring core staff • Seeking committee assignments • Attending official orientation programs and party organizational meetings	QUADRANT II • Planning for the term • Developing relationships with colleagues • Creating an office management structure • Drafting a first-year budget
Not Important	QUADRANT III • Responding to any routine requests by the media • Answering a constituent letter or dealing with casework problems	QUADRANT IV • Visiting Smithsonian Museums • Taking official photo for press kit • Having committee staff brief Member on upcoming legislation • Obtaining additional office furniture

It's also important to remember that just because an activity is urgent does not necessarily make it important. A reporter's request for an interview or a constituent letter both have a sense of urgency to them. A reporter has a deadline and a constituent is expecting a reply. But are performing these activities now contributing to your first-term effectiveness, and is it worth pushing aside other critical tasks in order to devote time to them? Most often in these cases, the answer is no.

The Critical Transition Tasks

While each new Member must determine his or her own list of critical tasks for the transition, there are three activities which should appear on everyone's list. These are the activities which will be vital to any Member's successful management of the transition, although the amount of time, attention and resources devoted to each may vary according to the Member's priorities.

Critical Activity #1: Decisions About Personal Circumstances

Becoming a Member of Congress means ending one career and lifestyle and establishing a new one. It's like taking a new job in a new city. All of the details involved in a move apply here as well.

Most decisions regarding your personal state of affairs will be just that, personal, and should be decided based upon your needs and those of your family. You'll have to leave your current job, and you'll need a place to stay in Washington. Other circumstances will vary greatly from Member to Member. Your spouse may have to leave a job. You may need to find child care for your young children. You may want to resolve potential conflicts of interest regarding your investments. And you may need to let organizations to which you belong know that you could be quite busy for a while (e.g., probably unable to continue on as the chairman of the board or head of the PTA).

One crucial decision that each new Member faces is whether to relocate to Washington. Members may want to keep a primary residence in the district or state and commute to Washington during the weeks that Congress is in session. Alternatively, they may move their families to Washington and travel back home on weekends and during district/state work periods. Unless your personal situation makes the choice obvious, it can be helpful to discuss these options with freshman and veteran Members who have already made and lived with their decisions. One word of warning: most new Members are startled at the high cost of housing in the Washington area.

MANAGEMENT FACT
In 2010, a decent one-bedroom apartment on Capitol Hill costs between $1300 and $1700 a month.

Personal circumstances qualify as a vital transition activity primarily because they will contribute to, or distract from, your emotional and physical well-being, which could significantly influence your job performance. Personal decisions have the potential of consuming a large quantity of your time and attention, so it's worth choosing which decisions you want to make during the transition, and which can be postponed.

Critical Activity #2: Selecting and Lobbying for Committee Assignments

This is a critical activity for November and December because of the significant role committees can play in a Member's success and because the entire assignment process is almost always over by swearing-in day. Committees are the primary means of moving legislation to the House or Senate floor. They also provide an opportunity, through hearings, for Members to bring issues to the forefront of the congressional agenda. Not all committees are alike, however, making it imperative for a Member to choose committees which will be able to assist in the pursuit of his or her goals. Some committees are geared towards specific policy areas or regions of the country, while others allow a Member to be more of a generalist and national legislator. Some committees carry more clout, and others are associated with the leadership.

The formal committee assignment process begins during the early party organizational meetings held during the first week Members are in Washington. The informal lobbying, however, often starts the day after the election, as Members-elect jockey for position for open committee seats along with returning Members who are looking to switch committees. In December and January, the party's decisions are usually finalized.

"The formal committee assignment process begins during the early party organizational meetings held during the first week Members are in Washington."

We should emphasize that it is common for Members to try to switch panels mid-career, so while choosing and lobbying for committee seats are critical decisions, they are not irreversible. Still, if you are clear about your goals, it is preferable to get on the committees of your choice as a freshman.

Chapter 2 will provide you with a comprehensive description of the committee assignment process, and tips for selecting and lobbying for committee seats.

Critical Activity #3: Setting Up Your Office

There are an incredible number of decisions which encompass the setting up of a congressional office, but some decisions are clearly more important than others. Your goal for the first 60 days should be to determine your staffing and equipment needs, and office management policies, for at least two offices (Washington and district/state). They will allow you to: (1) take care of routine business from opening day, and (2) create a foundation that will provide a smooth climb to a fully functioning operation that reflects your values and priorities, and is capable of accomplishing the strategic objectives you've set for your first term.

We have identified five tasks that are necessary for setting up a congressional office. We'll only briefly describe them here, as they are covered in great detail in Chapters 3-7. The five critical tasks are:

Creating a first-year budget (see Chapter 3). Many of the major decisions you'll make in the first 60 days, such as hiring a core staff and establishing district/state offices, will have budget implications. Without a budget, you'll have a difficult time allocating your resources in a way that will help you reach your goals. With a budget, you'll be able to test whether your goals are feasible, and make educated trade-offs to stay true to your priorities.

Creating a management structure and method of communicating between staff and Member (see Chapter 4). A freshman office cannot be effective unless the Member and staff have a clear, shared understanding of how the office will operate: who has decision-making authority and over what issues, who supervises whom, and how staff and the Member should communicate with each other. Unless these choices are made in November and December, staff will be hired without a clear understanding of their roles in the office. Down the line, ad hoc policies will evolve that create staff confusion and frustration, impair productivity and diminish accountability.

Hiring a core staff (see Chapter 5). Your staff will be your most valuable resource, greatly influencing your success in Congress and ability to accomplish what you set out to do. You will need a core staff on opening day that can keep your Washington and district/state offices functioning: answering phones, answering mail, scheduling your time, doing basic legislative research, preparing speeches and talking points, and processing casework. You'll also want this staff to bring the skills and expertise necessary to help you accomplish your longer-term goals.

Evaluating your technological needs (see Chapter 6). Technology is a necessity in today's fast-paced, information-based world of Congress. Computer equipment that is inadequate will hurt office productivity and may not even allow your staff to keep up with routine business. Depending upon your predecessor's purchases, the equipment you inherit may be top-notch, barely sufficient or somewhere in between (if something doesn't meet minimal standards, you won't even be allowed to inherit it). You should evaluate this equipment in November and December to see if it will meet your most immediate needs. If it won't, you'll want to minimize the disruption to your office by being ready on opening day to place your order to upgrade.

Establishing district or state offices (see Chapter 7). Every Member of Congress will have at least one district or state office; some Senators will have as many as eight or nine. While veterans say that it is important to establish one district/state office by the first day of the new Congress — to demonstrate that you're "open for business" — it is also important to draw up the plans for all of your proposed offices by the time you're sworn-in. How many offices you'll eventually want, where you'll locate them and the work you'll expect to be performed out of them, will impact your early decisions on budgeting, management structure, staffing and technology purchases. Also, many decisions regarding district/state offices are difficult to reverse (or at least not without political or financial penalties) if you later discover they do not contribute to achieving office goals or do not fit into a larger game plan. Planning now will save time and money later.

Of course, setting up your offices and deciding which committee assignments to pursue will require some basic understanding of how Congress operates, both formally (rules/regulations) and informally (norms/practices). You will likely be figuring out "how the place works" well into your first year. In the short term, your best sources of information will be orientation programs run by the House/Senate and your party's leadership. CMF strongly recommends that you and an aide attend these orientations. You can also pick up quite a bit of advice by talking with veteran Members and their Chiefs of Staff. We provide an overview of the orientation and early party organizational meetings later in this chapter. Chapter 8 in Part II will provide Members-elect with helpful background information on the culture of Congress, which will assist you in both pursuing committee assignments and setting up your office.

Guiding Principles for the Transition

Develop and Base Decisions Around Your Strategic Goals

As we discuss throughout this book, one of the common attributes of successful Members is the ability to set clear goals and develop a workable plan for achieving them. Without clear priorities, offices quickly become overwhelmed with the pressures of work and events. Members become crisis managers putting out an endless series of fires with little time to actually decide upon, or pursue, their priorities.

Many Members-elect make the mistake of deciding that they can put off planning until later in the year when they have completed the Herculean activities described earlier. More often than not, they end up making a range of critical decisions in November and December with too little strategic thought about their long-term effects. The result can be regrettable decisions; regrettable because many of these early decisions cannot be easily rectified if it turns out you need to change course. Planning should precede or accompany decisions such as:

- Which committee assignments to seek
- Who you should hire for your key staff positions (e.g., Should you hire an outstanding Press Secretary or an outstanding Legislative Director? Should you hire four Legislative Assistants and two Constituent Services Representatives, or the reverse?)
- How many district/state offices you should open and where you should locate each one

Developing goals for your first term requires that you balance three primary factors: your personal interests; the interests or needs of your district/state; and the political environment within which you are operating. Your goals should be targeted to achieve strategic ends that you intend to achieve, such as becoming a national leader on medical fraud issues or being seen throughout the district as the champion for addressing a sewage treatment problem. And because goals are the top strategic priorities of the office, you should have no more than six. Any more indicates that you have failed to make the hard trade-offs, leaving you with too many priorities to pursue effectively.

"Developing goals for your first term requires that you balance three primary factors: your personal interests; the interests or needs of your district/state; and the political environment within which you are operating."

With clear goals established early on in your transition, you will be in a much better position to make wise decisions about setting up your offices and positioning yourself for a successful first term. Freshmen should also read Chapter 11, "Strategic Planning in Your Office" in Part III of this book. There you'll find a complete discussion about planning, as well as a step-by-step process for setting and evaluating goals.

Recognize: "Less is More"

You will quickly discover that the critical activities we discussed earlier do not come close to encompassing the potential tasks to which you could be devoting time and energy during the first 60 days. In fact, we routinely use as an orientation training tool a list of about one hundred possible tasks Members-elect and their aides can undertake during the transition. All seem urgent and important, and that's where you can get tripped up.

In fact, only a handful of tasks need to receive the bulk of your attention in November and December because they are critical to your first term. The topics in Part I of this book cover most of them. You may add a few more to reflect your specific goals and priorities. But remember, the more items on your list, the less effective you will likely be at accomplishing any of them.

We're not saying that you should ignore the other tasks, but rather that you should keep a sense of perspective. You don't need to spend weeks organizing the VIP list, or selecting the catering and souvenirs for your swearing-in party. Similarly, it is probably not worth devoting heavy resources to scouting the best Washington office suite available through the "office lottery." You'll have a swearing-in party and select an office, to be sure, but neither a memorable bash nor a prime office location will have much effect on whether you're a successful first-term Member.

By keeping your attention focused and doing the essential tasks well, you can lay the foundation for later achievements. If one of your goals is to be a leader on senior citizen issues, for instance, you may see good reason to spend time during the transition drafting legislation dealing with elderly issues so it can be introduced on opening day. Or maybe you'd want to get together your

> **Early Member Tasks**
>
> ✓ Decide first-term strategic goals
> ✓ Select Chief of Staff
> ✓ Target/lobby for committee assignments
> ✓ Attend orientation and party caucuses
> ✓ Determine number and location of district offices
> ✓ Set up office management structure ∎

biography and official photo so you can hand them out when seniors visit. But neither of these activities is the best use of your time.

You will be much more effective in the long-run by thoughtfully and strategically completing critical tasks such as creating a first-year budget, hiring a quality core staff and evaluating your technological needs. With this groundwork, you'll be in a position not only to introduce legislation, but to promote it and guide it through Congress. You will not only have material available when seniors come to visit, but you will be able to use technology to reach out to them.

Learn to Delegate

A final consideration as you think about what needs to be done is who should get it done. New Members are often reluctant to delegate, but being effective requires it. Delegating involves identifying which tasks should be performed by the Member, and which can be entrusted to staff. It also entails creating a reporting or communications structure that allows the Member to oversee and direct the transition staff without actually having to do the work.

Certain activities should only be done by you, the Member, or by a Member with staff input. These include deciding on first-term strategic goals; selecting a Chief of Staff; deciding which committee assignments to seek and lobbying for them; attending Member orientations and party caucuses; deciding how many district/state offices to open and where to locate them; and deciding on an office management structure. In contrast, a flock of other tasks can easily be delegated to competent staff, such as: sorting through resumes, invitations and casework requests; working with House and Senate support offices to negotiate a district/state office lease; evaluating your inherited computer system and recommending whether to upgrade; and coordinating your swearing-in celebration and Washington office suite selection.

You'll need a transition team for the first two months, at which time you'll be able to bring your core staff on the payroll. Two to four aides should be enough. The single most valuable aide would be someone whom you trust, and who can be designated as the transition team leader. This person can attend some orientation programs, contribute to strategic planning, assist with media requests and manage the details of setting up your office. Ideally, you would pick someone who would eventually become your Chief of Staff. The second most useful person on the team would be someone with administrative skills to manage the paper — invitations, resumes, letters — and provide personal assistance to you and the team leader.

You'll have to decide how to compensate transition staffers. Senators may put only two staffers on the payroll and House Members may hire no one until January 3. You can either recruit volunteers or pay some or all of your transition staff out of campaign funds. Volunteers are free, but they may have competing demands and loyalties that limit their ability to give you their complete attention. On the other hand, using campaign funds enables you to quickly assemble a team exclusively dedicated to serving your needs. However, you may have to defend your choice to spend these funds for something other than their original purpose.

> *"Senators may put only two staffers on the payroll during transition and House Members may hire no one until opening day."*

Finally, as you delegate during the transition, you'll need a system that ensures that decisions are being made in accordance with your wishes. No single system will work for everyone. One Member-elect had his transition team leader provide him with daily memos. Other Members-elect relied upon oral briefings every few days. The key factor is your level of comfort and confidence that tasks are being carried out pursuant to your goals and priorities. Develop a simple reporting or communications structure that meets your need for information without bogging down the decision-making process.

Orientation and Organizational Meetings

At separate House and Senate orientations, new Members are provided handbooks that describe the official rules they must follow in setting up their offices and conducting their business. Presentations amplify and expand upon the written materials. The topics usually covered in these sessions include: budgets allocated to hire staff and run your office, use of the congressional frank, use and availability of computers, internal congressional services, employment benefits and congressional ethics. Additional sessions describe legislative branch support offices (such as the Congressional Research Service), introduce and explain the duties of the officers of the chamber, and discuss options for setting up a congressional office.

Orientation programs are generally taught by Members in each chamber and are helpful in providing "lessons learned." Social events are also held for both Members and their spouses. These orientation programs provide Members with their first opportunity to make impressions on their colleagues and to begin the important process of establishing coalitions. It is also one of the few times that party leaders will both make presentations and provide new Members the opportunity to ask questions.

Simultaneous with the orientation programs, the Congressional Management Foundation (CMF), in conjunction with the House Chiefs of Staff Association, conducts a one-day specialized training program for one designated House staffer accompanying the Member-elect to Washington. This program enables key staffers to quickly develop a detailed working knowledge of administrative and legislative procedures in the chamber, and to meet other top congressional staffers. Veteran congressional staff and CMF staff lead workshops on planning, budgeting, setting up an office, and hiring staff.

Immediately following orientation, which usually lasts two or three days, veteran Members join the freshmen for early organizational meetings, which are conducted independently by each party in each chamber. Whereas the official orientation provides general information, the party leadership programs are more likely to provide Members with advice on how to effectively use available resources to meet political objectives. This program is more partisan in nature, as party positions and strategies are decided.

The culmination of the orientation and early organizational meetings are party organizing meetings, at which the organization of the new session of Congress is determined. During these meetings, the parties select their floor leaders and committee leaders, and begin the process of making appointments to committees. Social events held during this period offer Members, particularly new Members, valuable opportunities to interact with senior Members and party leaders.

Outside organizations also conduct policy-oriented programs, primarily for new Members. The Congressional Research Service (CRS), the American Enterprise Institute, the Heritage Foundation, and Harvard's Institute of Politics all hold seminars early in December and January. These programs focus on policy and ideological topics facing the new Congress. In addition, the CRS program covers legislative and budget procedures.

Conclusion

Managing the first 60 days after the election is the first real test for a new Member of Congress. Your decisions and choices during the transition will have a long-lasting impact on your first term, and quite possibly your career. You must recognize that some tasks will be critical to overall first-term effectiveness; these should receive the bulk of your attention and resources. You should also develop a handful of goals to guide your early decisions. Thoughtful decisions now can save time and resources later, and start you down the path towards achieving your objectives. And, finally, you should put together a transition team and delegate certain prescribed tasks to them.

The other chapters in Part I take a closer look at the critical tasks we've identified in this chapter and provide advice on how best to accomplish them. We'll examine selecting and pursuing committee assignments, creating a first-year budget, creating a management structure and method of Member-staff communication, hiring a core staff, evaluating your technological needs and establishing district/state offices. We hope this advice will allow you to chart a course toward a successful first term.

Chapter Summary
The DOs and DON'Ts of

Navigating the First 60 Days: November and December

Do...

- **concentrate most of your energy on three critical activities:**
  - making decisions about your living and other household arrangements;
  - selecting and lobbying for committee assignments; and
  - setting up your office.
- **use your strategic goals to shape critical early decisions, such as:**
  - creating a first-year budget;
  - establishing/selecting a management structure;
  - hiring a core staff;
  - evaluating your technology needs; and
  - establishing a district or state office(s).
- **learn to delegate.** A Member should focus on those tasks which only he or she can perform, and delegate the rest to staff.

Don't...

- **try to do everything.** Set priorities so you can do essential tasks well, rather than an overwhelming number of tasks only adequately.
- **put off strategic planning until later in the year.** If you do, you'll make decisions that cannot be easily reversed.
- **skip the House/Senate orientations and party organizational meetings.** They provide invaluable opportunities for networking and learning the intricacies of Capitol Hill.

CHAPTER TWO

Selecting Committee Assignments

This Chapter Includes...

☆ The importance of committee assignments to freshmen
☆ How the committee assignment process works
☆ How to choose and lobby for committee assignments

Perhaps the most important event for a freshman that occurs between the election and the first day of the new Congress is the allocation of committee assignments. These assignments often determine the character of a Member's first term, if not his career. Indeed, they are often the key to successful congressional careers and successful policy-making. For this reason, the attempt to obtain the best possible committee assignment often begins the day after the election. Your timing is critical because the process intensifies during the early organizational meetings your first week in Washington, and decisions are almost always finalized by the parties before opening day.

This chapter describes how the committee assignment process works and offers advice on how best to secure an assignment.

Importance of Committee Assignments

Because of the prominent role committees play in Congress, committee assignments can play a central role in shaping the character of a Member's career.

Committees are a key structural component of the work of Congress. They are the principal vehicles for initiating and shaping bills to be considered on the House or Senate floor. Moreover, leadership usually respects committee jurisdiction when referring bills, allowing committees to exercise great power within their spheres of influence. Committees also provide forums, through hearings, for Members to raise awareness on issues, which can have quite a dramatic effect when administration officials or experts are called to testify.

> *"It's the most important decision you can make. If you're on a good committee, you'll enjoy legislating and accomplish something. If you're on a bad committee, you won't enjoy it here."*
>
> *Senator Charles Schumer (D-NY)*

Not all committees are alike, and some are clearly more powerful than others. A seat on a powerful committee gives a Member clout and may lead to other political and legislative opportunities. Some committees lend themselves well to development of an expertise in an issue or two, while others tend to promote Members who are generalists. Still other committees are tied closely to the leadership.

It should be noted that committee choices in the first year are not forever binding, and it is common for Members to try to switch panels mid-career. However, given the predominance of the seniority system, it is preferable for freshmen to try to land a committee seat of their choice from the start. Your ability to do so will be affected, however, by how clearly you've defined your strategic goals.

How the Committee Assignment Process Works

Before each party can begin placing its Members on committees, the number of seats that each party will receive on each committee must be determined. Traditionally, the respective party leaders, occasionally with input from committee leaders, negotiate individual committee sizes and party ratios prior to the early organizational meetings. However, this process can continue well into January.

CHAPTER TWO Selecting Committee Assignments

Committee sizes tend to remain fairly constant year after year. When committee seats are increased, it is usually done to accommodate an individual Member's request to serve on a particular panel. In the Senate, the overall ratio on committees generally reflects party strength in the chamber. That is, a party with 60 percent of a chamber's seats will have roughly 60 percent of the committee seats, although the composition of individual committees may, in some instances, diverge from the overall ratio of the parties in the chamber. In the House, the majority party controls the ratio of committees and it may not reflect the ratio in the chamber — a practice that usually causes disputes with the minority party at the beginning of each Congress.

Once committee sizes and party ratios are fixed, the process for a Member receiving a committee assignment has three formal steps: (1) party recommendation, (2) approval by the party caucus or conference, and (3) a House or Senate floor vote on the entire roster of assignments created by each party's leadership, for pro forma acceptance.

By far the most important step is party recommendation. Recommendations are made by a "committee on committees," sometimes referred to as "party committees." Membership on these party committees may vary with each new Congress, but it's generally designed to give each leadership considerable influence. The party committees are:

- *House Democratic Steering and Policy Committee* — comprised of regionally-elected Members (usually 12), top party and committee leaders (recently 24), a representative of the freshman class, and up to 16 Members appointed by the Speaker. Each Member has one vote.
- *House Republican Steering Committee* — comprised of party and committee leaders, regional representatives (recently 10), a representative of the sophomore class, and a representative of the freshman class. The Republican Leader has five votes, the Republican Whip has two votes, and other Members have one vote each.
- *Senate Democratic Steering and Coordination Committee* — Senators appointed by the floor leader. Recently there were 25 Members with one vote each.
- *Senate Republican Committee on Committees* — Senators appointed by the floor leader. Recently each of the eight Members had one vote.

In making their recommendations, these party committees take into account a number of factors, including: the number of vacancies on each committee, the number of Members competing for those vacancies, and the chamber and party rules governing the number and types of committees on which a Member may serve. They also consider each Member's seniority, background, ideology, election margin and leadership support. In addition, they may seek to achieve geographic balance by ensuring a committee's membership represents a cross-section of the United States.

Respective party committees vote by secret ballot to arrive at individual recommendations for assignments. The party caucus or conference then votes to ratify the recommendations, as does the full House or Senate.

Committee Categories

A combination of chamber and party rules govern how many, and what types, of committees a Member may serve on. For convenience, committees are grouped into categories. The process is different in each chamber, so we'll discuss each separately.

House

Each party committee in the House determines its own categories and which committees it wants to place in those categories. The lists are printed in the respective party caucus rules (see Figure 2-1). House Members can serve on no more than two standing committees and four subcommittees of those committees. However, waivers are often granted by the respective party to serve on additional committees and subcommittees. Both parties limit service to one exclusive committee, although a Democratic Member can serve on the Budget or House Administration panels while on an exclusive committee. A Republican Member may take a leave of absence from a standing committee allowing Members to serve on the Rules Committee without losing seniority on the standing committee. Both parties allow service on two nonexclusive committees.

For both Democrats and Republicans, service on the Standards of Official Conduct ("Ethics") Committee is exempt from assignment limitations. House rules limit service on the Ethics Committee to three Congresses in the last five. Further, service on the Budget Committee is generally limited to no more than four Congresses in the last six, although this limitation was waived in recent Congresses. Finally, service on the Intelligence Committee is also limited to four Congresses in the last six.

Senate

Senate committees are categorized according to Senate rules as either "A," "B," or "C" (see Figure 2-2). Each Senator may serve on two "A" committees, one "B" committee, and one or more "C" committees. However, waivers are often granted to permit service on additional panels.

In addition, each party designates certain committees as "Super A," and prohibits Senators under party rules from serving on more than one of these committees. Currently the list of "Super A" committees is the same for both

Figure 2-1

House Committee Categories

Category	Democrats	Republicans
Exclusive	Appropriations * Energy & Commerce ** Financial Services Rules Ways & Means	Appropriations Energy & Commerce Rules Ways & Means
Non-Exclusive	Agriculture Armed Services Budget Education and Labor Foreign Affairs Homeland Security House Administration Judiciary Natural Resources Oversight and Government Reform Science and Technology Small Business Transportation & Infrastructure Veterans' Affairs	Agriculture Armed Services Budget Education and Labor Financial Services Foreign Affairs Homeland Security Judiciary Natural Resources Oversight and Government Reform Science and Technology Small Business Transportation & Infrastructure Veterans' Affairs
Exempt	Select Energy Independence and Global Warming Select Intelligence Standards of Official Conduct Joint Economic Joint Library Joint Printing Joint Taxation	House Administration Select Energy Independence and Global Warming Select Intelligence Standards of Official Conduct Joint Economic Joint Library Joint Printing Joint Taxation

* Applies to Democratic Members named in or after the 104th Congress.
** Applies to Democratic Members named in or after the 109th Congress.

parties: Appropriations, Armed Services, Finance, and Foreign Relations. Republican Senators from the same state are prohibited from serving on the same committee by Republican Conference rule. Democrats adhere to the same prohibition, but by tradition rather than party rule.

Rules Governing Committee Chairs and Ranking Members

Both parties in both chambers designate a formal leader for each committee, with the leader chosen by the majority party serving as chair. Seniority can play a role in these selections. There are limitations on the number and type of chairmanships a Member may hold, although exceptions are allowed.

In 1995, House Republicans adopted a House rule that limits chairs of committees and subcommittees to three consecutive terms (six years). The rule was retained by the new Democratic majority in 2007 but repealed in 2009. Republican Conference rules apply the term limit to ranking minority leaders when the party is in the minority. In 1996, Senate Republicans adopted a similar six-year limit on committee chairs. After control of the Senate changed hands in 2001, Senate Republicans became Ranking Members of the Committees, and this rule was modified in 2002. The Senate Republican Conference changed their rules so that Senators' service as Ranking Member would not count against their six-year limit as chair. Another new rule required that chairs be elected by secret ballot within each committee and by the full Republican Conference, thereby making the chairs accountable to all Republican Senators and not just those on the committee. Senate Democrats have not adopted term limits for their committee leaders.

Figure 2-2

Senate Committee Categories

"A" Committees	"B" Committees	"C" Committees
Agriculture, Nutrition and Forestry	Budget	Select Ethics
Appropriations	Rules and Administration	Indian Affairs
Armed Services	Small Business and Entrepreneurship	Joint Library
Banking, Housing, and Urban Affairs	Veterans' Affairs	Joint Printing
Commerce, Science, and Transportation	Special Aging	Joint Taxation
Energy and Natural Resources	Joint Economic	
Environment and Public Works		
Finance		
Foreign Relations		
Health, Education, Labor, and Pensions		
Homeland Security and Governmental Affairs		
Select Intelligence		
Judiciary		

Advice for Choosing and Pursuing Committee Assignments

There is no one right way to decide which committees to pursue, nor one right way to lobby for them. Members have different needs and strengths, which should govern their choices and their strategies for gaining leadership support. Veteran observers of the process, however, offer the following time-tested advice:

Start early. The attempt to obtain the best possible committee assignment for freshmen often begins the day after the election. You should learn where the openings are, learn the jurisdiction of each committee, talk with other Members about the working atmosphere of each committee and the operating style of the committee chair, and plot strategy for obtaining the best assignment. If you think this is too early, consider that for returning Members, the process of changing committee assignments actually begins long before the election.

Gather information. Members are generally advised to talk with "their" representatives on the party committee (i.e., those who represent your region, class or other grouping) about their choices. It's also recommended that Members talk with other Members from their district, state, or region about ways to influence the party machinery to obtain the best committee. Members from the same group, such as women, conservatives or progressives, should also be consulted for advice and support. There are excellent opportunities to gather information at the orientation programs and early organizational meetings.

Select committees that will help you achieve your goals. Do you want to focus on constituent services or be a national legislator? Will you become an expert in foreign affairs, health care, financial services or the environment? Are you from a "safe" district or will you likely face a difficult re-election battle in two years? The answers to these types of questions, combined with the information you've assembled about the committees, should help you narrow your choices.

If you know precisely where you want to go, or if your district or state has a few dominant interests, your best choices may be easy to identify. As one south Florida freshman said, "We know what's important for our district: crime and immigration. That's why we went after [the] Judiciary and Foreign Affairs [Committees]. We've got heavy Cuban and Jewish populations and needed to represent their interests." Similarly, Members representing rural districts will probably want to consider the Agriculture Committee even though they might personally prefer another assignment. One freshman told us, "Listen, if you're from my state, you don't select the Agriculture Committee, you're sentenced to it."

Make your case. You should let your colleagues know why a particular committee assignment is important to you (e.g., representation of the needs of the district/state, or electoral concerns) and why you are qualified to serve (e.g., prior experience in the subject while serving in the state legislature).

> *"Listen, if you're from my state, you don't select the Agriculture Committee, you're sentenced to it."*

But you should also demonstrate why your desired assignment is important to your colleagues; in other words, why it is in their best interest to grant you a seat. As a House Democratic Member explained to us:

> "I didn't understand the value of exploring and exploiting the leverage I had available. I came [to the process of selecting committees] with a resume — my professional credentials. I thought that was the primary basis of the committee selection process. What I learned was that the resume by itself was clearly insufficient. You have to be able to figure out how you can best leverage your assets so that leadership feels motivated to meet your needs."

A prime time for lobbying is the orientation and organizational meetings. The way you conduct yourself during these sessions may influence your ability to get a good committee assignment, and may shape other Members' perceptions of you. These meetings also allow you to start the long-term process of forming relationships and building coalitions with your colleagues.

Consider leadership requests. Leadership may recommend to a Member where he or she should seek assignment. The composition of committees is important to party leaders who organize the chamber. Doing what the leadership wants early in a career often pays great dividends in future years.

Assess your chances. Many Members seek assignment to the most prestigious committees such as Appropriations, Energy and Commerce, and Ways and Means in the House, and the Appropriations and Finance Committees in the Senate. Appointments for freshmen and junior Members on these panels are rare, especially for House freshmen. Only when an extraordinary number of new Members are elected does the leadership show a willingness to demonstrate a commitment to appointing some freshmen to these committees. Further, only when their numbers are large are freshmen emboldened to demand their share of top assignments.

This does not mean you shouldn't try for a top committee; you'll never get it if you don't try. But you should consider your chances of obtaining a top spot, and perhaps have a second choice in mind.

Conclusion

Choosing and securing committee assignments will be one of your first major decisions as a Member-elect. It's a critical task for your first 60 days. The process may begin as soon as the election is over, will heat up during the orientation and organizational meetings, and will likely be concluded by the time you're sworn-in to office. Landing the right assignment, one that fits your needs and can help you achieve your goals, will put you on the path towards a successful first term.

Chapter Summary
The DOs and DON'Ts of
Selecting Committee Assignments

Do...

- **recognize the importance that committee assignments play** in the success of your first term.
- **become well-acquainted with the formal rules and processes that govern the assignment of committee seats.** Pay particular attention to your party's committee on committees. Pursue committee assignments that can advance your goals and which reflect your priorities.
- **start early.** Gather information on the seats available and your chances of getting them. Make your selections, and make your case to your colleagues as to why you should be granted a particular assignment.

Don't...

- **be discouraged if you do not get your first choice for committee assignment.** The appointment of freshman members to the most prestigious committees is rare. It is common for Members to try to switch panels after two or four years.

CHAPTER THREE

Creating a First-Year Budget

This Chapter Includes...

☆ An introduction to the rules of House and Senate budgeting
☆ The Member's role in budgeting
☆ A four-step process for developing a first-year budget
☆ Advice from veteran offices in putting together a first-year budget

On the Covey Matrix described in the first chapter, budgeting is a Quadrant II activity. It is an important, but not urgent, task for a new Member of Congress to undertake between the election and January. No one is demanding that your office put together a budget. Without one, however, your goals are little more than a wish list. A budget sketches out how you will allocate resources in a way that will help you reach those goals. Of course, this assumes you've set down some goals for your first term. If you haven't done so yet, we urge you to. For guidance in goal setting, see Chapter 1, "Navigating the First 60 Days," and Chapter 11, "Strategic Planning in Your Office."

Crafting a budget early, even if it's only a rough estimate of how you plan to spend your money, has a number of advantages to just winging it as you go along. First, it will help you avoid making fast and loose commitments which you may later regret. Without the big picture in mind, it may be difficult to see that promising $100,000 salaries to three inexperienced campaign workers, or telling your constituents that you'll visit every town in the district or state in the first year, might not be the best use of your limited resources. Second, it will give you confidence that large commitments of money you do make will fit into a larger spending plan. Hiring staff, buying computers and signing district/state office leases may use a good portion of your budget, and decisions once made are not easily undone.

Early budgeting also lets you know if your goals are feasible. If you've promised to turn back some of your allocation, or to stay in close touch with constituents through newsletters and surveys, you will get an idea of whether you can afford to do so. Moreover, you will have a good basis on which to decide if the costs are reasonable and justified by the anticipated benefits. It may also alert you to expenses over which you'll have little control. Rent in Manhattan is expensive. So is traveling from Washington, DC to a state without major air hubs. Now is a good time to consider whether it's worth opening an extra district office or flying home every weekend.

This chapter is designed to help you get that first budget in place. Chapter 12, "Budgeting and Financial Management," contains a more detailed discussion of the strategic uses of budgeting, the challenges of planning for year two and beyond, the importance of sound accounting practices and a list of cost-saving and budgeting tips. For now, we'll cover the basics.

Congressional Budget Primers

This section provides an overview of official House and Senate allowances and their uses. It will be especially helpful for any Member or staffer with limited experience in managing congressional funds. For additional information, House Members should review the *Member's Handbook* (found at http://cha.house.gov), and consult with staff from the House Finance Office (202-225-7474) and the Committee on House Administration (Democrats: 202-225-2061; Republicans: 202-225-8281). Senators may seek advice from the *Senate Handbook* (available on Webster, the Senate Intranet), the more extensive *Senate Manual*, and from the staffs of the Disbursing Office (202-224-3205) and the Senate Rules and Administration Committee (202-224-6352).

While each chamber sets its own spending levels and regulations on the use of their funds, they share some budgeting characteristics. **House and Senate offices** should keep in mind that:

- **Allocations are fixed.** Unlike campaign funds, you cannot raise more.
- **Members are personally responsible for finances.** If an office overspends its allocation on official expenses, the Member, personally, must pay the difference.
- **Funds are *not* actually *given* to you.** Your office will not receive a check at the beginning of each year. The money is held by the U.S. Treasury. The House Finance Office and Senate Disbursing Office track accounts, process payment requests (known as *vouchers*), and remit payments and reimbursements to vendors, Members, and staff. As an employee of the

MANAGEMENT FACT
If an office overspends its allocation on official expenses, the Member, personally, must pay the difference.

CHAPTER THREE Creating a First-Year Budget

Senate Disbursing Office described it, "We're not sitting around with bags of cash."

- **Funds are authorized annually.** Any funds not obligated by the end of the year for which they are authorized are lost for your use. But if you obligate within the year, the payment can come up to two years later. This situation occurs quite regularly, as when items are purchased at the end of a year and the bill doesn't arrive until the following year, or when staff find long-lost travel receipts. Many offices use funds still unexpended near the end of the year to stock up on supplies, upgrade or pay off existing equipment, and give staff bonuses. It's important to note that the House uses a legislative year (January 3 to January 2) and the Senate a fiscal year (October 1 to September 30) in authorizing funds to Members.

- **Funds have limited uses.** They cannot be used for just any expense that you choose, but only for those categories of expenses sanctioned as "allowable" (i.e., "reimbursable"). The Senate goes further than the House and reserves certain pots of money for specific expenses (see the next page).

- **Your office doesn't pay for employee fringe benefits.** Your staff salaries are deducted from your account, but your office is not charged for the government's share of payroll taxes, pension/retirement plans, or health, life, disability and unemployment insurance. These expenses are picked up by House and Senate-wide accounts.

- **Your office is not charged for *Washington* office space, standard furniture, a limited number of parking spaces and many support services.** Each Member is assigned one office in a House or Senate office building. Many, but not all, Senators have a second "hideaway" office in the Capitol. These offices, along with furnishings and support services (e.g., housekeeping, maintenance and trash removal), are provided at no cost to your operating allowance.

House offices have two additional rules to remember:

- **There is a single account (called the Members' Representational Allowance or MRA) from which all expenses are paid.** In order to simplify congressional office budgeting and give Members more flexibility in managing their offices, in 1995 the House replaced its system of separate allowances (staff, franking, office expense) with one consolidated account. This makes budgeting an even more versatile tool for achieving a Member's strategic goals.

- **All Members do not have the same MRA.** There are three variables that affect the amount of a Member's MRA: distance from Washington to the Member's district, the cost of office space in the district, and the number of postal drops (i.e., households, post office boxes, etc.) in the district. The House Administration Committee does the calculations and will inform you of your MRA; there is no work to be done on your part. Recently, the MRA has ranged from $1.4 million to $2 million, with an average of $1.5 million.

The budget accounts for **Senate offices** are organized differently:

- **Senators have many accounts, each with a different sum of money and limitations on how it can be spent.** Not surprisingly, the allocations available to a Senator are in most cases determined by the population of the state that he or she represents. States are grouped into categories, such as "fewer than 5 million people" or "28 million and more." The accounts described below are ordered from largest to smallest in size, on average:

- **Senator's Official Personnel and Office Expense Account (commonly referred to as the Senator's Account).** This is the big one, ranging from $3.1 million to $4.9 million, depending upon state population, distance from Washington, DC and number of postal addresses in the state. The Senator's Account is used for staff salaries and all other "official office expenses," including travel, subscriptions, some telephone charges, franked mail or delivery charges, stationery and office supplies. This account includes $50,000 for mass mailings (though that money can also be used for other expenses).

- **Economic Allocation Fund.** After you are elected or re-elected, your office will receive an Economic Allocation Fund that can be used anytime during your six-year term. The fund is for the purchase of information technology equipment and office equipment in your DC and state offices. The fund is given to offices in two three-year allotments. Unspent balances from the first three-year allotment may be carried over into the remainder of your six-year term. The total amount of the fund is based on each office's state population.

- **Constituent Services Systems (CSS) funds.** This funding is allocated for the six-year term and is based on state population. The CSS funds are only to be used for CSS hardware, software purchases and maintenance.

- **Home State Furniture and Furnishings.** Your office will receive a lifetime allowance for furniture, drapes, carpeting and other furnishings for all your state offices. The amount ranges from $48,000 to $68,000, depending upon state population.

- **Senator's Allowance.** For each six-year term, an amount of $5,000 is allotted to each newly elected/re-elected Senator for the purpose of

CHAPTER THREE Creating a First-Year Budget

furnishing a personal office, reception room and conference room with non-standard items in the Washington office. This amount cannot be rolled over to future terms.

- **Other accounts available to Senators allot things rather than money.** Again, a specific Senator's allotment is often based on state population. This is just a sample:

  State office rent. You may lease as many state offices as you wish, as long as (1) the total square footage is under the maximum allotment (currently 5,000 to 8,200 square feet); and (2) the rent in each office is less than the maximum per square foot lease rate set by the General Services Administration for that city. Rent is approved and paid through the Sergeant at Arms.

  Long distance telephone service. There's no separate bill for domestic long distance calls made on pooled WATS lines, though the calls are itemized on your phone records. Again, these charges are paid by a Senate-wide account.

  Paper and envelopes. Each office receives a substantial quantity of blank and letterhead paper, and blank and franked envelopes.

  Printing and folding services. The Senate Sergeant at Arms has facilities to print, fold and mail constituent mail and outreach mass mail.

"Officially related expenses" may be paid out of excess campaign funds. Generally speaking, this category includes expenses incurred in connection with official duties which are not reimbursable under Senate rules, such as refreshments provided at official events. If you have any questions about whether an expense falls under this category, contact the Ethics Committee for guidance. A reminder that this rule is for the Senate only; House Members may not pay for any official expenses with campaign funds.

The amount of money allotted to House and Senate offices is based on the distance from D.C. to their district/state and number of postal drops. In the Senate, state population is also part of the calculation.

Senate budgets are prorated for partial years. Because newly elected Senators do not take office until three months into the fiscal year, they receive three-quarters of their usual allotments to cover January through September. Similarly, Senators who retire or are not re-elected have one quarter of a yearly budget to carry them from October until they leave office in January. Check with the Senate Disbursing Office to confirm exactly what your allocations will be your first year.

The Member's Role in Budgeting

The vast majority of budgeting and financial management decisions can be delegated to staff, but you, the Member, must take an active role in three areas: defining goals and setting guidelines for spending decisions; determining your level of involvement in the financial management of your office; and assembling a financial team.

1. **Goals and Guidelines.** Do you want to use every dollar at your disposal, or do you want to demonstrate maximum economy with the public funds over which you have direct control? Do you want to maintain visibility and a dialogue with your constituents or do you want to focus more energy on Washington-based coalition building and rely on an active press program to keep constituents informed of your activities? These types of decisions are fundamental to budgeting. You have fixed resources. More of one option means less of another. You must provide general guidelines about where you wish your resources to be targeted. No one can do this for you. Your choices here must be consistent with your office goals and, in many cases, will be dictated by them.

2. **Your Involvement.** Do you want to decide which photocopier to buy, or will you leave that decision to staff? Who will set salaries and subsequent merit pay adjustments? How often do you want to be briefed on your office finances? Monthly? Quarterly? You need to delegate, but you also need to establish clear limits on your staff's authority to commit funds for which you ultimately are responsible. We have run across Members whose preferences vary widely on these matters, from those who want to know how every penny is spent, to those who get involved only when big decisions are made.

3. **Your Financial Team.** The less involved you are, the more important your financial team will be. Responsibility and authority for money matters in your office can be divided in any number of ways. It is vital that all parties absolutely understand their responsibilities and their authority. Candidates for membership on your financial team should include the Chief of Staff, the Administrative Director or Office Manager, and the District/State Director. You may also want to consult with other staff on expensive or important purchases, such as with the Systems Administrator for IT-related purchases. Of course, in the two months between the election and opening day, you may have only a few transition aides with which to work. Strongly consider giving one staff person the direct, day-to-day responsibility for managing your office finances.

Although you will delegate specific financial management activities to individual staffers, there are benefits to treating everyone on your staff as part of the financial team. The more staff are involved in the budgeting aspects of the planning process, the more they will understand the trade-offs of each spending decision. A freshman Chief of Staff in a recent Congress, for example, selected a very expensive computer system after seeking staff input. The staff understood that the choice meant either fewer people to help with the constituent correspondence or lower salaries for themselves. Of course, everyone in the office anticipated that using advanced technology would lead to increased staff efficiency.

Your decisions about the three elements discussed above form the foundation for all of the financial decisions that your staff will undertake in your name. After you have established general ground rules and broad strategies, your staff can fine-tune the details of the budget and the financial procedures that will be used to meet House or Senate regulations, and monitor your financial standing.

Developing a First-Year Budget

Your first-year budget will be the hardest to put together. Never again will you have to develop a budget with so little staff support, relevant information, or time. Seasoned veterans advise that it is nearly impossible to develop an accurate, detailed budget until at least six months into your first term. Still, as we discussed earlier, it is important to start putting figures down on paper as soon as possible. We therefore recommend that you follow the most commonly stated advice of Chiefs of Staff: err on the side of caution. With that wisdom in mind, we offer a four-step process for developing a first-year budget: (1) collect expense information; (2) make major allocations; (3) compare major allocations to your strategic plan; and (4) build a month-by-month budget.

Step 1: Collect expense information.

Below is a list of resources that freshman Chiefs of Staff have found useful in compiling data specific to the unique characteristics of their district or state. In addition, Figure 3-1 on the next page lists the average spending by freshman House offices, which may also be useful.

Sources of Office Expense Information

Your predecessor's budget(s). This is the best possible source of information tailored to *your* district/state. Unless a no-holds-barred campaign has completely poisoned relations, your predecessor will likely share his past years' budgets with you. It is important to review more than one year, since

Figure 3-1

Average Spending By Freshman House Offices in 2009

Category	Spending	% of MRA
Franked Mail	$72,381	4.89%
Personnel Compensation	$828,578	55.80%
Personnel Benefits	$907	0.06%
Travel	$59,165	3.98%
District Office Rent, Communication & Utilities	$93,778	6.31%
Printing and Reproduction	$80,877	5.47%
Other Services	$53,904	3.64%
Supplies & Materials	$35,979	2.42%
Equipment	$17,039	1.15%
Average Expenditures	**$1,242,608**	**83.72%**
Unspent Funds	$244,472	16.28%
Total Allocated Funds (Average MRA)	**$1,487,080**	**100.00%**

Note: These figures represent an analysis of the 55 full-year freshman offices' spending in 2009 as reported in the Statement of Disbursements of the House.

---

election year and retiree budgets can differ significantly from off-year budgets or those for non-retirees. This information source can be a gold mine, provided that you understand how your priorities differ from those of your predecessor.

The budget(s) from an adjoining district or similar state. If you cannot obtain your predecessor's budget(s) easily, that of a district or state with similar demographic and geographic characteristics will provide much of the same information.

Statement of Disbursements of the House (compiled by the Chief Administrative Officer) and Report of the Secretary of the Senate. These massive multi-volume official reports, as required by law, publicly disclose every expenditure of every office in detail. The House report is published quarterly (disbursements.house.gov) while the Senate report comes out twice a year.

Combined Airlines Ticket Office (CATO) or Airline Congressional Desks. If none of the preceding sources are helpful for estimating travel expenses, consult the Combined Airlines Ticket Office (CATO) (House: 703-522-2286; Senate: 202-224-5886; www.catotvl.com) or the congressional desks run by most major airlines. You'll need to know how often you plan to travel back to your district/state.

CHAPTER THREE Creating a First-Year Budget

House Information Resources (HIR) and Senate Sergeant at Arms (SAA) Office Support Services. Given the ongoing rapid improvements in technology, computer equipment may be a big ticket purchase during your first year or two. HIR (202-225-6002) and the SAA (202-224-0821) can help you estimate what an upgrade is likely to cost.

Congressional Management Foundation (CMF). CMF, which produced this book, can answer your questions on a range of budgetary and management issues. CMF is an expert on congressional staff compensation and benefits, having produced several reports on House and Senate employees between 1990 and 2004. Contact CMF at 202-546-0100 or cmf@cmfweb.org for guidance.

Outside third parties. Several off-the-Hill organizations, such as the Sunlight Foundation, LegiStorm and the National Taxpayers Union, analyze House and Senate expenditures, using publicly available data from the official House and Senate reports discussed earlier. Their analyses tend to focus on salaries, travel expenses, franked mail, or simply overall spending and receive a good deal of press attention, bringing additional scrutiny on your expenditures.

Step 2: Make major allocations.

With expense information and office goals in hand, your financial team (e.g., Chief of Staff, Administrative Director/Office Manager, and District/State Director) can assign general dollar amounts to major spending categories. By grouping expenses into broad categories, your team can quickly develop a usable budget. It is important that *all* of the people on your financial team participate in this step because they may be able to contribute valuable insights into the allocation process, based on their prior work experiences in Congress or elsewhere. They will also be charged with modifying the budget as necessary during the year.

Working with veteran Chiefs of Staff, we have developed budget worksheets to assist freshman House and Senate offices (see Figures 3-3 and 3-4). Again, because of the differences between the chambers, we'll discuss each separately.

Each **House budget category** has special characteristics that you should bear in mind:

Compensation. By far, your largest expenditure will be for staff salaries. Determine how many staffers will be needed to carry out your strategic plan, which positions are necessary to execute your plan, and what salary ranges will be set for each position. You are limited in the number of staff you may hire (18 permanent and 4 temporary), but you have a great deal of freedom in the salary levels you select. You are constrained only by the national minimum wage and maximum annual staff salary levels ($168,411 in 2009). To

---

MANAGEMENT FACT
Freshman Members spent 84% of their budgets in 2009, approximately $244,472 less than allocated.

Source: Statement of Disbursements of the House

Figure 3-2

Average Salaries of Congressional Staff

House

Washington Office
Chief of Staff	$134,307
Legislative Director	$84,273
Senior Legislative Assistant	$61,622
Press Secretary/Communications Director	$60,452
Office Manager/Executive Assistant	$59,618
Scheduler	$48,110
Legislative Assistant	$45,105
Legislative Correspondent	$35,177
Staff Assistant	$30,521

District Offices
District Director	$85,779
Field Representative	$47,713
Constituent Services Representative/Caseworker	$44,850
Staff Assistant	$30,633

Senate

Washington Office
Chief of Staff	$151,767
Deputy Chief of Staff	$121,571
Legislative Director	$116,952
Counsel	$95,210
Communications Director	$95,050
Administrative Director/Office Manager	$78,266
Executive Assistant	$68,060
Legislative Assistant	$66,789
Press Secretary	$66,027
Scheduler	$63,634
Systems Administrator	$60,955
Director of Special Projects/Grants	$52,995
Assistant Admin Dir/Office Mgr	$43,416
Mailroom Supervisor	$41,443
Deputy Communications Director/Press Secretary	$40,802
Assistant to Chief of Staff	$38,300
Data Entry Clerk/Mailroom Assistant	$33,921
Legislative Correspondent	$32,802
Receptionist/Staff Assistant	$29,664

State Offices
State Director	$104,748
Constituent Services Representative/Caseworker Supervisor	$61,575
Field Representative	$50,742
State Scheduler	$49,886
State Office Manager	$48,639
Constituent Services Representative/Caseworker	$38,631

Source: Chief Administrative Officer's *2009 House Compensation Study* and the Secretary of the Senate's *2006 U.S. Senate Employment, Compensation, Hiring and Benefits Study.*

assist you in setting salaries, the CAO's *House Compensation Study* (found on HouseNet) provides detailed profiles of every typical staff position. The average salaries are provided on the previous page in Figure 3-2. This is also the time to consider organizing your office to share staff with other Members to get specialized experience on a less than full-time basis, such as with a financial specialist or Systems Administrator. In addition, you should take into account that most freshman offices are not fully staffed on swearing-in day. Finally, do not forget to budget for staff overtime pay or bonuses, if applicable (see Chapter 5 for guidance on hiring your core staff).

Franked Mail. Look at your predecessor's budget and determine whether you plan to mail more or less frequently than he or she did. The National Taxpayers Union also publishes data on franking for every House Member. Because many mass mailings involve outside printers and other contract services, don't overlook your "Printing and Reproduction" expenses when budgeting for franked mailings.

Equipment. This category includes computers, computer services, photocopiers, fax machines and similar types of equipment. This category may be the most difficult to estimate because there are so many options. Your computer system is likely to be the largest expense. It may take time for you to develop a feel for Washington and district office work flow and communication needs. Veteran Chiefs of Staff strongly recommend that you talk to several friendly offices in addition to House Information Resources before purchasing equipment (see Chapter 6 for advice on evaluating, purchasing and using information technology in your office).

District Office Rent, Communication and Utilities. The important variables affecting expenditures in this category are the number of offices you will open, the number of staff and interns in each office, typical office rents in your district, whether utilities are included in the rent, and the telecommunications system you choose for your office(s) (see Chapter 7 for information on establishing district offices).

Travel (Member and Staff). Estimate the number of expected trips to your district in accordance with your office objectives. Erring on the side of caution in this case means estimating on the high side — many Members travel home more than 40 times a year. Take into consideration the expenses that are incurred when traveling — hotels, dining, and car rental, to name the most obvious — and budget for the unexpected. Determine how often district staff may need to be in Washington and vice versa. Explore the option of leasing a car for official use rather than constantly using rentals. And finally, remember that special government fares are available to you for official travel; these are usually the cheapest and most flexible options available.

Supplies and Materials. This broad, surprisingly expensive category includes costs as disparate as office supplies, bottled water, food and beverages for meetings with constituents, newspapers, online subscriptions and reference books.

Printing and Reproduction. This category includes newsletters, printing, photography, and other related expenses. As with franking, your best guides are the Statement of Disbursements, your predecessor's budget(s) and the extent to which your plans differ from his practices. You should be aware, however, that the number of variables is quite large. The size of a newsletter, the quality of paper stock, the use of colors in printing, whether you are mailing to all postal patrons in a zip code or are using individual addresses, how much folding and stuffing your staff will do in-house, and many other factors will affect how much you spend in this category. As soon as you have a well-developed communications plan, have your staff produce detailed cost estimates for printing and reproduction, as well as franking.

Other Services. This miscellaneous category includes several relatively small items. Examples of "other services" are: janitors for district offices, news clipping services, room fees for town hall meetings, and staff training.

Returning Money to the Treasury for Debt Reduction. Many Members, to be consistent with their fiscal philosophy or to keep campaign promises, decide to spend less than their entire MRA. If you fall into this category, we encourage you to explicitly include this decision in your budget and set aside the money accordingly. In 2009, freshman Members spent an average of 84 percent of their MRAs, approximately $244,472 less than each was allocated. Note that all MRAs are funded from a single appropriation, so there is not an account at the Treasury with your name on it; all unspent MRA funds are applied as a lump sum toward reducing the national debt. Also note that this debt reduction takes place after three years (the year the funds were authorized plus two additional years when they remain available).

Contingencies. Veteran Chiefs of Staff keep at least $5,000 in reserve; freshmen may want to increase this figure as an extra margin of safety. There has never been a congressional office that had no unforeseen expenses. If every cent is already allocated, you will find yourself with limited options when you encounter a surprise expense. This is especially important to remember at the end of the year, when the only option if an office has overspent its MRA is for the Member to pay the difference from his or her own pocket.

One of the tricks of **Senate office budgeting** is figuring out how best to use your allocations of space, equipment and services so that you can better use your allocations of money. While this makes budgeting in Senate offices a simpler procedure than it is in House offices, it also makes it less of a strategic tool. You don't get to make as many choices, nor do you have to make as many

CHAPTER THREE Creating a First-Year Budget

trade-offs as House offices do. You cannot decide to forgo new state office furniture and use that money instead to make more trips to the state. You cannot decide to forgo replacing your copier machine for one more year so you can give staff bonuses.

Figure 3-3

House Budget Worksheet — Legislative Year 20___

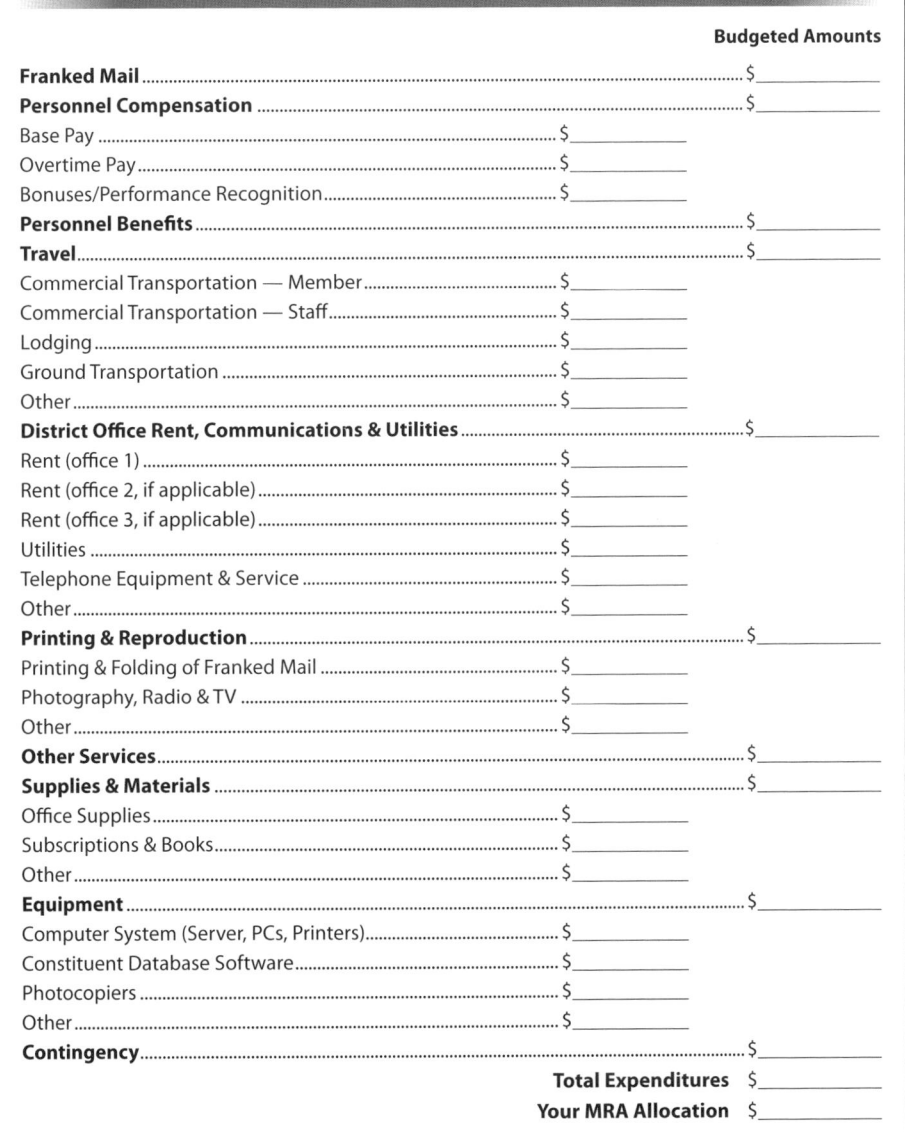

Budgeted Amounts

Franked Mail .... $_____
Personnel Compensation .... $_____
    Base Pay .... $_____
    Overtime Pay .... $_____
    Bonuses/Performance Recognition .... $_____
Personnel Benefits .... $_____
Travel .... $_____
    Commercial Transportation — Member .... $_____
    Commercial Transportation — Staff .... $_____
    Lodging .... $_____
    Ground Transportation .... $_____
    Other .... $_____
District Office Rent, Communications & Utilities .... $_____
    Rent (office 1) .... $_____
    Rent (office 2, if applicable) .... $_____
    Rent (office 3, if applicable) .... $_____
    Utilities .... $_____
    Telephone Equipment & Service .... $_____
    Other .... $_____
Printing & Reproduction .... $_____
    Printing & Folding of Franked Mail .... $_____
    Photography, Radio & TV .... $_____
    Other .... $_____
Other Services .... $_____
Supplies & Materials .... $_____
    Office Supplies .... $_____
    Subscriptions & Books .... $_____
    Other .... $_____
Equipment .... $_____
    Computer System (Server, PCs, Printers) .... $_____
    Constituent Database Software .... $_____
    Photocopiers .... $_____
    Other .... $_____
Contingency .... $_____
                                Total Expenditures $_____
                                Your MRA Allocation $_____

MANAGEMENT FACT
Senate offices spend 75% - 90% of the Senator's Account on salaries.

Source: Report of the Secretary of the Senate

In fact, it is likely that you will spend 75-90 percent of your Senator's Account on staff salaries (see Figure 3-2 for average salaries). As a result, personnel is one of the few areas in which you can really budget strategically. This is where you will make decisions that will fundamentally affect your ability to meet your goals. You will staff your office, and pay salaries, according to the priorities you have set for your term. For example, if one of your goals is to become one of the top Senators on environmental policy, you may want to hire an experienced environmental lawyer as one of your Legislative Assistants, or hire a Legislative Director with environmental experience, or hire several junior staff who studied environmental politics in college (see Chapter 5 for guidance on hiring your core staff).

Another potentially large budget category is travel, especially if your state is far from Washington, DC and doesn't have major air travel hubs. With a larger staff and more territory to cover than a House Member, staff travel, as well as your own, will likely take up a good portion of the budget.

It is also important to remember that the Senate budget runs on a fiscal year rather than a calendar year. Although the last month of your first-year budget is September, it is likely that some of the choices you make will commit your office through December. You may want to start a separate, second-year budget now to evaluate the long-term impact of your decisions.

Figure 3-4

Senate Budget Worksheet — Fiscal Year 20___

	Budgeted Amount
Salaries	$_____
Senator's Travel	$_____
Staff Travel	$_____
Additional Telecommunications Equipment and Services	$_____
Additional Office Equipment	$_____
Stationery Room Certifications	$_____
Books, Newspapers, Magazines, and Online Information Services	$_____
Recording & Photography	$_____
Stationery & Other Office Supplies	$_____
Postage Certifications	$_____
Recording & Photo Studio Certifications	$_____
Franked Mail Certifications	$_____
Mass Mail Certifications	$_____
Other Official Expenses	$_____
Unallocated Funds	$_____
Total	$_____

Step 3: Compare major allocations to your strategic plan.

Now that you have a rough budget, compare it with your allowances and your goals. Have you over-budgeted? Is the plan too ambitious for the available resources? This step is important in adjusting the plan to financial realities, further clarifying priorities, or developing creative ideas to meet your goals more economically. You may find that a major overhaul of your budget or plan is necessary or that just a few adjustments will do the trick. (A list of cost-saving and budgeting tips can be found in Chapter 12.)

If you are still over-budgeted after using the cost-saving tips and other minor adjustments, here are some guidelines for doing what is necessary, whether it's an overhaul of your budget or of your goals.

1. **Involve your entire financial team.**
2. **Look for creative ways to meet your goals.** For example, could you achieve your district/state outreach goal by locating your Press Secretary in the district/state, instead of hiring an extra Field Representative at $46,000? Several House offices have done this because the Press Secretary can generate more local press by being in the district. Evaluate the benefits of these types of moves against the costs (e.g., loss of access to the Member and the legislative process). A Member may want to be involved in this creative budgeting process by reviewing a list of alternatives for achieving office goals.
3. **If you cannot find creative ways to meet your goals within budget, you will need to reassess your goals.** See Chapter 11, "Strategic Planning in Your Office," for information on how to do this, especially the section on "Evaluating Potential Goals." It is obvious that a Member must be personally involved in this very important process.

Step 4: Build a month-by-month budget.

Finally, your office should allocate your budgeted expenditures month-by-month. Estimate as best you can when periodic expenses will be incurred, in addition to providing for fixed items that will appear each month. Each month, this process will yield the following: monthly expenditure figures, year-to-date expenditures, committed funds figures, and a net balance. This is one of the most valuable steps in the budgeting process because you are creating a means of determining if you are on the right financial track as the year progresses. This comprises the early warning system that can prevent end-of-the-year horror stories.

After completing these four steps, you will have a basic budget to guide you through the year. In one of your early staff meetings in January, we recommend that you share this information with the entire staff. The budget is an integral part of your office plans and will affect the way in which the staff is expected to conduct the business of the Member. Giving your staff knowledge of the financial structure of the office has four benefits: (1) it will clarify what the Member intends to accomplish this term; (2) it will clarify the staff's role in achieving the Member's goals; (3) it will give staff a greater sense of ownership and accountability in meeting the goals; and (4) it may generate cost-saving ideas from staff.

Veteran Office Advice on Developing a First-Year Budget

This last section contains advice on putting together a first-year budget that we've picked up from veteran Chiefs of Staff and Office Managers. Suggestions listed first apply to both House and Senate offices. The ones that follow are divided into those which may be useful to one specific chamber.

Advice for House and Senate Offices

Learn the rules and regulations, and when in doubt, ask for help. This seems like basic advice, but sometimes the rules are counterintuitive. When one Senate Office Manager tried to submit a voucher for bottled water in a state office, he discovered the expense could not be paid because the "cooler" also provided hot water. Availability of hot water meant hot beverages could be served, and hot beverages in the Senate count as non-reimbursable food expenses. The solution was to turn off the hot water option.

Keep your options open when it comes to spending leftover funds. Many offices have a multi-purpose cushion fund that can be used for contingencies, to pay off computer equipment, stock up on supplies at the end of the year, to give staff year-end bonuses or performance awards, or simply to be left unspent. Each option has benefits: paying off computers frees up money in the next year; giving staff bonuses could boost morale; not spending your entire allowance can be trumpeted in a press release.

Still, it's a good idea to have some proposals in mind ahead of time as the year draws to a close or you'll be, as one Chief of Staff put it, "scrambling right before Christmas trying to figure out how to buy $20,000 in office supplies or whether to give your staff another round of bonuses." Remember, you use it or lose it.

Get to know the employees of the House Finance Office and Senate Disbursing Office, especially the ones assigned to work with your office. They know the tricks of the trade.

CHAPTER THREE Creating a First-Year Budget

Use the buddy system. Almost every staff member with whom we spoke recommended that a new office team up with a friendly veteran office to help get them through the first year. There are also House and Senate staff associations which can help.

Estimate your transportation costs as soon as possible. Distance from Washington does not always correlate with transportation costs. For example, roundtrip airfare from DC to a hub such as Los Angeles is generally less expensive than DC to a smaller market such as Mobile, Alabama.

Budget at the highest level of detail that still allows you to keep sight of the big picture. For instance, a single budget category called "subscriptions" may not provide enough information to help you decide whether to subscribe to a news service online or in hard copy. Breaking it down into subcategories to get a sense of how much each format costs will help you weigh the advantages of each. But don't go overboard. You could probably divide telephone service or transportation into a dozen or more subcategories, but there is a point where the extra information is not worth the time to put it together.

Advice for House Offices

District offices are expensive. Research what it takes to run a district office before you commit to one. More than one office has been surprised by unanticipated costs. Remember that you will pay for virtually everything associated with a district office out of your MRA. And once you open a district office, it may be politically and contractually difficult to shut it down.

Pay attention to freshman specials that won't last. One budgeter recalled, "We had budgeted $20,000 for publications, but we didn't realize that the price for one subscription was an introductory offer. I about died when the next year we had to fork out an additional $12,000 we hadn't budgeted for."

Advice for Senate Offices

Learn all you can about allocations of things to which your office is entitled. Don't make the mistake made by one office of buying copier paper when the paper allotment may give you millions of sheets.

Purchase computer equipment out of the Senator's Account in the first year, when there is likely to be an office surplus, rather than deplete your Economic Allocation Fund, which has to last several years.

Decide early if you're going to send out mass mailings and whether you'll spend up to the $50,000 franking limit. One Office Manager told us a story of a Senator who decided to use this money for priorities other than franking. She continued, "Then one day the Senator walked out and said, 'I think we'll do some mass mailings.' I said, 'What?!?' That money was already committed for someone's salary."

MANAGEMENT FACT
Managers must be ready for changes to office budgets, even after they've been "finalized." Government shutdowns, mid-year rescission bills, and end-of-year continuing resolutions all can change budget allocations.

Pay close attention to budgeting in August. August is near the end of the fiscal year and the time of a traditional month-long congressional recess when a lot of staff travel to the home state takes place. Don't let surprise travel expenses upset the budget.

Be aware that changes in allocations can influence the rest of your budget. Let's say that the Senate decides to make a popular $5,000 per year information service standard (that is, the product will be made available to all Senators, and the Senate as an institution rather than individual Senators will pick up the tab). It may follow that every office budget is cut $5,000 the following year, which is just fine for offices which had been paying for the service that is now "free." But if your office made the strategic choice to use that money elsewhere, you will be down $5,000. It's tough to predict these changes, but at least be aware that they can occur.

Conclusion

Creating a budget is more than simply learning the House or Senate rules, although this is important. It's more than making sure you don't overspend, although that too is essential. Budgeting also means translating your office goals — the reasons you wanted to serve and what you intend to achieve while you're here — into tangible assets which are capable of achieving those goals. It involves balancing needs, alternatives and trade-offs — in other words, making all the pieces fit together. It leaves open the possibility that your list of goals is too ambitious and needs to be modified.

It is certainly possible for a freshman to survive his or her first term without putting together a budget during the first 60 days following the election. You'll have access to your office resources on opening day whether or not you've planned how you will spend them. But we don't recommend this ad hoc approach. Devoting the time during the first 60 days to create a first-year budget will allow you to make more informed decisions on hiring staff, opening district/state offices, purchasing computer equipment and other critical, early tasks. That, in turn, will contribute to a more successful first term.

Chapter Summary
The DOs and DON'Ts of
Creating a First-Year Budget

Do...

- **spend the time to write a first-year budget** before making decisions on management structure, core staff, district/state offices, and technology.

- **learn the rules and regulations for House and Senate allowances, and when in doubt, ask for help.** Develop good working relationships with staff from the House Finance or Senate Disbursing Offices, who know the tricks of the trade.

- **determine the Member's involvement** in financial management, and how responsibilities and authority will be delegated to staff on the financial team.

- **create a first-year budget by:**
  1. collecting expense information;
  2. making major allocations;
  3. comparing major allocations to your office goals;
  4. building a month-by-month budget.

- **have a plan for spending leftover funds.** Consider your goals for the next year so you aren't scrambling to spend funds at the end of the year.

Don't...

- **make commitments that might have financial repercussions** for staff or constituents without first devising a rough budget.

- **forget to set aside reserve funds** — particularly in your first year — to handle unforeseen expenses.

- **overspend the office budget.** If the office goes over budget, you must personally pay the difference.

- **forget that as an elected official, your expenditures are public information and are easily found online.** Spend appropriately.

CHAPTER FOUR

Creating a Management Structure and a System for Communicating with the Member

This Chapter Includes...

- ☆ The most common management structures used on Capitol Hill
- ☆ The advantages and disadvantages of each management model
- ☆ Guidance for designing a system for Member-staff communications

For a freshman office to operate effectively, staff and the Member must have a clear, shared understanding of how the office operates. How will decisions be made in this office? Who has decision-making authority and over what issues? Who supervises whom? How should staff communicate with the Member and the Member communicate with the staff?

Many freshman offices are inclined to let the answers to these questions evolve over the first term with little direction. Over time, the thinking goes, the Member's operating style emerges and the office can then cobble together a management structure and communication system that reflects these preferences. We believe this is a mistake for several reasons.

First, lack of clarity early on will create staff confusion and encourage freelancing, which in turn will impair office productivity and blur lines of accountability. Staff should not be left to figure out on their own "how the place works" and how they should operate. Second, basing an office's management structure and communications practices solely on the Member's preferences will likely not result in a productive work environment. Many Members will choose practices that are familiar and comfortable to them but make the office inefficient and ineffective. Finally, decisions about how you want the office to function should influence, and therefore precede, your early hiring decisions. For these reasons, freshman offices should carefully address and decide these operational issues in the first 60 days.

Selecting a Management Structure

The term "management structure" is a catch-all phrase generally describing the structure an organization uses to manage its operations and oversee each employee.

Larger public and private organizations frequently depict their management structure visually in an organizational chart that shows the hierarchy used to manage the organization. While few congressional offices draft such diagrams, the questions of authority, responsibility, and accountability are central to their operations as well. Consequently, the subject deserves careful consideration by Members and management staff. Specifically, freshman offices need to address basic structural questions such as:

- What role will the Member play in office management?
- Who will report directly to the Member?
- Who will report directly to the Chief of Staff (CoS)?
- Who will report directly to the District/State Director (DD/SD)?
- Will the DD/SD report directly to the Member or to the CoS?
- Will the House LD supervise the LAs or simply provide them guidance when needed?
- Will the Senate LD supervise the LCs or will that function be left to another supervisor?
- Should the office hire a Deputy CoS or Deputy DD/SD to help manage the office or can an Office Manager or Administrative Director assist with these duties?
- Which other staff will have supervisory responsibilities?
- Which, if any, staff will report directly to more than one person? (e.g., Member and CoS)
- Will the district/state offices be managed by region (or geography) or by function (e.g., casework vs. outreach vs. Member schedule and travel)?

The answers to these questions should influence your early hiring decisions. For example, will you hire as District/State Director the person with the best political skills or must this hire also have good management skills? The answer to this question should be partially based on how you choose to structure your district/state offices and if the Chief of Staff or the District/State Director is responsible for managing the district/state offices. In selecting your Legislative Director (LD), the relative importance of management skills should be determined on the basis of what management duties the LD will be expected to assume. Similarly, you may choose one Press Secretary over another because your Chief of Staff wants to supervise this activity and one of your candidates insists on reporting solely to the Member.

The answers to these questions will also quickly shape the way your office operates. And once patterns are established, whether through clear deliberation or benign neglect, they are very difficult to change. It is very difficult and painful to take responsibility away from staff once they become comfortable with their duties. Similarly, it is difficult to persuade a Member that decisions that she has become accustomed to making should now be decided without her input. So, make these decisions carefully and deliberately.

A Review of Personal Office Structures

There is no single best organizational structure. The key is to select one that best suits the mission, goals and personnel of the office, taking into account the management styles of the Member, the Chief of Staff, and the District/State Director; their respective management skills; the demands on the Member's time; the experience of the staff; and the amount of supervisory attention and oversight needed.

House and Senate offices tend to use three basic management structures, though a number of offices create hybrids from these main types. This section describes these structures from most to least centralized, and the advantages and disadvantages of each (summarized in Figure 4-4). This analysis should help freshman Members and their senior management staff determine which structure is best suited to their office. Veteran offices can also use this discussion to analyze their present structure and identify possible ways of improving their operation.

The most common structure in both the House and Senate is the centralized model (Figure 4-1). *The vast majority of House and Senate offices* use management structures that resemble this model. This model has all staff reporting to the Chief of Staff, with the Chief of Staff reporting to the Member. In this model, other staff also may report directly to the Member. However, its defining characteristic is that the Chief of Staff has a great deal of responsibility for managing the office.

Figure 4-1

Model 1: Centralized Structure

MEMBER

COMMUNICATIONS DIRECTOR

OFFICE MANAGER

SCHEDULER

CHIEF OF STAFF

LEGISLATIVE DIRECTOR

DISTRICT/STATE DIRECTOR

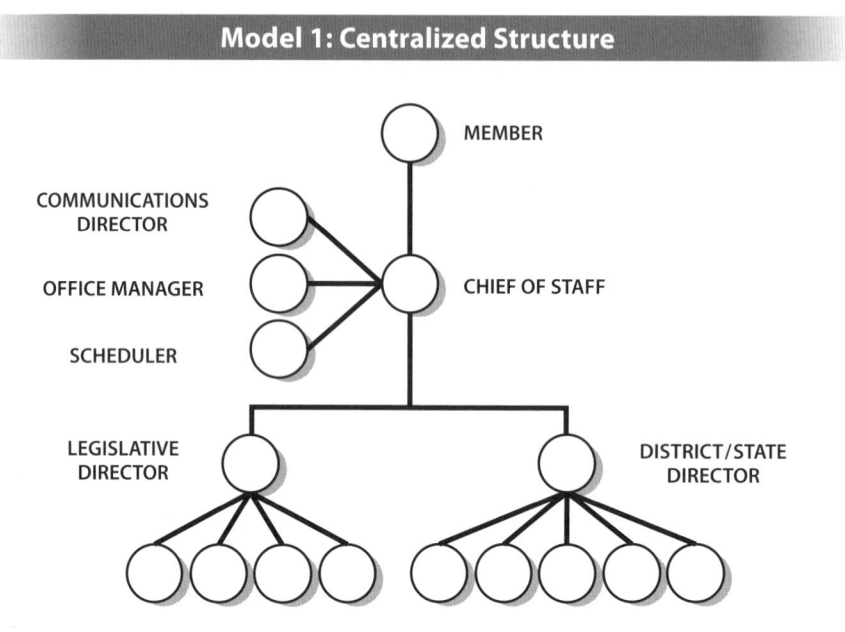

This model has several advantages that explain why it is so commonly used. First, it is simple and clear. If the Member or staff has a question, needs clarification, or has a problem, it is abundantly clear who they should see about it. Second, because virtually all relevant office information flows to the Chief of Staff, it allows one person to efficiently coordinate the activities of the entire staff. Third, by making the Chief of Staff the office gatekeeper, this model provides well-controlled access to the Member, thus protecting the Member from unnecessary interruptions and allowing him to focus on Member-only activities.

However, CMF has found through its research that this model has some clear drawbacks to consider. First, such a structure places a tremendous burden on Chiefs of Staff. Few are actually capable of staying on top of all of the office activities and supervising all of the staff. Consequently, success using this structure tends to require a Chief of Staff with very good management and interpersonal skills, and a good, experienced staff that requires minimal assistance and supervision. This combination is unusual in congressional offices. Second, this structure makes the Member and the office very dependent on one staff person. If the Chief of Staff leaves the office, it may be difficult to find a replacement capable of immediately and comfortably taking over the job. Third, this model tends to make it more difficult for a district/state staff person to effectively represent the Member

CHAPTER FOUR   Creating a Management Structure and a System for
                Communicating with the Member

back home. Under this model, there is no district/state staffer with ready access to the Member or the authority needed to make decisions. For some offices this is a liability; for others it is insignificant. Fourth, this centralized structure can sharply limit staff access to the Member if the Chief of Staff chooses to take on the role of staff liaison, which often hurts staff morale.

The parity structure (Figure 4-2) is used by *17 percent of House offices and several Senate offices.* Under this structure, all of the Washington staff generally report to the Chief of Staff while all of the district or state staff report to the District/State Director. The defining characteristic of this model is that the Chief of Staff and District/State Director share responsibility for the management of the office and each reports directly to the Member. They generally decide which other staff meet with the Member and when.

This model has several strengths: First, decentralizing authority allows for shared management responsibilities within the office, which can result in greater management oversight and control. Second, it provides the District/State Director with authority to actively and visibly represent the Member in the district/state. For some offices, this is especially desirable if the District/State Director is politically savvy and has close ties to the community, and the Chief of Staff is not from the district or state. Third, it provides controlled staff access to the Member by using the Chief of Staff and District/State Director as gatekeepers.

The model also has some weaknesses. First, unless the Chief of Staff and District/State Director work well together, this model can lead to competing agendas, conflicts between managers, and competition among staff. Second,

Figure 4-2

Model 2: Washington–District/State Parity Structure

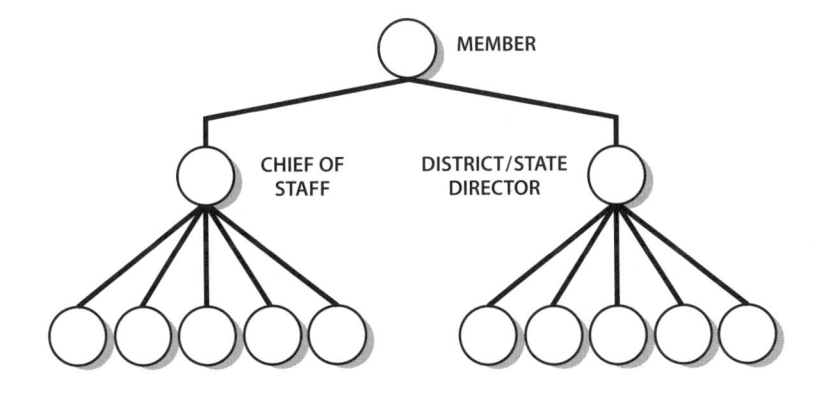

this model, like the centralized model, can limit staff access to the Member if the Chief of Staff and District/State Director choose to be the primary liaisons for their respective offices.

The functional structure (Figure 4-3) is used by *9 percent of House offices and several Senate offices.* In this model, all staff responsible for independent functions of the office report directly to the Member. Thus, the Member may

Figure 4-3

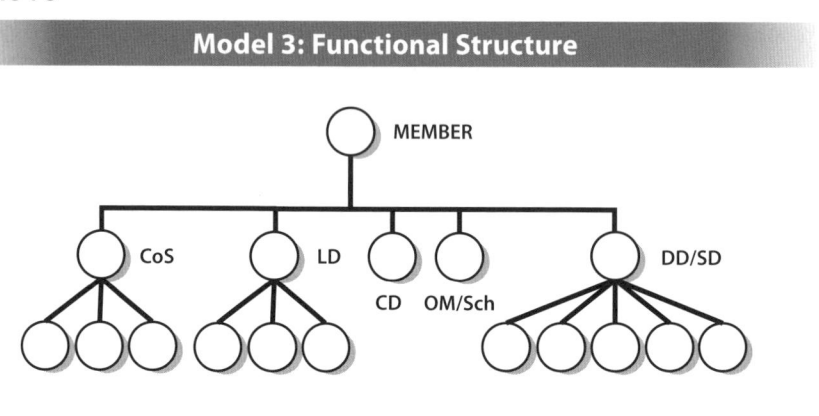

Model 3: Functional Structure

have as many as five direct reports: the Chief of Staff, District/State Director, Legislative Director, Communications Director, and maybe even the Scheduler or Office Manager. In this structure, however, the Chief of Staff usually retains responsibility for the overall management of the office. Thus, the other functional heads generally report both to the Member as well as to the Chief of Staff.

On its face, this structure makes sense. It creates a group of managers, each responsible for his or her functional areas, and thus reduces office bureaucracy and the dissemination of information from one level to the next. It also provides those Members who want to keep track of office activities ample opportunities to do so, while providing some limits on staff access. This structure can also foster the development of a management team, which reduces the Member's reliance on any single person.

For this structure to work well, the office must have a Chief of Staff who is comfortable working collaboratively with the other management staff. The Chief of Staff's power and effectiveness in this structure does not come from his or her position in the hierarchy, but from the ability to earn the respect and trust of the other function heads.

The primary downside of this structure is that it is more complex than the others and requires more attention and maintenance. Because several staff share responsibility and accountability, the Chief of Staff and functional heads must work hard to ensure that office activities are properly coordinated. Failure to coordinate creates confusion and mistakes due to unclear and overlapping responsibilities. In addition, this structure places greater management responsibilities on the Member than does either of the other two — responsibilities that Members frequently find they cannot or do not want to manage.

Finally, *7 percent of House offices and several Senate offices follow "other" structures,* typically combinations or hybrids of these basic models. Due to their larger staff sizes and the number of state offices they manage, Senate offices have more options and flexibility when defining their management structure. The occurrence of hybrid models illustrates the need for managers to carefully consider the pros and cons of each structure (summarized in Figure 4-4) and implement a structure that best meets the needs of the office.

Once a management structure has been selected, every staffer must clearly understand how the office will operate and how decisions will be made, including the chain of command and the expectations for, and responsibilities of, each manager and employee. Equally important, offices should expect to make modifications in the structure based on first-year feedback about what is working and what is not, what is clear and what is causing confusion.

The consequences of not selecting a management structure, or not defining it to employees, can cause significant problems in staff productivity and morale. CMF has found that when offices have not clearly defined or communicated their office structure, the managerial role essentially defaults to the Member. Any staff person with a decision to make must see the boss.

" The consequences of not selecting a management structure, or not defining it to employees, can cause significant problems in staff productivity and morale."

The obvious disadvantages of this situation far outweigh the advantages. Staff access is maximized, but usually at the expense of effective office coordination and order. Members tend to develop good working relations with their staffs, but are overwhelmed by the work they take upon themselves. In short, this situations tends to lead, at best, to controlled chaos.

For these reasons, CMF recommends that the Member play a minimal role in managing day-to-day operations. As leader of the office, he or she should be heavily involved in setting the overall direction, strategy and goals of the office and should be consulted on all major decisions. However, the Member should leave the daily operational decisions to key management staff.

Figure 4-4

Pros and Cons of Management Structures

Model	Basic Characteristics	Advantages	Disadvantages
Centralized Structure	• All staff report to CoS • Only CoS reports to the Member • CoS has a great deal of responsibility for managing the office	• Simple and clear • Allows one person to efficiently coordinate the activities of the entire staff • Provides well-controlled access to the Member	• Large burden on CoS • Requires CoS with strong management and interpersonal skills and best for experienced staff who need minimal assistance and supervision • Very dependent on one staff person • More difficult for district/state staff to effectively represent the Member back home • Limits staff access to the Member
Washington–District / State Parity Structure	• CoS and DD/SD share responsibility for the management of the office • Each reports directly to the Member • CoS and DD/SD generally decide which other staff meet with the Member and when	• Allows management responsibilities to be shared within the office • Provides the DD/SD with authority to actively and visibly represent the Member in the district/state • Provides controlled staff access to the Member by using the CoS and DD/SD as gatekeepers	• Can lead to competing agendas, conflicts between managers and competition among staff • Can limit staff access to the Member
Functional Structure	• All functional heads report directly to the Member • CoS usually maintains office management responsibility	• Reduces office bureaucracy and the relaying of information • Provides Members opportunities to more closely track activities • Develops a management team, making office less dependent on one person	• Complex and requires more attention and maintenance • Shared responsibilities require proper coordination • Increased management responsibilities on the Member • Requires CoS committed to collaboration with the other management staff

CHAPTER FOUR   Creating a Management Structure and a System for Communicating with the Member

Designing a System for Member–Staff Communications

One of the most important issues facing all personal offices is how to effectively manage Member-staff communications because, in Congress, access to the Member is power. Areas which must be addressed include:

- What should be communicated in writing and what should be communicated orally?
- Which matters should be brought to the Member's attention and which can be handled by the Chief of Staff or LD?
- Should someone in the office play the role of gatekeeper and screen staff requests for time with the Member, or should your office maximize staff access to the Member?
- Should the Member meet with staff individually or in small groups (which could affect the total number of meetings the Member will attend)?
- Who should initiate most meetings — Member or staff?
- Should the purpose of Member-staff meetings be to convey information, engage in analysis, or both?

These issues are vitally important because information is the lifeblood of a Member in Congress, and most of it comes from the staff — the Member's eyes and ears. Staff who have regular access to the Member can operate more effectively than staff who have to wait days to get Member input. In addition, the methods that evolve for managing the Member-staff communications will significantly shape the way the office functions and its organizational culture (see Chapter 10, "The Member's Role as Leader of the Office" in Part II).

For example, we have found through our work that Members who tend to meet primarily with staff individually throughout the day tend to create offices that discourage teamwork. Everyone has projects they are working on with the Member, and no one is responsible for or capable of coordinating all of the activities or identifying issues in which working collaboratively makes more sense than working individually. In offices in which the "open-door" policy is the predominant method of communication, Members often face an above average workload, while the work and authority of the Chief of Staff and LD is diminished.

Offices that communicate with the Member largely in writing tend to be less creative than offices that regularly kick around ideas with the boss. On the other hand, these writing-oriented offices also tend to free up more time for the Member to pursue other important activities like reading and reflecting, meeting with other Members, or getting home earlier and spending more time with the family.

Although the system by which offices manage communication is critical, most offices give little active thought to the subject. Instead, communication practices tend to evolve over time without directly addressing the question: What communication practices best suit the needs of our office?

Often, freshman Members just hang out their shingles in early January, and begin operating and interacting with their staffs in the manner in which they are most comfortable. Members' styles of communicating are usually a melding of their general preferences (e.g., hates interruptions, prefers to talk rather than read) and previous experiences. The problem is that communication habits that prevailed in the large law firm, the family business, or the state legislature may not serve the Member well in his congressional office.

This section will help you analyze your communication practices and design a Member-staff communication system that most effectively meets your needs and those of your staff.

The Member Binder

Many congressional offices create standardized binders for their Member—one for workdays (provided the night before) and one for the weekend. The contents typically include the Member's current schedule, upcoming floor and committee action, background materials, legislative and informational memos, constituent mail to approve, personal notes to be drafted, and the latest news/press from the district/state. ■

Methods of Communication

There are six primary communication methods used in congressional personal offices:

1. Open-door or unscheduled meetings initiated by staff
2. One-on-one meetings initiated by the Member
3. One-on-one appointments scheduled by the staff
4. Group meetings
5. Written communications (primarily memos, notes, and faxes from district and state offices)
6. E-mail

Freshman Members and their Chiefs of Staff should devise a Member-staff communication system for their offices that addresses our 10 objectives (next page) and uses a full range of these communication methods. Each method has strengths when used in moderation but shows weaknesses when overused.

For example, a Member who insists that most communication from staff should come in writing to her through the Chief of Staff will effectively meet several of the key objectives: ensuring important information gets to the Member; screening out unnecessary information; creating regular and

CHAPTER FOUR Creating a Management Structure and a System for Communicating with the Member

Communication Objectives

1. Essential information deserving of Member attention gets to the Member.

2. Information that doesn't require the Member's attention is handled by others.

3. Staff has sufficient access to the Member to effectively represent the Member.

4. Staff convey simple, factual information to the Member quickly and concisely.

5. Opportunities for creative and analytic thinking when appropriate (e.g., problem-solving, brainstorming, strategizing — not just exchanging information).

6. Meetings between the Member and staff efficiently utilize the Member's time.

7. Rapport, trust, and good working relations are built between the Member and the staff.

8. The Member responds to staff requests for input and decisions promptly and effectively.

9. Relevant decisions or important information discussed with the Member reaches other relevant staff when appropriate (e.g., Chief of Staff, Scheduler).

10. The Member and Chief of Staff have opportunities to clarify expectations and provide both positive and constructive feedback to staff about their performances. ∎

reliable communication routines. If this is the primary mode of Member-staff communication, however, it will fail to meet several of the other objectives: allowing staff sufficient personal access; allowing staff to communicate basic information quickly; and permitting creative, analytic meetings.

On the other hand, an open-door policy that encourages unscheduled meetings will maximize staff accessibility, improve morale and foster in-depth, analytic discussions. If relied on predominantly, this method runs the risk of not screening out non-essential, non-urgent matters, potentially overwhelming the Member with information and taking up too much of the Member's time.

Additionally, it excludes supervising staff (e.g., Chief of Staff, LD) from the information loop, thus harming office coordination and generally weakening the office's management. Similarly, group meetings can encourage teamwork, provide staff access to the Member and foster analytic discussions, but can be very time-consuming and inefficient in getting the Member essential information.

Finding the right balance for your office will require regular review. After a few months, make an assessment by asking these questions:

- Which methods are most used by your office? Might they be over-utilized?
- Which methods are rarely used? Might they be under-utilized?
- Which specific communication objectives do your present practices meet effectively?
- Which specific key communication objectives are not effectively met given your present practices?
- What changes would enhance your Member-staff communications?

General Advice for Designing Your Communication System

In designing a system for your office, there are several key points you should keep in mind:

First, employ a full range of methods to create more effective communications. As we stated earlier, Members tend to over-rely on one or two of these methods to the overall detriment of good Member-staff communications. House Members tend to over-utilize open-door policies. It is the simplest practice to put into place because it requires no "system." Just leave the door open and let staff who have questions walk in. It also tends to be stylistically preferable to many House Members who are uncomfortable putting barriers between themselves and their staffs. But Members who grow frustrated with the amount of time they spend in meetings with staff frequently take drastic measures to solve the problem — like terminating their open-door practices. Unfortunately, this solution only creates a new set of problems. Instead, Members could reduce open-door access to one to two hours a day at regular times.

In contrast, Senate offices, because they are bigger, tend to discourage open-door policies and Member meetings with staff and, instead, over-rely on written communication. Consequently, Senate offices tend to be far more formal. Senators are often too sheltered from their staffs, and staff are often frustrated with the cumbersome communication practices, lack of access, and lack of understanding of their boss' needs and preferences. In fact, one Senate Chief of Staff recently told us, "the number one thing staff complain to me about is lack of access to the Member."

> *"The number one thing staff complain to me about is lack of access to the Member."*
> — *Senate Chief of Staff*

Conducting Effective Meetings

1 **Meet at regularly scheduled times** when possible so that the effort of securing a time that works for everyone does not have to occur each week.

2 **Designate a meeting facilitator.** Most Chiefs of Staff believe that it is more effective for them to run a meeting than for the Member.

3 **Have a clear purpose** (e.g. information-sharing, coordination, problem-solving). Without it, meetings try to accomplish too much, go too long and diminish the energy of the participants.

4 **Operate from a written agenda** so everyone knows what is to be discussed. Whenever possible, distribute it in advance to allow staff to prepare.

5 **Establish a starting and ending time (and stick to it!).** Ideally, each agenda item would also have a starting time, which requires the facilitator to think through how long the meeting should take.

6 **Inform staff of their responsibilities ahead of time** (bringing their calendars, briefing other staff on relevant issues, note-taking, etc.).

7 **Everyone should participate but no one should dominate.** Staff comments and questions should be encouraged so the meeting is not just about top-down management direction.

8 **Adhere to a standardized format.** If staff understand the format and what is expected of them, the meetings will operate more efficiently.

9 **End by summarizing the results and next steps.** Review who is going to do what by when. Afterward, promptly circulate this summary to all staff, including the major topics discussed, decisions made and assignments.

10 **Assess their effectiveness.** Even effective formats can grow tiresome over time. Ask staff for feedback and suggestions that would improve future meetings. ■

Second, draft a memo that specifies how the office intends to manage Member-staff communications. Don't allow practices to just evolve over time. Freshman offices should specify in writing *before* the end of January:

- Which matters or issues should be put in writing before being submitted to the Member for comment or decision?
- What types of matters should be taken up during the Member's open-door time and which should be handled through other means?
- How often the Member will meet with the legislative staff, and what the objectives are for these meetings?
- What types of Member-staff meetings the Chief of Staff, LD and/or Press Secretary should attend?

The entire staff and the Member should comment on, discuss and eventually agree on the points in the memo.

Third, evenly enforce the agreed-upon ground rules and practices. Members cannot expect their Chiefs of Staff to manage an orderly office when the Member breaks the rules regularly. Staff who neglect to go through channels must be reminded by the Chief of Staff and especially by the Member of the ground rules. Of course, real crises and urgent matters do occur in congressional offices that will occasionally require setting aside the agreed-upon practices. That is to be expected. But offices must police themselves to make sure that not every unexpected event is turned into a crisis justifying a disregard for the office's communication practices.

Finally, conduct regular office-wide discussions about your communications to identify problems and consider ways of fine-tuning the system to address them. It is almost impossible to get this balance right on the first try, but through discussions an office can create a system that meets everyone's needs.

Conclusion

This chapter has provided freshman offices guidance on designing an office management structure and a Member-staff communication system. Both of these tasks should be undertaken in the first 60 days after your election. Addressing these decisions in November or December will allow your office to make better hiring decisions and provide clarity to you and your staff about how the office is to operate. This will help your office get off to a good start. It will enhance productivity and morale, promote accountability and instill a sense of professionalism throughout the organization. Delaying these decisions will invite problems and the development of ad hoc practices and expectations that will be difficult to change down the road.

CHAPTER FOUR — Creating a Management Structure and a System for Communicating with the Member

Chapter Summary
The DOs and DON'Ts of
Creating a Management Structure and a System for Communicating with the Member

Do...

- **address basic questions in management structure, such as:**
  - what role should the Member play in the management of the office?
  - who will report directly to the Member?
  - who will report directly to the Chief of Staff?
  - who will report to whom (don't forget about the district/state office staff)?
- **create a management structure** that reflects the styles and abilities of the Member, Chief of Staff, and District/State Director and takes into account the office's mission, goals and personnel.
- **design a system of Member-staff communications that employs a range of methods.**
- **conduct regular office-wide discussions to fine tune the communication system.**
- **create a monitoring system or establish a checklist to track all requests requiring the Member's attention.**

Don't...

- **let the office management structure and methods of communicating** between staff and Member "just evolve" over your first term.
- **base an office management structure solely on the Member's preferences.** Many Members will choose procedures comfortable to them, which may not necessarily be good management practices.
- **cut off access to the Member completely, but preserve the Member's time for high-value activities.** As the most valuable resource in the office, the Member's time should be spent wisely.
- **neglect to include in your communications procedures a system for creative and analytic work.** Problem-solving, brainstorming, and strategizing require time.
- **ignore the importance of regular, well-run staff meetings.** Have a clear purpose and written agenda for each meeting. Establish firm starting and ending times.
- **overlook district/state office staff when developing communications and access procedures.** They also need conduits for communicating with the Member.

CHAPTER FIVE

Hiring Your Core Staff

This Chapter Includes...

☆ The pressures new Members face to hire staff quickly

☆ The benefits of hiring only a core staff in November and December

☆ The office functions that a core staff need to perform and the number of staffers needed to perform them

☆ The importance of fitting your core staff to the mission and goals of your office

☆ Hiring the rest of your staff

☆ A process for interviewing and hiring candidates

New Members are under enormous pressure to hire a full staff as soon as possible, and they frequently try to assemble that staff in the two months between the election and swearing-in day. The results are often poor hiring choices that do not contribute to the Member's success, as well as a neglect of other critical tasks which must be accomplished before swearing-in day. The long-term effects can be low staff cohesion and morale, staff talents which do not match office needs and priorities, high staff turnover and wasted resources in hiring and training new staff.

This chapter lays out an alternative approach that we believe will help you assemble an office team capable of achieving your goals. We believe Members-elect should interview and offer jobs in November and December only to a core staff who will be in place on opening day to perform the essential functions of a congressional office. Individuals should be hired who can become part of the larger office team dedicated to achieving your office goals. The remainder of your staff should then be hired when you have finalized your goals and you have the time and resources necessary to hire the right candidates.

Note: For specific legal guidance on interviewing and hiring, contact the Office of the House Employment Counsel (202-225-7075) and the Senate Chief Counsel for Employment (202-224-5424).

Importance of Hiring Only a Core Staff in November and December

Members-elect frequently believe they must put together a full staff as quickly as possible. They may fill typical office "positions" from a list compiled by talking with veteran Members. They will hire eager campaign workers, long-time friends, business partners or the first experienced Hill staffer that walks through the door, all with a vague notion that "we'll find places for them somewhere." And they do all of this before they even take the oath of office.

The pressures you face are real and should not be ignored. But if you hire too many staff too soon, you may find that you've squandered precious time and resources during the transition that were needed for other tasks. Moreover, you may find that you've assembled a staff that lacks certain skills critical to the pursuit of your goals.

Pressures to Hire a Full Staff Quickly

There are a number of reasons why Members-elect feel the need to hire their entire staff in November and December. Some are quite altruistic and sincere. For instance, Members might value staff to such an extent that they fear highly qualified candidates will be snatched by other offices if they aren't hired right away.

Freshmen may also have very high expectations for their first terms, and believe that having a full staff is absolutely essential in order to "hit the ground running." The media and constituents back home may contribute to these expectations. They may be looking for signs that their freshman is preparing well for the rigors of representing the district or state.

New Members may also hire quickly in an effort to stop the flood of job requests from all those eager to become part of the new team. After an election, a new Member can expect to hear from friends, supporters, campaign staff, business partners, experienced Hill staff who work for defeated or retiring Members and countless others looking for jobs (2,000 resumes is not unheard of). It's not comfortable to have to put off supporters and campaign staff who worked long hours and demonstrated great loyalty in support of your election efforts. The easiest way to resolve this situation, the new Member rationalizes, is to fill the roster.

Finally, some freshmen come to Washington lacking management experience, and so turn to the last model they saw for setting up a political operation, i.e., their campaigns. They hire for a congressional office as they would a campaign, by favoring the short term, focusing on a single goal (for the campaign, it was election victory; for the office, it's survival), and aiming to keep a team together only long enough to achieve that goal.

Benefits of Hiring Only a Core Staff

You will be in office for at least two or six years, and judging by history, probably far longer than that. You owe it to yourself and to your constituents to build an office structure that is capable not only of serving in January, but over your entire career. This means making the right decisions early on that will allow you to achieve your longer-term strategic goals. Granted, it's difficult to concentrate on the long term when faced with so many short-term demands, but that's what most successful offices do. With this framework in mind, there are two major benefits to hiring only a core staff in November and December:

Scarce time and resources during the transition can be directed towards accomplishing other critical tasks. Opening day is less than two months after the election, and until you are sworn-in, you have very little resources. Your energies during this time must be used to make strategic decisions outlined in this part of the book: not only hiring core staff, but setting up a district/state office, putting together a first-year budget, selecting and pursuing committee seats, and evaluating your technology needs.

Even if you are absolutely sure of your first-term priorities and know precisely the staff you need, you still don't have the time to properly locate, interview and hire an entire well-qualified staff in two months, while still taking care of your other duties. Neither you, nor anyone else, should be expected to undertake such an important task under these conditions.

Moreover, a congressional office can operate effectively with a core staff for six weeks or so after opening day. This news comes as a shock to some freshmen, who are overwhelmed during orientation by the myriad tasks required just to get an office up and running. But the reality is that January is usually a slow legislative month, so you really won't need more than a basic legislative shop for a while. You will also probably not be generating large press or mail outreach, so these functions can be reactive rather than proactive. All in all, our experience shows you can survive fairly well for a month and a half with a core staff.

> *"A congressional office can operate effectively with a core staff for six weeks or so after opening day."*

Chances of hiring the right staff are increased. Staff turnover rates are incredibly high among freshmen. It's not uncommon for a freshman office to experience 20 to 40 percent turnover in their first year. Staff leave for a variety of reasons, to be sure, but poor hiring decisions are arguably first among them.

The indirect and direct costs of turnover are high. It is time-consuming and costly to hire and retrain new staff, office productivity and staff morale suffers, and opportunities can be missed while new staff get up to speed. In the extreme, poor hiring may cost you your congressional seat. The people who work in your Washington and district/state offices are your most valuable resource, greatly influencing your success in Congress. A high-caliber, sharp, creative, productive team who work well with you and with each other will be key to achieving your goals. Conversely, you will show little progress on your strategic objectives if you are burdened with an ill-fitting or constantly changing staff. You can still make mistakes in hiring your core staff, but you're much less likely to make bad hiring decisions if you hire eight staffers, rather than 16, in the 60 days between the election and swearing-in.

Which Functions To Hire as Part of Your Core Staff

For more than 60 years, a barnstorming *four-person* softball team called the King and His Court has been soundly defeating full, 10-player teams. They win mostly because they are superb athletes and because the four play the key positions needed to cover a softball field: catcher, first baseman, outfielder, pitcher (the pitcher also acts as an infielder when pitching from second base — did we mention they are great athletes?). It's a perfect combination of the right people standing in the right spots.

This section is designed to help you emulate the King and His Court by identifying the core functions in your congressional office and the number of staff needed to perform them. Through our work and experience with numerous congressional offices, CMF has identified the following vital functions that must be performed by any congressional office from opening day:

Answering the phones/greeting visitors. Whoever performs this function will be the first contact constituents and others who walk through the door or call on the phone will have with your office. Staff who handle this function should be helpful and convey professionalism.

Beginning to manage the mail. You may not have the capacity to keep up with (or dig out from) the postal mail that's been piling up since the election and the e-mail likely to arrive soon after you open an account. You may not have firmly established all of your mail policies. Still, you have to start organizing and categorizing your mail right away and developing some basic responses to constituent letters, even if it is a general acknowledgment of their concerns and opinions.

CHAPTER FIVE Hiring Your Core Staff

Conducting basic legislative research. As we've said, January tends to be a slow legislative month, so you won't need to do any heavy lifting in this area. But you'll need someone who can generate talking points, or explain your positions on key issues to whomever might need them. You will also need some legislative support for the few floor votes that do take place.

Maintaining the computer system. You'll want someone who can keep your current computer systems functioning. You'll also want someone who can help decide if the office should upgrade, and if so, which new system to purchase.

Handling scheduling requests. Someone has to organize, help prioritize and respond to the many requests you'll receive to attend this or that function, both in DC and in the district/state.

Providing Member with personal assistance. In Washington, if you need a list of names and phone numbers, a thank-you note drafted, or travel arrangements made, you, the Member, should not be doing it yourself. Staff should be designated to help you in Washington. In the district/state, a variety of administrative tasks go along with attending an event. Whether you will require assistance may be a matter of personal preference and style.

Handling casework. You will most likely inherit cases from your predecessor, and many constituents will call your office to inquire about the status of their cases. In addition, publicity surrounding the election will generate new cases. You will need to respond professionally and knowledgeably to these constituents, even if you won't start working immediately on their cases.

Handling press inquiries. Even if you don't actively court the press, they will call you looking for comments on various issues and doing profiles of the "new faces." Someone needs to be able to speak on your behalf, assist you in managing these requests and draft basic press releases.

Day-to-day management. This function includes tasks like advising the Member, solving problems that arise, coordinating activities of the Washington *and* district/state offices and staff, as well as coordinating hiring, spending and other office decisions.

Coordinating Office Move (Senate only). You will first have a temporary Washington office, but soon thereafter you will have the opportunity to select a permanent suite. Usually, all moves are completed by the end of March. Somebody, preferably somebody with experience, needs to be in charge of getting everybody and everything smoothly from one office to the other while the daily work continues.

How many core staff people do you need to cover these functions? There is no single right answer, but CMF recommends that you hire as few staff as possible, especially if you are as yet undecided about your office goals.

MANAGEMENT FACT
A House Member may employ up to 18 permanent staff and 4 additional staff (designated as paid interns, part-time employees, shared employees, temporary employees, or employees on leave without pay). The Senate has no staff limit.

Remember that you are looking for people who will fit an overall office strategy. It is useful, however, to have staff who are flexible and capable of performing many roles.

A new Senator should consider the population of his or her state when staffing certain functions. For example, a Senator from California may require a few more people to handle casework, answer constituent mail or just answer the phones than a Senator from Montana. On the other hand, some core functions can be handled by a single person whether the Senator represents 1 million or 30 million people (e.g., day-to-day management, coordinating office move, basic legislative research).

With those caveats, below are core staff lists for typical House and Senate freshman offices. (See Chapter 3 for the average salaries of these positions.) You will notice that a number of critical players are not on these lists. CMF research shows that historically, each fully-staffed Representative averages 15 staffers (8-9 in DC and 6-7 in the district), while each Senator averages 35

Figure 5-1

Sample House Core Staff (7-10 people)

COMMON TITLE	FUNCTIONS
Chief of Staff	day-to-day management, press
Scheduler	scheduling, personal assistance
Legislative Assistant	legislative research, mail
Systems Administrator	computer maintenance, mail
Staff Assistant (DC)	answering phone, greeting visitors, mail
Staff Assistant (district)	answering phone, greeting visitors
Constituent Services Rep (district)	answering phone, casework, personal assistance at district events (optional — may not be needed depending upon Member's style)
District Director (district)	day-to-day management, press (optional — may not be needed if DC Chief of Staff handles these duties)
Scheduler (district)	scheduling, personal assistance (optional — may not be needed if DC Scheduler handles these duties)
Field Rep (district)	personal assistance at district events (optional — may not be needed depending upon Member's style)

Figure 5-2

Sample Senate Core Staff (13-14 people)

COMMON TITLE	FUNCTIONS
Chief of Staff	day-to-day management
Scheduler	scheduling, personal assistance
Communications Director	press
Administrative Director/Office Manager	coordinating office move, assisting day-to-day management
Legislative Assistant	legislative research, mail
Systems Administrator	computer maintenance, mail
Legislative Correspondents (2)	mail
Staff Assistant (DC)	answering phone, greeting visitors
State Director (state)	day-to-day management
Staff Assistant (state)	answering phone, greeting visitors
Constituent Services Reps (2) (state)	answering phone, casework
Field Rep (state)	personal assistance at state events (optional — may not be needed depending upon Senator's style)

staffers (22 in DC and 13 in the state). In the House, you may be thinking how nice it would be to have a Communications Director and Legislative Director on board from day one. In the Senate, you might feel that an LD and Legislative Counsel could contribute to your team. But remember, they are not critical to your success in January or February, and it is far better to hire confidently than to fill slots quickly. If you are not sure yet whether your legislative focus will be health care, taxes, the Great Lakes or foreign aid, then you don't know the role the LD will play or the skills required for the job. Even if you've settled on an issue, you do not have the time or resources to do a thorough LD search.

Although it is listed as an office function like any other, a special word needs to be said about the role of the Chief of Staff. This person will be responsible, to a large degree, for the work output from your office. In so many ways, this position is more than the sum of its parts. A Chief of Staff is often described as the Member's alter-ego. Both Members and top aides emphasize that the Chief of Staff must be someone whom you trust. He should both complement and reinforce your management style, be able to transmit your values and expectations to the rest of the staff and the public at large, and excel in areas that are not your greatest strengths. For example, if you are a big-picture person, you may want a Chief of Staff who is good at detail. If you are inexperienced in management, you may want to hire a Chief of Staff who is a strong and experienced manager. Your choice ideally should be someone with whom you can feel comfortable working intimately for years to come. He or she should be someone who can help you build an effective organization over time.

In fact, we recommend that, if possible, the Chief of Staff be the first person you hire. A good Chief of Staff will be very helpful in the early days, as you set out to broadly assess your needs. He or she will also be able to serve in other useful capacities: as the gatekeeper, to ensure outsiders and your own staff don't unwisely monopolize your time or attention; as the Jiminy Cricket on your shoulder offering a fresh perspective on difficult choices, and preventing you from making unwise commitments; and as the "bad guy" who can deliver unpleasant news or break commitments made in haste. Of course, the critical nature of this position dictates that you hire only when you are absolutely sure of your needs and can find a candidate who meets them.

Fitting Core Staff to Your Mission and Goals

A central theme of all the chapters in Part I of this book is that new Members should base early decisions, especially those involving office resources, on their strategic goals. Hiring a core staff is no exception. The clearer you are about your goals for your first term, the more likely you'll be to hire a staff that will help you meet them.

Your aim and challenge is to put together a core staff that will allow you to function in the short-run, while preparing your office to thrive in the long-run. For example, let's say a freshman House Member decides that constituent outreach is a top goal, and that his District Director must have political savvy, local connections and know how to communicate a message effectively. The Member's immediate concern is who should run the district offices in January. This decision, however, should be made with his larger objectives in mind. If the perfect candidate for a District Director lands on his doorstep, the choice is easy. Hire him or her. But if no such candidate appears, and recruiting one is going to take a good deal of time, then the Member must choose another route: let the Washington Chief of Staff oversee the district offices; hire a risky District Director now; or let a Constituent Services Representative manage the office on an interim basis and delay the District Director search. Each choice gets the district offices up and running, but some choices will make it easier to reach the longer-term goal of having district offices with top-notch constituent outreach capability.

Unfortunately, there are many examples of offices doing it the wrong way. One office we encountered hired a Legislative Director very early without clarifying her duties. She quit a few months later when she was told she had to answer some of the office's constituent mail. Another office hired a Press Secretary before the Member had decided whether he planned to focus on Washington or the home district media. The Press Secretary was replaced when the office later settled on pursuing favorable district press because, although she was quite talented, her expertise was in the DC media market.

The bottom line is that, to the extent possible, think about how well each staff candidate will contribute to your long-term goals. In addition, try to assess whether each candidate is likely to fit in well with your management structure and your budget priorities. Some offices we've known were unable to make these assessments to their satisfaction for the candidates available, and therefore hired temporary workers to cover the vital office functions. If you take this route, make those you hire clearly aware of their temporary status.

Hiring the Rest of Your Staff

When should you hire the remainder of your staff? Recall that a core staff can carry the workload for about six weeks after opening day. Most House offices have a full or near-full staff in place by late April to early May. Some Senate offices may take a bit longer, especially if the move to a permanent suite doesn't take place until February or March.

Within these time constraints, however, you have some discretion as to when you hire for each remaining staff position. If you know the type of staffer you need (i.e., what functions he'll perform and what skills he'll require), start the hiring process early, even before the initial six weeks is up. This situation might occur if you've been sure of your needs since the Fall, but you rightly delayed hiring because you didn't have the time or resources during November or December to find a superior candidate.

If, on the other hand, you do not have a clear vision of your needs, it is wise to take some time to settle on your goals before expending energy on the hiring process. Above all else, we urge that you emphasize quality, not speed. For example, you may be looking to hire someone to accompany you on district or state trips, but are not sure exactly what role you'd like that person to play. You have a few options. You could simply hire a "driver" and be done with it. However, it makes more sense to take some time and gather additional information to help in your hiring decision. You ought to run "tests," perhaps having different existing staffers travel with you. You can then decide on the types of logistical or legislative skills you'll require in an aide.

It will be equally important to move slowly if you were once sure of your needs and goals, but changed circumstances have necessitated that you reevaluate them. One could imagine, for example, a Member who hoped to make health care a priority, until a natural disaster hits his state, leaving constituents clamoring for help. Where he might have earlier planned to start a search in January for an LD with expertise in health issues and the legislative process, he must rethink his agenda and the staff he'll require. Maybe his new focus will be securing private and government assistance to rebuild his district's battered infrastructure.

Recruiting the Best Candidates

1 Design a standard application that solicits basic information and job experience. Include questions to help you assess a person's "fit" with the mission of your office. Ask candidates to sign the application attesting to the accuracy of the information provided.

2 Develop a customized job posting with the unique attributes of the vacant position and your office. Clearly state your requirements to eliminate candidates you would not consider.

3 Utilize district/state-based job boards to attract candidates. For example, contact local universities in your district/state to find exceptional students interested in Capitol Hill.

4 Create a balance in your office between staff from your district/state and Hill professionals. The combination of district/state understanding and Capitol Hill know-how will give you the perspectives and knowledge needed for a more successful term.

5 Seek out applicants with a broad range of backgrounds and skills. Both the House and Senate have launched diversity initiatives to assist offices with recruiting and placement. Contact Senate Majority Leader Harry Reid's office or the Committee on House Administration for guidance.

6 Take advantage of Capitol Hill resources. Both chambers maintain resume banks and post job vacancy announcements. Due to high volume, a separate "resume drop-off" location for newly elected Members is usually set up during the transition period. Check with the Senate Placement Office (202-224-9167; www.senate.gov/employment) and the House's FirstCall Customer Service Center (202-226-4504; B-227 Longworth HOB) for more information. ∎

CHAPTER FIVE Hiring Your Core Staff

A Process for Hiring the Right Staff Candidates

Now it's just a matter of finding the right candidate for each job. No matter how well you've assessed the needs of your office, both immediate and long-term, it all means very little if you then hire people with the wrong qualifications. CMF's experience is that the hiring process used by most congressional offices falls short in a number of areas. We will review the approach taken by many offices on the Hill, discuss the weaknesses of their approach and then describe a better process for finding the right candidate.

Typically on the Hill, a Chief of Staff would start by identifying a position in the office to be filled, such as the Scheduler. He would then review the stack of resumes which have been accumulating on his desk looking for "likely candidates" based upon some minimum criteria. For instance, he may take a closer look at those with at least a bachelor's degree, home state ties and scheduling experience. He may also call or e-mail other Chiefs of Staff asking if they know of anyone seeking a scheduling position.

After whittling down the list to a few names, the Chief of Staff will call in each candidate for an interview. The interview would likely begin with the Chief of Staff saying, "Let me tell you a little bit about the office" or "Tell me about yourself and why you want to work for Congressman X?" Talk might turn to the candidate's career goals and previous experience. The session would seem more like a casual discussion than an interview, with the Chief of Staff trying to get a sense of whether the candidate would be a "good fit" in the office. He may also give a writing test.

Following each interview, the Chief of Staff would decide whether the candidate is worth further consideration. He may mark the candidate's resume "yes," "no," or "maybe." After all interviews are completed, the Chief of Staff will choose the final candidate(s). The finalists may have final interviews with the Member before one is offered the job.

Congressional Accountability Act

Though House and Senate staff are "at-will" employees, they are still guaranteed certain protections under the Congressional Accountability Act (CAA). Members of Congress and staff responsible for managing personnel should familiarize themselves with the 12 civil rights, labor, and workplace safety and health laws applicable to the Legislative Branch.

The CAA also created the Office of Compliance (OOC), which educates congressional offices and employees about their rights and responsibilities and investigates alleged violations. More information on CAA and OOC is available at www.compliance.gov.

The Office of House Employment Counsel (202-225-7075) and the Senate Chief Counsel for Employment (202-224-5424) provide legal guidance on personnel policies and practices and represent employers in litigation arising under CAA. ■

> **Six-Step Process for Hiring Staff**
>
> 1. Develop a job analysis for each position.
> 2. Design interview questions and other tests that assess the candidate's skills as identified in the job analyses.
> 3. Present the same key questions and test to each candidate.
> 4. Involve other staff in interviews and testing processes.
> 5. Conduct further interviews or tests as needed.
> 6. Check candidate references. ∎

What's wrong with this approach? Plenty, according to research on hiring. The Chief of Staff started off looking at the available resumes rather than first developing a sense of the requirements and skills needed to do the job, combined with the unique priorities of his office.

The Chief of Staff should have been able to construct a profile of the hypothetical perfect candidate. Instead, he was resigned to choose from among the best of what was immediately available.

Moving on to the interview, the Chief of Staff was handicapped by not knowing which skills and traits he was looking for, and therefore was unable to formulate questions targeted towards determining if a candidate had those skills. He may have known which skills were needed to perform the job "generically." What he didn't know were the skills and experiences required to do the job well in his office, for his boss, and in pursuit of his office's goals.

This Chief of Staff's evaluations were also unreliable because of the subjectivity of his approach. First, he tried to sum up an entire interview with a global assessment that boiled down to a "yes," "no" or "maybe." Such a simplistic appraisal would, at best, reflect how well the candidate and Chief of Staff had gotten along together. Second, he made this global assessment after the interview ended. Studies have shown that memory alone is not reliable; managers in test conditions were not able to recall what a candidate said even 20 minutes earlier. Third, the Chief of Staff injected potential bias by being the only one in the office conducting the interviews, although the Member may have done a final interview before making a job offer.

Can an office locate an acceptable staffer this way? Probably. But the goal is to hire not those who can merely perform the job adequately, but those who can do so superbly and as vital contributors to achieving the office's goals. It is the inattention to these details which leads to high staff turnover, low morale and an inefficient use of resources. We believe there is a better way to evaluate a candidate's suitability, and we describe below a process to improve your chances of selecting an excellent candidate for each job.

We recognize that Members-elect and their one or two aides during the transition will be hard-pressed to complete our entire multi-step process when hiring each core staffer. Your limited time and resources just won't permit it. However, the more you can incorporate these steps, or at least the principles underlying the steps, in choosing your staff, the better off you'll be. Then, starting in January, you can be much more thorough in hiring the remainder of your staff.

Staff Candidate Selection Process

1. Do a job analysis for each position.

The first step in any attempt to fill a staff position is to put down in writing the principal duties and functions of the job, and the *skills required to perform those functions*. Those duties and skills can start with the common, Hill-accepted job description, but must take into account your office's goals and priorities and the particular needs of the Member. Only you know what you want each staffer to do; only you know what additional skills are important to you.

> *"The first step in any attempt to fill a staff position is to put down in writing the principal duties and functions of the job, and the skills required to perform those functions."*

For instance, depending upon the office, a Scheduler may be required to organize incoming scheduling requests by date, their potential contributions to the office's legislative goals, or their importance to the Member's political prospects. She may be required to present and defend her recommendations at scheduling meetings with other senior staff. She may be asked to anticipate the logistical and political needs accompanying a district or state event, or the Member's frequent appearances on the national television news show circuit. Or, in some cases, a Scheduler may be expected to perform all of these functions. Each of these duties would require different competencies, so you should assess the applicant's professionalism, organizational skills, and technical abilities, rather than rely solely on previous Hill experience.

It is important at this stage to differentiate between critical and non-critical job skills. Your office may want every staff member to be very knowledgeable about the district or state, but you should assess whether this expertise is absolutely necessary for every position. For a Scheduler and Chief of Staff, perhaps yes. For a Systems Administrator, perhaps not.

Fully defining a job saves an office time and resources by allowing a candidate to remove himself from contention if he doesn't believe he can meet the requirements and qualifications. For those who do interview, it may help to explain a typical day or week on the job to the candidate, including the undesirable elements. It's better to have the candidate admit he may not be able to handle the job or that the job doesn't sound as good as he thought, than to end up having to repeat the hiring process three months later.

Finally, job analyses help address whether campaign staff or a predecessor's staff should be hired, common occurrences among freshmen. Most often, a staffer is being considered for a job similar to that which he held during the campaign (i.e., a Campaign Manager is considered for Chief of Staff). Job analyses may reveal which congressional positions utilize skills similar to those of their campaign counterparts, and which require a different set of abilities. (Schedulers and Press Secretaries may transfer well from campaign to congressional office; Campaign Field Representatives may have a tougher time adapting to the role of Legislative Assistant.) Similarly, it may bring to light that you have different expectations for a Legislative Director than did your predecessor. We are not recommending that a campaign or predecessor's staffer not be given the chance to compete for an official position, but only that both the office and the candidate will benefit from a better understanding of the job requirements. However, we do recommend that offices not carelessly create a position for or structure their office around a person they want to hire. Rather, the requirements of the position should be determined first, then the best candidate should be identified.

2. Develop interview questions and other tests which will elicit information about whether the candidates have the skills identified in the job analyses.

It seems logical, but you'd be surprised how readily interviewers can get distracted with interesting, but irrelevant points. Essentially, you are trying to predict how a candidate will perform in the job, based on an interview. Each question or test should help pursue that end.

Asking a Scheduler candidate to "tell me a little about yourself" might be the beginning, but should not be the end, of the questioning. It will give the candidate the opportunity to put her best foot forward, which might give you insight into what the candidate deems most important (i.e., personal values), or what the candidate thinks you think is most important (i.e., perception). These basic requirements can be assessed in a 15-minute telephone interview, making efficient use of your time. However, this approach may not give you relevant information about the candidate's qualifications in scheduling, political awareness, professionalism or any other critical skills you have identified.

> *"In addition to open-ended questions, construct problem-solving questions which give you a chance to learn how the candidate thinks and makes judgments."*

In addition to open-ended questions, construct problem-solving questions which give you a chance to learn how the candidate thinks and makes judgments. To do this, you can ask about past experiences or use hypothetical situations. For instance, if you're seeking a Scheduler who works well with others, has a keen political sense and can think proactively, the interview might include the following:

CHAPTER FIVE Hiring Your Core Staff

- Tell me about a time when you disagreed with a former employer (Chief of Staff or Member, if candidate worked in a congressional office) over a scheduling priority. What was the disagreement about, and how did you handle it?
- Suppose you are asked to turn down the request of a large civic organization that's been trying for months to get the Member to address their group. What would you do or say?
- Taking into account what you perceive to be the Member's strengths, weaknesses, interests and electoral situation, what are some of the events in the state he should attend this year?

It is also useful to see how the candidate performs under pressure and under realistic conditions. For instance, some offices ask candidates to answer a hypothetical letter from a constituent. The result may show how well the candidate understands a particular issue, or how much confidence he portrays in writing a response. It may also simply confirm that his writing skills are up to par.

Tests can also be tailored to the specific job at hand. Writing constituent responses may take different skills than writing press releases. As such, an office might want Press Secretary candidates to write a sample release based on materials provided by the legislative team. Or perhaps the candidates could be asked to develop a list of further information they would request to improve the quality of a release. All of these tests would indicate whether a candidate has the specific skills needed to get the job done well.

Finally, ask the candidate about their strengths and areas in need of improvement. If they are unable to identify any areas for development, you should carefully consider whether that person is open to learning and growth in the job, which are essential attributes of successful Hill staff.

3. Ask the same key questions of, and give the same test to, each candidate. Use a rating system and tally the scores, deciding on the scoring system ahead of time.

Interviewing is not an exact science, but studies show that numerical ratings are more useful than "gut feelings." Also, resist the temptation to assign a single score to the entire interview at the end from memory. This isn't reliable. Instead, rate the answer to each question during the interview and use that raw data to arrive at a single score. Also, you may want to weight some questions more heavily than others to reflect which issues or questions are most important.

By developing a scoring system and deciding *ahead of time* the types of answers which will receive specific scores, you will greatly reduce subjectivity and bias on the part of the interviewer. For example, an office Legislative Assistant applicant might be asked, "The Member wants to take the lead in Congress on transportation issues. How should she do that?" If this office

MANAGEMENT FACT
The Congressional Accountability Act (CAA) forbids asking questions about gender, race, religion, disability, parental or marital status, national origin, health, or other protected characteristics.

seeks an LA who is creative and energetic, but also sensitive to political realities and the requirements of the legislative process, the following ratings might work (based on 1-10 scoring).

Sample Answer by LA Candidate:	Score
"Create a task force in the district/state, develop legislation with a 2-3 year goal for passage, invite Transportation Committee Chairman to join Member on fact-finding trips, pursue speech opportunities at transportation conventions, advocate for Washington hearings and field hearings."	10
"Give one-minute floor speeches on transportation issues, send out press releases after transportation-related votes, develop legislation and pressure Transportation Committee chairman and leadership to bring up bill this year."	1

In this example, the office concluded that the answer demonstrating enthusiasm for the work and an understanding of constructive activities likely to raise the Member's profile deserves a "10." In contrast, the answer revealing the applicant's timidity and recklessness receives a "1." This rating system uses only two sample answers, but your system can include additional middle-ground answers which merit, for instance, a "3," "5," or "7."

4. Involve other staff in the interview and testing process.

Studies show that using a panel of interviewers better predicts a candidate's job skills than does an interview by one staff member. This makes sense. The chance of bias is reduced if a candidate is rated by a number of interviewers as opposed to just one.

Involving staff may also provide another perspective on whether a candidate would be a "good fit" for your office's culture. It would convey to the candidate that he is joining a team rather than just filling a position. Just as important, it would convey to your existing staff that you value their input.

5. Don't hesitate to conduct further interviews or tests with each candidate.

You are hiring people to be part of a relatively small, close-knit team, and you shouldn't feel obligated to make a final judgment after one meeting. Often additional time is needed to make successful hiring decisions. In addition, the willingness of a candidate to participate in multiple interviews gives you valuable information about his commitment to your office.

6. Check references.

Checking references is absolutely essential and frequently overlooked in the rush to hire. You want to make sure that the candidate's background information and professional accomplishments are accurate. Talk to previous supervisors and current or former co-workers, clients, or peers. Ask pointed and detailed questions. Also, be aware that how something is said, and what is not said, can be equally important.

You should also protect yourself from unexpected discoveries by conducting an online search of your candidate. Ensure that he presents himself professionally, particularly on social networking sites. You may also request that the U.S. Capitol Police (USCP) conduct a criminal background check on your candidate, or on all new hires as part of your office policy, which would require fingerprinting. Contact the USCP Badging & Fingerprinting Office (202-593-1545) for more information.

Conclusion

You will likely not have the time necessary to assemble a full staff and complete all of your other critical tasks by the opening day of Congress. You may also not have a clear idea of your strategic priorities, the type of staff you'll need, and the skills you'll want them to possess. You may also not have the perfect applicants standing neatly before you. Our recommendation therefore is to choose a core staff who can begin in January and perform the vital functions of the office, and who will also fit into your long-range plans. Then, hire the rest of your staff over the next couple of months as you finalize your needs and are able to devote the necessary resources to finding quality candidates. In this way you'll increase your chances of building an effective team which will help accomplish your office goals.

Chapter Summary
The DOs and DON'Ts of
Hiring Your Core Staff

Do...

- **select your Chief of Staff first,** if possible. A good Chief of Staff is instrumental in setting up your office and must be someone you trust to make critical decisions during the transition.

- **pick a core staff that will be able to perform the essential functions of your office for about six weeks.** January is a slow legislative month, and it's more important to answer phones and greet visitors than to research legislation.

- **hire the remainder of your staff between January and May,** as you become sure of your needs.

Don't...

- **only review the stack of incoming resumes in seeking potential staff.** Find other candidates so you aren't resigned to hiring only those people who have contacted you.

- **choose a full staff before January,** even though there is enormous pressure to have a lot of staff in order to "hit the ground running."

- **hire staff without a written job description for each position**.

- **hire someone you cannot fire.** For example, don't hire the child of a prominent politician or another key stakeholder from the district/state unless you're absolutely certain that you want this employee for the long term.

CHAPTER SIX

Selecting and Utilizing Technology

This Chapter Includes...

☆ Guidance for purchasing hardware and software
☆ Key considerations for making technology decisions
☆ Steps to purchasing the right hardware and software
☆ How to keep systems running smoothly

The Internet, intranets, and e-mail have enhanced Congress' ability to conduct legislative research, provide constituent services, and enhance press operations. Correspondence Management Systems (CMS) in the House and Constituent Services Systems (CSS) in the Senate have enabled offices to integrate all constituent interactions into one, readily accessible database. BlackBerry devices, laptops, and remote access to House and Senate networks allow staff to be fully connected, even when they aren't in the office. Technology has provided congressional offices with new opportunities and new strategies for conducting legislative work, and delivering more effective and efficient constituent services. Constituents, reporters, and interest groups now expect congressional offices to implement new technologies quickly and seamlessly to provide greater access to legislative information and the legislative process.

Balancing constituent expectations and limited resources, however, has become one of the most difficult management issues for offices. Like any business, each congressional office is responsible for making most of its own information technology (IT) decisions, which can feel like a daunting task. Before you can determine the appropriate technology for your office, you will need to have a clear sense of exactly what you'll want it to do for you. Don't worry — the House and Senate have extensive assistance available to help ensure a smooth transition for the Member and staff. This chapter will guide you through this process.

MANAGEMENT FACT
More information is available from CMF at www.cmfweb.org and through our Partnership For A More Perfect Union at pmpu.org.

The Basic Congressional System

While the Senate tends to have a more standardized electronic workplace, almost as many different hardware and software configurations exist in the House as there are Members. However, there are some things that can be found in most congressional offices — House and Senate — because they have proven invaluable. These are:

- **Staff computers.** Most offices have one PC for each member of the staff in both the DC and district/state offices, though a few offices are using Mac operating systems instead of Windows. Desktop computers are most common, but increasing numbers of offices are providing staff with laptop computers for greater mobility and/or the option to access office information from home or on the road. Some offices are purchasing unassigned laptops for staff to use when they need to work remotely. In the House, all freshman Members in the 112th Congress will receive at least 10 workstations and one laptop.
- **Networks.** The Senate provides a high speed network connection for the DC office and all of the Senator's state offices. The House provides high speed network connections for the DC office and between the DC office and primary (flagship) district office. Each office is responsible for the networks within each district/state office, as well as the connection between the secondary district offices. Network options, speed and performance can be affected by the configuration of the network, and your staff's use of the network. Be sure to ask vendors to explain how to optimize your network performance, and what steps would be involved to ensure optimization, before you purchase from them.

    The Senate also supports Virtual Machine Infrastructure (VMI) that provides a virtual network infrastructure in offices to minimize the need for additional internal hardware. Additionally, both the House and Senate support virtual private networks (VPNs) that enable remote access to office information via a secure connection on the Internet, but in most cases individual staffers are responsible for the necessary broadband Internet connections in their residences.
- **File servers.** Most Senate offices have a server in the DC office for storing centralized documents and files, and some also have a server in the primary state office. In the House, freshman Members are provided a virtual file server, securely hosted in the House's data center. The server, care and maintenance are provided at no cost to the office. The primary district office also stores and shares files on this House-provided virtual file server.

MANAGEMENT FACT

Freshman may inherit their predecessors' equipment, unless the House and Senate determine that the systems are no longer adequate.

CHAPTER SIX   Selecting and Utilizing Technology

- **Network access.** House and Senate offices use Microsoft's Active Directory structure for the creation and maintenance of user accounts and e-mail access. Senators can choose to host and maintain a server in their office for these functions, join the enterprise system maintained by the Senate, or compromise with a hybrid of the two. Your assigned CSA can walk you through the pros and cons of each option. All House Members are supported by the institution, so no additional server in the office is required.
- **Printers.** In House offices, there is usually one high-speed printer, one or two average printers in the DC office, and one or two average printers in each district office. The House provides guidance to the maintenance providers on how to install printers securely. You may consult with your TSR

Glossary of Technology-Related Offices and Staff

CMS/CSS Providers — A vendor that is responsible for CMS/CSS software and associated hardware, technical and software support services. Most vendors offer their products for purchase or for use in a hosted environment. House offices can find more information on HouseNet.

Customer Support Analyst (CSA) — A representative of the Senate Sergeant at Arms who is specifically assigned to provide Senate offices with technical support, advice and assistance with requests for purchasing, and guidance using and operating computer hardware and software.

Maintenance Provider — A vendor who is under contract with the House to provide Member offices with services to ensure that the office's hardware and software are effectively integrated and functioning correctly. More information can be found on HouseNet.

House Information Resources (HIR) — An office of the Chief Administrative Officer (CAO) that oversees all House information technology (IT) systems.

Office Coordinator — A representative from CAO Office Services assigned to House offices to provide assistance with purchasing and/or leasing equipment, establishing maintenance agreements, furnishing district offices, and maintaining inventories of equipment and certain software in both the DC and district offices.

Senate Sergeant at Arms Office (SAA) — Institutional office that oversees Senate information technology and network systems.

System Consultants — A vendor assigned to each Senate office that provides limited technical support to the systems administrator and helps coordinate the technical support between the office, CMS/CSS vendor, and Sergeant at Arms staff.

Technical Support Representative (TSR) — A representative of HIR who is specifically assigned to provide Member offices with technical support, advice and assistance with requests for purchasing, and guidance using and operating computer hardware and software. ∎

or vendor on the proper installation of a networked printer. In the Senate, offices typically have one high speed printer for every 7-8 staffers and an average speed printer for every 3-4 staffers. In addition, it is common for congressional offices to employ multi-function machines that print, copy, scan and fax.
- **Correspondence Management System (CMS)/Constituent Services System (CSS).** In many ways, the CMS/CSS is the most important software in a congressional office. It is also the most specialized. CMS/CSS packages are databases specifically designed for the congressional environment that enable your staff to record, process, track, and manage constituent correspondence, casework, and any other interactions your office might have with constituents. The CMS/CSS package that an office chooses or inherits will often dictate many of its hardware and software choices.
- **Scheduling software.** The Member's time is the most valuable and most limited resource a congressional office has, so using the scheduling software that best meets your needs is crucial. The functions that most offices believe essential are those that enable them to update the schedule in real-time, search for keywords, present the schedule in a variety of formats, report on the office's scheduling trends, share the Member's schedule with all staff online, and view scheduling information on handheld devices. Most House and Senate offices use the calendar function in Microsoft Outlook, but some use the scheduling module in their CMS/CSS packages. Benefits to using Outlook include the ability to easily identify the availability of the Member and staff, and integration with handheld devices.
- **E-mail management.** House and Senate offices are on the Microsoft Exchange e-mail system, so most staff are using Outlook. Most often, offices are managing the flow of e-mail to and from constituents through their CMS/CSS databases, which can be configured to interact with Exchange/Outlook.
- **BlackBerrys and handheld devices.** Almost all staff on the Hill use BlackBerrys or other portable devices to stay in contact with their offices virtually 24/7. These devices have steadily increased in sophistication and now allow staff to access nearly all of the information and tools that used to only be available to them when they were in the office. While BlackBerrys are most commonly in use, the House is expanding support to other devices, such as iPhones.
- **Web browser.** Not only is a web browser imperative for congressional research, but some CMS/CSS packages are web-based, dictating the browser and version staff must use.
- **Intranets.** Each chamber maintains its own intranet that provides detailed information on the administrative services available to your office.

HouseNet (the House intranet) and Webster (the Senate intranet) also connect to several legislative resources that your staff will rely on, including the Legislative Information System (LIS), a Library of Congress intranet designed to provide Members and staff with the most current and accurate legislative information possible. Some Senate offices and a smaller number of House offices also create and maintain their own private intranet for staff use.
- **Budgeting and accounting.** Each House and Senate office is responsible for — and accountable for — its own budget. House offices use PeopleSoft, FinMart, and the Congressional Accounting and Personnel System (CAPS), while Senate offices use the Financial Management Information System (FMIS).
- **Social media tools.** The rise of social media tools like Twitter, Facebook, Flickr, YouTube, and blogs have created new opportunities and challenges to congressional offices. Keep two important things in mind when it comes to their use. First, always follow House and Senate rules about how you can and cannot use these tools. Second, don't feel compelled to use all of these tools. Begin by determining what your communications goals are and then assess which tools can help you best achieve them.

A range of other hardware and software tools — video conferencing systems and graphics design software, for example — can be found in offices on Capitol Hill. These provide offices with very useful communications and productivity options, but none of them has become ubiquitous yet. They are still largely being used by offices to support targeted goals or specialized needs, or by offices with more technically savvy staff. Be cautious, at first, about purchasing hardware and software that is not common on Capitol Hill, especially if it falls into the "gadget" category. In the complicated House and Senate technical environment, it can end up costing much more, both in terms of money and productivity, than it is really worth.

Determining When to Upgrade

Shortly after you are elected, you will receive an inventory of any equipment you will be inheriting from your predecessor. Some freshman Members will find that their inherited system needs to supplemented to meet their needs while others will find an entire system of practically new high-end computers. Unfortunately, the amount of time and money you must budget for information technology in your first year also depends, in large part, on what your predecessor left behind.

The lucky freshmen who find complete systems of good computers that are completely paid for by their predecessors do not even need to read the rest of this chapter. They can afford to spend their time and money on other things until they get settled and have a chance to figure out if there's anything more they need. The unfortunate freshmen whose predecessors' systems had to be removed because they were not up to par should read this chapter carefully, because information technology is going to be one of the biggest budget items in their first year. For better or worse, most freshmen will find that they inherit systems somewhere in-between.

The first thing to do is decide whether or not you need to purchase new hardware, software and peripherals right away. The more time you dedicate to understanding your information management and technology needs, the better equipped you will be to make wise decisions. Unfortunately, many offices will not have the luxury of waiting to make technology purchases. To help you decide whether or not you need to make hardware and software purchasing decisions immediately, or whether you can wait a few months to assess your needs, consult with your TSR (House) or CSA (Senate) to determine which of the following categories best describes the system you will inherit:

1. **Incomplete.** House and Senate Members-elect are not allowed to inherit any equipment deemed inadequate by House Information Resources (HIR) or the Senate Sergeant at Arms (SAA). Any substandard equipment is removed from their inventories, requiring House offices to pay for new equipment out of their Members' Representational Allowance (MRA) and Senate offices to use their Economic Allocation Fund or Senator's Account. If your hardware or software falls into this category, you will need to quickly decide how to complete the system to meet your staff's immediate needs.
2. **Complete and sufficient to meet your short-term needs.** If your office inherits sufficient equipment to get through the first few months, consider putting off new technology purchases for a little while and spending your time and energy elsewhere. This will give you time to become familiar with congressional systems, policies, and procedures; determine which features and capabilities are important to you; identify and explore your options; and further evaluate the system you've inherited. As a result, you will be much better-equipped to make effective, strategic decisions in February or March.
3. **Complete and sufficient to meet your long term needs.** If you are one of the lucky offices to inherit a complete system of medium or high-end computers and software, you can take your time to discover what, if anything, you might want to add or upgrade in your first term. Set aside some of your budget for things that come up — things will

always come up — but you are in a position to use most of your time and budget on other priorities.

Once you know into which of these categories your office falls, you will have a better idea of the urgency with which you will need to make hardware purchasing decisions. The decisions you make will have a significant impact on your office productivity and budget. Be sure to approach them strategically and thoughtfully, using the following advice.

Critical Questions

As you settle into Congress, keep track of the capabilities you wish your office had. Consider having staff keep lists of their own, as well, so that everyone's needs are represented in the decision-making process. Offices that must make immediate purchasing decisions should develop a list by seeking advice from veteran staff and your TSR or CSA.

Once you have created your list, you will need to winnow it down to a realistic size before making your final purchasing decisions. Begin by answering the following critical questions:

- **Do you have a strong foundation on which to build?** The most important components of your system are your servers, PCs, printers, and communications networks. Every capability you want to add to your system must be built onto this foundation. If the foundation is weak, you will likely experience frequent problems and crashes that will hinder productivity and add repair costs. Some offices try to make do with foundation components that are not performing well in order to purchase new capabilities and peripherals, such as video conference equipment, scanners, and digital cameras. While these tools can be very useful, adding them to a weak system is akin to building a luxury home on a weak foundation. The investment will be wasted if the whole thing comes tumbling down.
- **What are your goals and priorities?** Choose technology and functionality that allows you to achieve your goals and priorities more easily and effectively. If, for example, you intend to be seen as a responsive and technologically savvy Member, you may want a CMS/CSS with advanced e-mail management features. If keeping in close contact with constituents is a priority, even while you are in DC, you may consider a video conferencing system.
- **What is your staff's — and your own — level of technical comfort and skill?** State-of-the-art equipment is waste of money if staff is uncom-

fortable using it. Consider your staff's abilities and the complexity of the hardware and software that you are thinking of purchasing. Training is always an option, but be realistic about the time your office is willing to commit to training, especially during the first few months in office.
- **What are the district/state unique issues with which your office will be contending?** Each district and state has challenges that will affect technology priorities. For instance, a Member from the Pacific time zone may have greater need for video conferencing capabilities to keep Washington and district staff on the same page than a Member from the Eastern time zone. Members from high-tech districts/states may feel more pressure to fully integrate and use technological tools than Members from lower-tech districts/states. Consider your unique district/state circumstances and factor them into your technology decisions.
- **How much money should you budget for your system?** Your system will be important to staff productivity, but the costs should be weighed against your other budget priorities. Purchasing congressional computer systems is expensive. House Members will also need to budget for telecommunications, installation, training, and maintenance fees. For information about the hardware and software other offices are buying, and the amounts you can expect to pay, contact your TSR or CSA.
- **Where do you want to spend the money you've earmarked for technology?** There are infinite ways to spend your money, and you need to figure out where to focus. Is your goal to enhance staff productivity? Improve constituent communications? Enhance your press, outreach, and social media capabilities? Foster the image of a high-tech office? Ensure you have the best available support for your system? Naturally, offices will want to use technology for all of these goals, but a congressional budget can only go so far, and you will need to make trade-offs. Conduct a thorough needs assessment and get input from all staff to help you decide what your technology budget should best be spent on.

> *"Each district and state has challenges that will affect technology priorities. Consider your unique district/state circumstances and factor them into your technology decisions."*

Key Considerations

Technology plays a critically important role in supporting the effective functioning of House and Senate offices. It has been increasingly utilized to ensure the safety, security, and continuity of operations on Capitol Hill. At the same time, e-mail, websites, and social media have become an essential means of communicating with and serving an increasingly "wired" public. They have also become essential for communications among staff and between the staff and the Member. As a result, congressional offices are exploring more options to be as accessible, effective, efficient, and secure as possible. The following key factors should be considered as you plan and budget for new technology:

- **Remote access and telecommuting.** Establishing the means, policies, and procedures to enable staff to access office information from other locations is critical for the continuity of operations and potential emergency situations. It also gives staff the ability to work from home or on the road. Both the House and Senate provide offices secure remote access systems. To set this up effectively, you will need to find out the technical requirements, establish management guidelines, and follow House or Senate security protocol. The Senate also provides Remote Data Replication (RDR) that allows offices to purchase hardware and software to replicate their office data to a remote location. Most Senate offices take advantage of housing the remote server at the SAA's Alternate Computing Facility (ACF) in case of an emergency.
- **BlackBerrys and handheld devices.** BlackBerrys are so widespread and popular that some Members and staff jokingly refer to them as "crackberrys." They can help busy Members keep in touch with their staffs and with each other on Capitol Hill, as well as while they are in the district/state. The House and Senate have different capabilities and policies regarding BlackBerrys and other handheld devices, so learn what they are before you invest. You also need to determine your office's policy on portable devices. Questions to consider include: Who should get one? How will you handle lost, broken or stolen devices? How accessible will staff need to be after hours and on vacation? What constitutes appropriate and inappropriate use?
- **Online communications management.** A user-friendly and informative website is an essential communications tool and constituent service. A variety of options exist for creating and managing congressional websites, ranging from doing it yourself to hiring a vendor to both design and support your website. Talk to other offices whose websites you admire to find out what they do. In the House, freshman Members in the 112th Congress will be provided a fully functioning website and maintenance service options at no cost. And, you can always find information about, and examples of, Capitol Hill's best websites through CMF's *Gold Mouse Project* at pmpu.org. Once you have a high-quality, official site, you'll also probably want to investigate which other social media tools will help you best achieve your goals.

- **Data security.** As the number of portable devices on Capitol Hill grows, the need to protect the data they contain and the networks to which they attach becomes ever more important. These devices help increase productivity and improve communications, but offices that are using them should apply best practices for ensuring that the information on them — and the information to which they have access — is well protected in the event that the devices are lost or stolen. Be sure to follow House and Senate policies and recommendations to ensure data security in your DC and district/state offices, as well. And if you are considering purchasing or using any communications device or software not on the House or Senate supported lists, find out why not before you invest. It could cause security problems for your office or for the institution.
- **E-mail management.** E-mail is one of the more difficult technological issues on Capitol Hill. The volume of e-mail received by congressional offices continues to increase dramatically. Constituents' expectations for quick responses to e-mail also keep rising. Due to limited resources and technical skills, however, congressional offices have had difficulty implementing solutions for more efficient and effective handling of e-mail. For more information on development and maintaining an effective constituent mail operation, refer to Chapter 14, "Managing Constituent Communications."
- **Rapidly changing IT environment.** Technology continues to advance at a staggering pace, and many new technological capabilities and processes are being investigated and implemented by the House and Senate to help offices in a variety of ways, from ensuring the continuity of operations to webcasting committee proceedings to managing e-mail. E-governance and the continued exploration of best technology practices for legislatures will also impact the IT environment on Capitol Hill. As a result, your office should focus on building a solid foundation that can support new capabilities as they become available. You should also be somewhat cautious in implementing technologies uncommon in the congressional environment. Keep abreast of the options being explored by the House and Senate, since it is possible that the capabilities you are seeking will become available to all offices in the future.

Six Steps to Making Wise Technology Purchases

Once you have identified your goals, needs and resources, you will be ready to make your purchases. The six steps that follow can help you evaluate the products and choices available to you and select those to best suit your needs.

CHAPTER SIX   Selecting and Utilizing Technology

Step 1: Conduct an inventory of your current hardware, software, and functionality.

To determine what you need, you have to figure out what you have. Conduct a physical inventory of the hardware and software in your office, rather than just relying on the inventory provided during orientation. You may be surprised to learn what you already own or what equipment is listed on your inventory but missing in your office. For example, hardware upgrades to individual computers — such as installing more memory, larger hard drives, or cable TV capabilities — may not appear on your equipment inventory even though you own

CMF Technology Resources

For more than a decade, the Congressional Management Foundation has researched the use of technology in Hill offices and has become a leading expert on information and communication technologies in the House and Senate. Our research has led to best practices in constituent communications and congressional websites. Some of CMF's resources are outlined below.

Communicating with Congress: How Capitol Hill is Coping with the Surge in Citizen Advocacy — This groundbreaking study explores the surge in communications to Congress, how offices are reacting to the increased workload and how they view constituent communications practices. It also provides a comprehensive analysis of the implications of this research to citizens, grassroots organizations and congressional offices.

Communicating with Congress: How the Internet Has Changed Citizen Engagement — This report discusses the results of groundbreaking research with over 10,000 U.S. citizens with regard to their methods, reasons, and expectations in communicating with their Members of Congress.

Communicating with Congress: Recommendations for Improving the Democratic Dialogue — The concluding report from the *Communicating with Congress* Project that puts forward recommendations and a concept for a new model to make communications between citizens and Congress more meaningful and manageable.

Online Town Hall Meetings: Exploring Democracy in the 21st Century — This report summarizes the findings and recommendations from a study of 21 online town halls between Members of Congress and their constituents that were facilitated by CMF and its academic research partners.

Gold Mouse Project — These extensive research projects identify best practices in congressional websites and recognize the best Member, committee, and leadership offices with Gold Mouse Awards.

The Partnership For A More Perfect Union Website — In addition to the publications above, the Partnership's website provides a wealth of information and guidance to help congressional offices manage technology, websites, and social media. Find the latest research and reports at pmpu.org. ∎

them. You should also consider the services provided by the House and Senate. For example, rather than purchase hardware and software to support capabilities such as video conferencing, high-resolution printing, and electronic message management (including voice mail, e-mail, and faxes), House offices can use services provided by the Chief Administrative Officer (CAO).

Step 2: Talk to the people who can help.

Abundant resources are available to help you explore your options and make your decisions, including a wealth of information on the House and Senate intranets and the Internet. In addition, talk to the following people:

- **House and Senate Customer Support.** All House Members are assigned a Technical Support Representative (TSR) by the Chief Administrative Officer (202-225-6002) and all Senators are assigned a Customer Support Analyst (CSA) by the Senate Sergeant at Arms (202-224-0821). These people are there to help you find the information and support you need to purchase and operate your hardware and software.
- **The Committee on House Administration and the Senate Committee on Rules and Administration.** These committees are responsible for overseeing information technology in their chamber and setting policies regarding its purchase and use. They can also provide information regarding the technological needs, challenges, and future goals of the House and Senate.
- **Systems Administrators' Associations.** The House and the Senate both have active Systems Administrators' Associations, whose members and leadership can provide insight into what other offices are doing.
- **Vendor Representatives.** CSS vendors (and, for House Members, CMS and maintenance vendors) representatives will be among the first people you meet on the Hill. Your office should develop relationships with them as you contemplate what you need. Ask them questions and solicit information and bids from several before you make decisions and purchases.
- **Other Personal Offices.** Staff are good sources of subjective information about hardware and software. You will get the clearest picture of the experiences of other offices with hardware and software if you speak with the Chief of Staff (House), Administrative Director (Senate), and the Systems Administrators.
- **Leadership Offices.** The leadership offices in both the House and the Senate are very involved in helping offices use technology to be more effective and can provide additional assistance and resources.
- **House Office Coordinators and Senate Customer Support Analysts.** These individuals can help you with the purchase of equipment, maintenance plans (in the House), and the development of inventories of your equipment and software.

Step 3: Shop around.
House offices are encouraged to contract with a maintenance provider to help install and support their systems, but they do not have to purchase only from their maintenance vendors. House offices can request bids for products from other vendors or comparison shop online or at discount stores.

Senate offices that use their Economic Allocation Fund to purchase items are required to use the Senate's Technology Catalog to order items. If they do, the installation and support is provided by the Senate's support vendor for these items.

Step 4: Try before you buy.
To the extent possible, test hardware and software you might purchase in an environment as close as possible to the one in which it will be operating. For example, if you are considering a CMS/CSS package, try it out in both the DC and district/state offices of a veteran Member if you can. The version the vendor uses to market the product does not have to operate under the same strain that the actual software will. You should also ask the vendor for congressional references, and be sure to check them. You will be much happier with your purchase if you have realistic expectations from the start. The same applies for all hardware and software. The "floor models" operate under ideal conditions, but your equipment will not. It is very difficult for the vendors to predict and replicate all of the variables that might impact performance, so be diligent in your testing. In the Senate, the Sergeant at Arms has a Demo Center where office staff can see and use most of the currently supported hardware.

Step 5: Be sure your planned purchase is compatible with your existing system.
Be attentive to the technical requirements of any hardware and software you are going to purchase. You must have at least the minimum technical standards required to run it, but having the minimum does not guarantee optimal performance. You should also discuss compatibility, not only with the vendor of the hardware and software you are considering purchasing, but also with your CMS/CSS vendor, your TSR or CSA, and, in the House, your maintenance provider. Always check with all of these people *before* you buy, because the complex technical environments in the House and Senate can impact the performance of certain hardware and software tools.

Step 6: Pay close attention to the installation and maintenance details.
Once you have decided what to buy, be sure to work out the specifics of installation, testing, follow-up, maintenance, support, and all associated fees and

timeframes before you commit to the final purchase. The purchase price is only part of the cost of most systems, and you should be fully aware of the bottom line. Additionally, installation of new hardware and software in a congressional office often takes time, and it will cause your office some degree of inconvenience. It also involves coordinating details and schedules with your staff, vendors, and House or Senate support staff. Work out the general schedules and details before you commit to the purchase, and be sure to flesh them out and monitor them after you commit to the purchase. The better planned and managed the process is, the easier it will be on everyone.

Keeping Your System Running Smoothly

Once you have a computer system that meets your needs, the next step is to get it to work effectively for you. For this to happen, you must have three things in place: solid maintenance support, a set of policies and procedures governing its use, and a well-trained staff.

Exploring Maintenance Options

Congressional offices depend upon their hardware and software for almost everything they do. When systems malfunction, you lose time and work. It is unrealistic to expect all systems to run perfectly one hundred percent of the time — functionality like that costs far more than a single congressional office can afford. When systems do go down, you will want to receive the service, support, and good advice you need quickly. Clearly outline your maintenance expectations and consider your options carefully. You need reliable resources to keep your system as functional as possible, to provide fixes and enhancements when you need them, and to provide good counsel when it is time to upgrade. Whether and how you rely on a skilled or shared Systems Administrator, a support or maintenance provider, or a combination of these is the choice you need to make. For Senate offices, the SAA provides the maintenance through a contracted support vendor and standard service levels apply to all offices in DC and the state.

Defining Policies and Procedures

To ensure that technology is utilized effectively and appropriately in your office, you will need to define policies and procedures concerning many different aspects of its maintenance and use. House Information Resources and the Senate Sergeant at Arms can provide guidance and sample policies, and much of this information can be found on their websites. At a minimum, your policies and procedures should clearly define your expectations regarding:

CHAPTER SIX   Selecting and Utilizing Technology

- **Ethics.** As technology on the Hill is constantly changing, so are the rules regulating it. Be certain that your office is aware of, and complying with, the latest rules regarding technology use from the Committee on House Administration or the Senate Committee on Rules and Administration. In addition, you may want to go further and require that staff not only follow the rules, but also conduct themselves in a way that will not give any appearance of impropriety. Policies should cover such topics as sending unsolicited e-mail, privacy of constituent information, and appropriate use of technology and social media.
- **Security.** The House and Senate both have clear policies about data security and recommendations for office data security policies. Be sure you are familiar with them. Once data enters your office system, the House and Senate cannot manage the security, so you must establish and communicate policies to protect your data.
- **System maintenance and upgrading.** To protect the data in your office and ensure staff productivity, it is important to perform routine maintenance on your server and staff computers. Clearly define a procedure for server backups and routine maintenance for your Systems Administrator to follow. The procedure should be clear so that other staff can perform maintenance when the Systems Administrator is unable to do so. You should also define policies about upgrading and replacing your hardware. The House and Senate follow industry standards and encourage a policy of replacing servers, laptops, and desktops every three years, so budget accordingly. This will ensure that your system remains current and will prevent your office from having to spend for an entirely new system in one outlay.
- **Emergency procedures.** What procedures must your office follow to ensure the safety and security of your office data in the event of an emergency? Who will shut down the system, if necessary? Do you have a recovery plan? How will you ensure that you have a proper and secure back-up of your office data? How will staff communicate, if at all? Will staff have access to office files? Will phones be forwarded to another location, such as the district/state office? How will your website be used in an emergency, if at all? Who on your staff will be designated the Office Emergency Coordinator (OEC)? Contact the House Office of Emergency Management (OEM) (202-226-0950) and the Senate Office of Police Operations, Security and Emergency Preparedness (POSEP) (202-228-6737) for more information and guidance.
- **Knowledge management and archiving.** If you hope to achieve easy access to important documents, this should be a key priority. Unless you want each staffer to devise his or her own electronic filing system, you should establish policies for file and data management. What is the most

logical, user-friendly filing system? Will documents be filed by issue? By document type? By date? Should only final drafts be stored on the server? What file naming scheme must staff follow to ensure that everyone understands what he or she has access to? When and how will files be deleted or archived? How will staffers share and collaborate on important documents or projects? The Senate Archivist and the House Office of History and Preservation both provide guidelines and resources to help offices create effective record keeping strategies.
- **Remote access and telecommuting.** Members and staff engage in a great deal of travel, and you will need to decide how you want to handle remote access to your office information. Which staff will have remote access? How should information be accessed? What precautions should be taken? Will your office support telecommuting staff? The Committee on House Administration and the Senate Committee on Rules and Administration can provide policy guidance in these areas.
- **District/state office operations.** Determine who will be responsible for the computers in your district and state offices, where that person should turn for maintenance and support when needed, and how they should interact with the DC Systems Administrator.
- **Member website.** How often will your website be updated and maintained? How will it be integrated into the day-to-day operations of your office? What content should be posted? How will it be formatted? Who will review it? Will you include links to other sites? Does your staff know what material is prohibited from being posted? Which staff will be authorized to post material?
- **Social media.** What social media tools is the Member comfortable using? Which tools will help the office to best achieve its goals? How will potential new tools be tested and implemented? Who in the office is authorized to post to Facebook or Tweet? Who is responsible for reviewing posts for accuracy and political sensitivity? Will the office respond to some, all, or no incoming posts? What will you do when people say inaccurate or negative things about your boss?
- **Constituent e-mail.** What is the procedure for processing constituent e-mail? Will e-mail responses be formatted differently from written responses? For more information on developing and maintaining an effective mail operation, refer to Chapter 14, "Managing Constituent Communications."

Once policies and procedures governing technology use are developed, it is extremely important that they are shared with staff, and strictly enforced. Offices that have failed to do this have found that staff create procedures of their own, which often leads to misplaced data, duplicated work, and inconsistent messages to constituents. Due to the high staff turnover on Capitol Hill, you should formalize these policies and procedures in an office manual, and communicate them to staff every six months or post them on your office intranet.

Training Your Staff

To get the most out of the system you purchase, you will need to be sure that staff know how to use it. Consider the following three key training needs your office will have:

- **Systems Administrator training.** House and Senate computer systems are becoming increasingly complex. If your Systems Administrator is well trained, your system will run much more smoothly, your data will be more secure, and time and materials maintenance fees will be lower. Both the House Learning Center and the Senate Office of Education and Training offer high-quality, free training that is adapted specifically to the needs of the House and Senate environments. Additionally, Systems Administrators — and indeed anyone on the frontline of managing constituent communications — can receive CMS/CSS training directly from their vendor.
- **District/state staff training.** Do not neglect the staff in your district or state office. In many ways, they are more in need of training than are your DC staff, because they typically have access to fewer support resources. The House Learning Center and the Senate Office of Education and Training offer a variety of options that district and state staff can use, including Web-based training, videos, paper-based instructions, and manuals. You can also arrange to have a training representative travel to your district/state office to train staff.
- **New employee training.** Turnover is high on Capitol Hill, and you will need to ensure that your new hires get up to speed with your system as quickly as possible. Even if you are hiring people who have worked on the Hill before, you will need to introduce them to your office policies and procedures and any software versions they may not have used before.

MANAGEMENT FACT
The House Learning Center and the Senate Office of Education and Training offer professional development and technical training opportunities and services to House and Senate staff.

Conclusion

Purchasing and using hardware and software is a lot easier and a lot more effective when you begin by deciding what you want to do with it. Don't get bogged down in the minutiae. Vendors will begin to approach you immediately, and they will make very convincing arguments about why you *need* their systems. You will begin to feel overwhelmed by the number of choices and decisions you need to make.

Relax.

Although outfitting your office with the technology you need to be successful seems daunting, these decisions will almost always sort themselves out once you know what you want your technology to accomplish for you. If approached methodically, the choices and decisions can be whittled down to a manageable few. Focus on determining the capabilities you'll need to help you accomplish your goals in Congress. You can then explore the options with the help of your Technical Support Representative (TSR) or Customer Support Analyst (CSA) to find the hardware and software that will provide those capabilities.

In November and December, you should assess the capabilities of the equipment you might inherit (or might not if it is deemed inadequate). This initial work will allow you to make an informed decision about whether your existing equipment will meet your needs. If it won't, you'll be able to decide when and how to upgrade. You'll also be able to bring your technology choices into your other early decisions (i.e. budgeting, district/state offices, hiring staff), all of which will contribute to your first-term success.

Chapter Summary
The DOs and DON'Ts of

Selecting and Utilizing Technology

Do...

- **address critical issues before you make final purchasing decisions.** Consider:
  - the technology required to fulfill office goals;
  - the staff's level of comfort and skill with technology;
  - whether your district/state has any quirks that could demand unique technological resources;
  - how much of your budget you want to earmark for technology.
- **follow the "six-step process"** when purchasing:
  1. Inventory your current hardware, software, and functionality.
  2. Talk to the institutional experts in the House and Senate who can help.
  3. Shop around.
  4. Try before you buy. Test the equipment in a similar environment.
  5. Be sure your planned purchase is compatible with your existing system.
  6. Pay close attention to the installation and maintenance details. Maintenance contracts, services and costs can vary significantly.
- **establish technology policies and procedures** for data management, district/state office operations, social media use, and constituent communications.

Don't...

- **get mired in the details** when purchasing hardware and software. What you want to accomplish is more important than how you will accomplish it.
- **plan just for today's needs.** With the rapidly changing environment and increasing demands from constituents, offices need to be prepared to expand their technological capabilities quickly.
- **treat technology as an afterthought.** Think of it as integral to every function of your office.
- **buy anything without consulting available resources** or other offices that currently use the system. House staff should consult with their TSR; Senate staff should discuss options with their CSA.
- **neglect training the staff.** Your system will run more smoothly and staff will be more productive after training.

CHAPTER SEVEN

Establishing District and State Offices

This Chapter Includes...

- ☆ The importance of decisions concerning district/state offices
- ☆ Selecting the number and location of district/state offices
- ☆ Determining which office to open first
- ☆ Obtaining furniture and equipment for district/state offices

"All politics is local," according to the late House Speaker Tip O'Neill. And nothing creates more visibility on the home front, especially for a freshman Member, than opening a district or state office. According to most veterans, opening one office on swearing-in day is important. It need not be fully staffed or adequately equipped, but the door should be open. Therefore, preparing to open one office should be a critical task to undertake between the election and the start of the new Congress.

In addition, there are great benefits if you begin now to plan for all of your district/state offices. First, your success as a Member of Congress will depend on ensuring that your combined DC and district/state resources are coordinated in pursuit of your office's goals. Also, decisions regarding the number, location and objectives of your district/state offices will influence other key management decisions, such as budgeting, management structure, staffing and technology purchases. Finally, many decisions regarding district/state offices are difficult to reverse (or at least not without political or financial penalties).

This chapter will help you through the process of planning your district/state offices and opening one by the start of the new Congress.

Additional Information
CMF has published an entire book on this topic, *Keeping It Local: A Guide for Managing Congressional District/State Offices*. Visit www.cmfweb.org or contact CMF at 202-546-0100 for more information. ∎

Importance of Decisions Concerning District/State Offices

You have just been elected. In contrast to the tasks awaiting you in Washington — lobbying for committee assignments, making a favorable impression upon your party's leadership and your state delegation, and attending policy seminars led by the best minds in the country — the task of opening district/state offices can seem mundane. Many Chiefs of Staff tell us, however, that your initial decisions in the district/state are at least as important as those in Washington.

Why? For starters, more federal government programs are affecting the lives of constituents, from Social Security to federally funded local projects. Additionally, states and cities have more control over how federal dollars are spent, which places demands on district/state staff to become engaged in how those funds are distributed. This results in a growing need for Members to become more involved in local matters.

Citizens are also becoming savvier about the legislative process through the explosion of information available. Whether it's televised floor or committee proceedings, 24-hour news channels or blog updates, what happens in Washington just doesn't seem so far away anymore. A congressional office may be able to distinguish between legislative activities in DC and casework or community outreach handled in the district/state, but constituents and local media might not. For many constituents and reporters, there is no difference between contacting DC or a district/state office — especially by e-mail. Next door is the same as across the country.

In addition, technology has made Members and staff more accessible. Congressional offices can communicate electronically with more constituents more quickly than ever before and can directly engage them in public policy. Citizens are also using technology to stay informed of what their Senators and Representatives are doing and to make their voices heard. This results in greater coordination and awareness at the grassroots level, and constituents are turning out in greater numbers at Member events and appearances in the district/state.

Setting up district/state offices deserves your full attention for other reasons too:

Intractability. According to many Chiefs of Staff, you may never overcome an early mistake in your district/state. Administrative decisions in the district/state take on an air of permanency. Did you hire staff with ties to your strongest supporters? If so, how difficult will it be to fire them if they don't perform adequately? Once you've established a district/state office, can you move it without sending an implicit message to the local community that other constituents are more important? In contrast, the political cost back home of changing committee assignments or firing legislative staff is a lot less.

Your initial choices, of course, are not permanent. You can change staff and move offices, and *should* if those steps will better enable you to achieve your goals. But be advised that such action will come at a price. It will create problems that will have to be dealt with. Invest time and energy up front and avoid costly mistakes.

Public scrutiny. Decisions about your district/state offices often seem intractable because, small as the fishbowl is in Washington, it is even smaller back home. In Washington, you are one of hundreds of Members of Congress, but back home, you are only one of three. Your first visible decisions about your district/state will be locating offices and hiring local staff. Expect intense interest from the local media and community groups.

Fewer resources. An infrastructure of support services for congressional offices is well-established in Washington. If the computer system in your Washington office isn't working properly, qualified technical support staff are minutes away. If your Washington office needs rewiring, you need do little more than ask. In contrast, your district/state office, especially one in a rural area, is generally on its own. Arranging for congressional support services or for locally contracted vendors to reach you is more complicated and may result in a charge to your office account.

Selecting the Number of District/State Offices

Q: How many district/state offices should you establish?
A: *Only as many as you need!*

This seems obvious, but many Chiefs of Staff report that one of the biggest mistakes they made was setting up district/state offices in areas "without a demonstrated constituent need." Chiefs of Staff described situations where "too many offices were promised during the campaign" and the difficulty of closing an office once it was opened.

Senators typically maintain three to six state offices (an average of 4.4), and House Members have one to three district offices (an average of 2.4). Part-time offices can be an option for House Members depending on the leasing and other arrangements you obtain. However, our research indicates

Figure 7-1

District/State Offices Maintained by Members

Number of District or State Offices	Percent of House Members	Percent of Senators
1	26%	10%
2	33%	12%
3	28%	12%
4	9%	15%
5	5%	18%
6	**	17%
7	**	11%
8	**	4%
9	**	1%

Note: total may not equal 100 due to rounding. ** House offices are asked if they have 5+ district offices.
Source: Congressional Management Foundation.

that it is usually very expensive to operate a part-time office when you consider the rent, telephone, and equipment expenses that are necessary to make the office operational. Another option is holding community or open office hours regularly in various locations. Post offices, municipal buildings, and libraries may make space available to you for this purpose. This is an excellent way to "test-market" the demand for constituent services in an area and allows the Member to serve remote areas and reach constituents who may be unable to travel. Prior to accepting any donated space, House Members should check with the Committee on Standards of Official Conduct (202-225-7103). Senators are not allowed to utilize donated space.

Criteria for Selecting the Optimal Number of Offices

Criteria you might consider in selecting the number of district/state offices you should establish:

Size of your district/state. A physically smaller House district usually will enable you to operate fewer offices. In the Senate, your state's population will determine your "aggregate square footage allowance" — you may open as many state offices as you wish as long as they total less than this allowance. This means Senators need to consider carefully not just how many offices to open, but *how big they will be*. Senators from vast but sparsely populated states take special note, as you've got the largest area to service and the smallest allowance.

Accessibility to constituents. Accessibility is obviously tied to the district or state size. If it is important to you that as many constituents as possible have quick and easy access to your services, you don't want them to spend several hours traveling to your office. Or perhaps you feel comfortable satisfying this need by installing a toll-free 1-800 line or maintaining a quality website so that constituents have easy access to the resources of your office.

Constituent expectations. Whether or not you created certain expectations, constituents have them. Generally they derive from two sources:

1. **Number of offices operated by your predecessor.** It can be difficult to reduce the number of district/state offices from four to two or three. It is not impossible, but for communities who have become accustomed to, or feel entitled to, a particular office location, such a cut undoubtedly reflects poorly on the new Member. Make sure you have a plan to address potentially angered constituents.
2. **Campaign promises.** If you promised six offices on the campaign trail and used it to your political advantage, chances are you will be expected to — and will want to — keep your promise once elected.

Competing budget priorities. Ask, "What else can I do with my allotted resources to accomplish my goals most effectively?" If this means opening another district/state office, great. If it means having a Press Secretary based in the district/state, maybe that's a better idea. This is more of a limitation in the House because you are going to pay for everything the office needs to operate (rent, furniture, supplies, equipment, staff, etc.). For Senators, this may be less of a concern because much of what it takes to run a Senate office is allocated to you and does not compete with other priorities (notable exceptions are staff and office supplies).

Urban/rural differences. It should come as no surprise that rural districts/states generally operate more offices. It is still important, however, to assess the volume of constituent use of offices before opening them.

Strategic importance of constituent services. Again, how important are constituent services in your overall plan? If it's crucial because you said you were going to offer the best constituent services ever delivered in the state or because a very tough race is expected in the next election, you may need to open that extra office.

Staff hiring limitations. A House Member may employ up to 18 permanent staff and 4 additional staff who must be designated as paid interns, part-time employees, shared employees, temporary employees, or employees on leave without pay. This total includes the DC and all district offices. If you open another district office, is there space under the cap to hire someone to staff it, or will you transfer someone from another office? Will one person be enough to cover the phones and meet with constituents? Numbers are not a concern in the Senate, which has no staff limit, but budgetary restrictions may be.

Office Location and Space Considerations

Deciding on office locations and the type of space can be very challenging, especially in the rush between Election Day and the start of the new year. It's certainly not necessary to have secured all your district/state offices by the start of the new Congress, but the decision process should be well underway. Use the following criteria to help shape your deliberation.

Criteria for Locating Offices

Proximity to:

1. **Constituents most in need of casework.** If casework is a priority for your office, locate at least one office near the segments of your constituency that most frequently seek assistance. Locations for this office might include economically depressed or high unemployment areas, or areas with large elderly and veteran populations, or large numbers of government employees. On the other hand, central locations can be a favorite "drop by" destination for people who only want to visit.
2. **Federal agencies.** Occasionally a visit to a federal liaison officer is necessary to get a case moving or to overcome a bureaucratic roadblock. Frequently, offices are located within walking distance of federal agency offices, which may help Constituent Services Representatives develop a personal rapport with agency officials and facilitate casework operation.
3. **Targeted groups.** If your strategic plan calls for building or strengthening ties to a certain group, an office located in its community can be a crucial part of that effort.
4. **Airport or train station.** It's important to remember your own needs when locating offices. Late-night and early-morning trips between Washington and the district/state might be made easier if at least one of your offices is easily accessible to a major transportation facility.
5. **Staff.** Recruiting and keeping a first-rate staff is always a challenge, and is made even tougher if your office locations create difficult commutes for your employees.

Visibility. How important is it that your office itself be visible? If a "presence" is important, a storefront office should win out over an office in a high-rise.

Campaign promises. As with promises about the number of offices, you should think twice before reneging on a campaign pledge concerning where you would locate an office.

Rental cost (House only). The more offices you are going to open, the more important it is to get "the best bang for your buck." Be sure to have the cost of renovations included in the rent.

Quality of the space. No one wants to work in dingy, claustrophobic surroundings or in an office that does not support the needs of the equipment used by staff every day. This doesn't mean every staffer has a private office, or there's a luxurious full kitchen. Still, the quality of the work environment may be an important factor in retaining good staff.

Ask up front, "Is it a pleasing environment? Is the office an adequate size? Do we have enough hard-wired electrical outlets for computer and copier needs? Can the copier be centrally located, while not drowning out conversations with constituents in the front office? Is it possible to renovate the office?"

Assess potential renovation needs early and determine what can be accomplished. It can be extremely frustrating to deal with an ineffective layout simply because you didn't negotiate for renovations when you signed the lease. In addition, compliance with the strictures of the Occupational Safety and Health Act or the Americans With Disabilities Act may require renovation work (usually a requirement of the landlord). Be sure your office is, or can be made, accessible to all of your constituents.

Number of staff and interns. As a rule of thumb, allow 135 square feet for each person working in the office. Include the Member if he will be working out of a district/state office regularly. Don't forget to include interns in your calculations. Crowding your paid staff or, even worse, turning away interns for lack of space is a lose-lose situation that can be easily prevented. Also, make sure you have plenty of storage space because casework files will grow quickly.

Parking availability. This is a crucial consideration for both staff and constituents, especially if there is a "walk-in" tradition in your district/state. Parking tickets are not the way to "win friends and influence people."

Safety of location. To the extent possible, make sure your offices are in neighborhoods where staff and visiting constituents will feel safe. If the neighborhood's safety is marginal, consider a "duress button" with a line to police headquarters.

Length of the lease. Before you get too far in your negotiations, make sure the building will accept a two-year (House) or six-year (Senate) renewable lease. All leases for district and state offices must be reviewed and approved before signing by the Senate Sergeant at Arms' State Office Liaison or the Administrative Counsel of the Chief Administrative Officer in the House.

Cleaning and maintenance. Cleaning arrangements are frequently overlooked, yet are very important to a professional office appearance. Staff should not be expected to vacuum and dust after a long day of serving constituents.

Office Options

Once you have decided upon the number and general location of your district/state offices, you still need a specific site. Your options include occupying your predecessor's offices, using federal office space, renting private facilities, and using a mobile office housed in a van.

Occupying Your Predecessor's Offices. In our surveys, Chiefs of Staff and District/State Directors had mixed opinions about taking over the offices established by the preceding Member. Some were very satisfied with the results; for others, it was a mistake.

If taking over the office space of your predecessor is a possibility for your office, consider the following questions:

- How does your strategic plan differ from your predecessor's?
- What were constituent perceptions of the preceding Member's offices?
- Were the offices adequate for constituent services?
- Are renovations needed? Are they possible?
- Can renovations commence between the election and the first of the year?

Using Government vs. Privately-Owned Space. Past surveys have shown the majority of Senators, and a significant number of Representatives, had one or more of their offices in a federal building. In fact, the law says that Senators must use federal space if it is available and suitable to their needs. Leasing in federal buildings offers several potential advantages:

- The General Services Administration's (GSA) Congressional Services Representative and the Senate Sergeant at Arms' State Office Liaison can tell you what space is available in the areas of interest to you.
- The other tenants in a federal building are federal agencies. Close proximity to agencies may facilitate casework and probably increase constituents' use of your office.
- Seeking private space may subject you to pressure from people you know to locate in their buildings. After all, a Member of Congress is a prestigious tenant. Be very cautious about renting from anyone you know. This includes friends, supporters, prominent local political figures, and certainly political foes. The press intuitively questions the ethical nature of any government contracts directed toward family and friends. Moreover, any dispute over the terms of the lease could readily threaten or compromise any friendship or association, probably a risk worth avoiding.
- For Senators, renting space in federal buildings may be simpler. Senators may not pay more per square foot for private space than the

current maximum GSA rate for the city in which the office is located. Additionally, the lease may not include agreements to pay any non-rent charges separately. This means parking, signs, maintenance, common area upkeep, renovations and repairs, etc. must be built into the rent. Federal landlords are used to this, while private landlords are not. This also means that, should you rent privately-owned space, the lease should not commit you up to the full GSA rate at the very beginning. You will want to have some room under the cap to pay for unanticipated costs associated with extra parking space, repairs or renovations.

Renting private space also has its advantages:

- On rare occasions, private space can be more accessible during evenings and weekends. Depending on the location, businesses may be open beyond the 9-to-5 weekday schedule. By contrast, because federal agencies are closed most evenings and weekends, a federal building may be closed during those times.
- Federal office buildings exist primarily to house executive agencies, reducing the availability of space to other tenants, including Members of Congress. Therefore, your choices of privately-owned office space may be greater.
- Sometimes the only spaces GSA has available are more square footage than you need at a higher cost than you want.

Using Mobile Offices. Mobile offices are an alternative to traditional district/state offices that a few Members use to good effect. Members who operate a mobile office say it increases visibility; provides a personal atmosphere for one-on-one meetings; demonstrates a commitment to "staying in touch;" enables the Member to serve remote areas and reach constituents who may be unable to travel; and facilitates initiating casework.

There are, however, other considerations that may make the use of vans less attractive. These include maintenance and operational costs; extreme weather that may discourage constituents from waiting to be served; unpredictable constituent turnout; and unproductive travel time.

Each Senator may lease one mobile office, with operating costs (excluding the cost of staff) paid for by the Senate Sergeant at Arms. A mobile office is charged against a Senator's allotment based on a formula that takes into account the actual cost of the lease, the operating costs, and the number of square feet remaining in the Senator's allowance. House Members pay for mobile offices out of their Members' Representational Allowance (MRA).

The Option of Senators Sharing Offices

House Members are not allowed to share district offices with each other, although they may share them with local officials. Senators from the same state may share office space, but there are statutory and Senate rules and regulations that must be adhered to. Because of the complications, you should discuss this option in detail with the Sergeant at Arms.

To help you decide if sharing offices is right for your office, consider the common features of those who do. They:

- Make excellent constituent services a top priority.
- Get along well together professionally and personally and are comfortable sharing the goodwill and credit generated by shared constituent outreach activities.
- Are from the same political party.
- Share only employees who perform non-political and non-legislative functions (administrative and casework staff are most common).
- Agree in advance on how to split *everything*: costs for resources (furniture, franking, square footage allotment), credit for casework (who gets to send out the press release touting a success story?), staff time and expertise (to whom do they report?), office attention (both Senators in the same part of the state at the same time holding different events could overtax office resources).

Which Office To Open First

Developing a plan for the number and location of all your district/state offices doesn't answer the most immediate question: Which one do I open first? As long as your overall plan is in place, it really doesn't matter. A major goal of opening your first office is simply to demonstrate that you're open for business. But some choices may be better than others, so you may want to take these factors into account:

"As long as your overall plan for establishing district/state offices is in place, it really doesn't matter which one you open first."

Symbolism Counts. The media will be paying attention, so if you want to convey a message beyond, "yes, we're open," this is your chance. If your grand plan calls for more or fewer offices than your predecessor, or in dif-

CHAPTER SEVEN   Establishing District and State Offices   111

ferent parts of town, now might be the time to "sell" the changes. Part of that sale can be conveyed by the symbolism of which office is opened first.

Make Sure the Office Can Carry the Load. One office will be representing you in the district/state for a while. Make sure it can handle the immediate onslaught of work, especially constituent contact. This may mean having private areas for one-on-one meetings and conference rooms for large groups.

Additionally, there will be pending cases from your predecessor (which you hope get transferred to you), and some of those people may call to see whether you still have their files. You don't need to start processing the work immediately, but you need the basic ability to field the questions and look competent.

Don't Do Anything Just To Look Good on Day One. You may want to make a favorable impression, but don't blow your budget or make decisions you can't undo. Think twice before hiring too many staff too quickly (see Chapter 5, "Hiring Your Core Staff") or buying expensive reception area furniture.

Furniture and Office Equipment

Another mundane but important task is outfitting district and state offices with furnishings and equipment: desks, chairs, tables, computers, staplers, telephones, garbage cans, and other essentials. Chiefs of Staff of freshman Members tell many stories of learning about rules only by breaking them.

Our first and best recommendation is to always check *before* making commitments. In the House, contact the Committee on House Administration (Democrats: 202-225-2061; Republicans: 202-225-8281) and CAO Office Services (202-225-3994); in the Senate, consult the Sergeant at Arms' State Office Liaison (202-224-5409).

Help is also available from the General Services Administration (GSA). GSA regional liaisons work closely with new offices. For both freshman House and Senate Members, liaisons can assist in selecting GSA furniture or finding local private discount dealers. Senate offices should be aware that *all* purchases, including those from private sources, have to be made through GSA, whereas House offices can purchase from GSA or directly from private vendors. House offices should also keep in mind that, if buying from private sources, most states exempt your purchases from sales taxes. Check to see if yours does, and if vendors will require proper documentation from the House. When purchasing through GSA, the regional liaisons will handle the tax exemption for you.

MANAGEMENT FACT
Most states exempt congressional offices from sales taxes.

Although the rules and budgets for outfitting district/state offices differ between the House and Senate, the process is roughly the same:

STEP 1: Compare the inventory of your predecessor's furniture and equipment with what is actually on hand. You'll get the inventory after the election.

STEP 2: Decide what you're going to keep and what you're going to return. Stories of battered furniture and worn-out equipment are common, particularly in the House. At the same time, a few minutes examination can save the office substantial expense. Serviceable secondhand furniture will be cheaper than buying new, and is available for immediate use.

STEP 3: Assess your needs. How many staff and interns will be using each office? How many desks and chairs do you need? How many rooms will be available for meeting with constituents? Will the Member have a private office? What level of quality is appropriate for the office furnishings in general and for the Member's office?

STEP 4: Consult with the appropriate institutional staff. Again, always check before making commitments. In the House, call the Committee on House Administration and CAO Office Services; in the Senate, contact the Sergeant at Arms' State Office Liaison.

STEP 5: Place your orders. Senate offices must purchase through GSA, while House offices can buy from a local vendor or GSA.

There are some additional things to keep in mind that are chamber-specific. On the **Senate** side:

Remember: you do *not* pay for furniture or other furnishings (carpets, curtains, etc.) out of your Senator's Account. You have a separate allowance for your offices based on your "allowable" square footage. Your allowance may already be all or partially "spent" by the value of your predecessor's furniture, which you will inherit. If you wish to return an item to GSA, your allowance will be credited with the item's original cost.

You may also want GSA to restore and refurbish older pieces. If it can be restored for less than half the cost to replace it, then the Sergeant at Arms will not charge the Senator's allowance for the work. For this reason, you may want to consider keeping some of your predecessor's big-ticket items, particularly desks, tables, and cabinets, even if they appear old, scratched, and decrepit. While restoration might be more cost effective than replacement, this option is allowed on a case-by-case basis. Contact the Sergeant at Arms' State Office Liaison (202-224-5409) for guidance *and* approval before proceeding.

Because all of your offices will be furnished out of one finite allowance, it is important that acquisitions from that allowance be monitored and approved so you don't end up with gross inequities among offices. It is helpful to develop a formula that accounts for square footage, number of employees, size and type of reception area, and any special needs (such as the amount of time the Senator will work out of that office) to use in establishing a budget for each office. You may wish to leave some money in reserve, especially in the first part of your term.

On the **House** side:

When assessing your needs, don't forget the little things such as phone lines for fax machines and garbage cans. Everything you need that's not inherited will have to be bought and paid for by your MRA. Even some items you inherit may not be paid off, in which case you'll have to assume the payments if you decide to keep them.

You have a choice of two payment plans for your purchases. Computers, office equipment, and furniture may be paid for in full or the charges may be spread over two years. Small-priced items and internal computer components such as hard drives must be paid for outright. Lump sum purchases must be kept on the Member's inventory for one year and those procured under the multi-year plan for the length of the contract. If you inherited little useful furniture and equipment from your predecessor, you may have no choice but to spread out the payments, especially if your office wants to maintain a significant presence in the district.

Conclusion

District/state offices offer an unparalleled ability for a new Member of Congress to meet constituent needs, complement DC legislative efforts with district/state events and achieve high visibility. But these offices are expensive to operate and once you've opened one, it's difficult to close down. Opening too many, or in the wrong locations, can be costly. Weigh your options, limitations and goals, and make your choices wisely.

Always check *before* you act to make sure you are complying with House/Senate rules. Most important, all leases for district and state offices must be reviewed and approved by the Senate Sergeant at Arms' State Office Liaison or the Administrative Counsel of the House before signing. If you agree to a lease that violates the rules, you could be *personally* financially liable. That's sure to ruin what should be an opening day celebration.

CHAPTER SEVEN

Chapter Summary
The DOs and DON'Ts of

Establishing District and State Offices

Do...

- **understand that setting up a district/state office is a difficult decision to reverse.** Give it your full attention because closing an office in your first term can have political repercussions.

- **weigh the advantages and disadvantages of using government vs. privately-owned space** for your district/state offices. Consider location, accessibility, cost, square footage, and other factors when making your decisions.

- **think creatively about how to best serve constituent needs.** Part-time offices and mobile offices are alternatives to the traditional district/state office, and holding regularly community and open office hours allows the Member to reach remote areas and constituents who might be unable to travel.

- **make sure the first district/state office you open is adequately prepared.** While it doesn't need to be fully staffed or equipped, the office will need to handle an immediate onslaught of meetings, scheduling requests and questions about ongoing casework.

Don't...

- **automatically decide to occupy your predecessor's office(s).** Consider how your needs and goals might necessitate a different city or a different space.

- **open more district/state offices than you need.** Use the following criteria to determine the number to open:
  – size of district/state;
  – accessibility to constituents;
  – constituent expectations;
  – competing budget priorities;
  – urban/rural differences;
  – strategic importance of constituent services; and
  – staff hiring limitations.

- **make any long-term commitments without first seeking guidance and assistance** from the Senate Sergeant at Arms' State Office Liaison or the Committee on House Administration.

- **overlook the role of technology** in increasing district/state effectiveness and efficiency.

Part II:
Defining Your Role in Congress and Your Office

Chapter Eight: Understanding the Culture of Congress:
An Insider's Guide 117

Chapter Nine: Defining Your Role in Congress 127

Chapter Ten: The Member's Role as Leader
of the Office 141

Icons Used in Setting Course

Notes a series of questions. Your unique answers can help you make decisions about managing an office and a career.

Alerts you to a situation which Hill offices have found to be problematic. Proceed with caution and pay close attention.

Notes a concept or recommendation that CMF has determined, through its research with congressional offices, to be helpful.

Identifies an office or organization which you may wish to contact for further information on the topic.

Notes a process or steps you can use in the operations of your office.

CHAPTER EIGHT

Understanding the Culture of Congress: An Insider's Guide

This Chapter Includes...

- ☆ Constants in Congress
- ☆ Three trends that have influenced recent Congresses: close party ratios, large influx of new Members and increased partisanship

Like all organizations, Congress has a culture, a context in which Members operate. This culture extends beyond formal rules and regulations to encompass the unwritten and often unstated norms, values, tensions, practices and taboos of the institution.

Culture can greatly influence a Member's official decisions by determining the scope of the choices a Member has available and how a Member defines success. Possessing insight ahead of time can help Members — especially new Members — maneuver and make choices without having to learn lessons the "hard way." This chapter is an overview of some of the trends we've observed.

Constants in Congress

Some things in Congress never seem to change, such as the pageantry of the House Sergeant at Arms carrying the mace into the chamber, or the continued presence of blotters and snuffboxes in the Senate. But these are only outer trappings. There are also some understood ways of doing business which have become ingrained in the culture of the institution, whether over two centuries or just in the past few decades. It is impossible to list them all here, but mentioning a few will give you the flavor.

First, nothing big gets done early or quickly. Policymaking in Congress can be, at times, partisan, slow, cumbersome, and frustrating. The rules and organization in each chamber exist equally for supporters and opponents of each proposition. Constituents, the media, the President and various interest groups all exert pressures. In fact, some scholars believe that Congress was created not to pass good legislation, but to stop "bad" legislation. An old maxim tells of the Senate having only two rules: unanimous consent and exhaustion. A House freshman understood the situation well: "You can have a cure for cancer and if you can't get 218 people in this body to agree with you, it doesn't matter because you can't get anything done."

> *"You can have a cure for cancer and if you can't get 218 people in this body to agree with you, it doesn't matter because you can't get anything done."*
>
> –House Freshman Member

Many state legislatures also exhibit this behavior, of course, but the effect is intensified by the diversity of interests represented at the national level. At the state level, there is usually some common understanding of, and even agreement on, at least which issues to address, if not the proposed solutions. A state legislator's concerns rarely extend beyond the other side of the state, and this is still relatively familiar territory. In contrast, Members of Congress must try to be knowledgeable about issues important to districts or states on the other side of the continent. Yet it may not be a natural inclination for a Florida Member to be sensitive to home heating fuel prices in winter, or a Kansas Member to worry if the New Jersey Turnpike has potholes. Deciding which issues to address, and how to address them, is often a gradual process.

There is also an inherent tension between a Member's individual autonomy and the efficiency of the institution. On the one hand, Members must advocate strongly for their constituents; on the other hand, they must be willing to negotiate and compromise if anything is to get done. Congress is often criticized for being both too parochial, and too plodding, to address the pressing needs of the country. Members can easily be caught in the crossfire and receive criticism whether they choose to promote institutional efficiency or exercise individual autonomy in looking out for their constituents.

Second, nothing on a schedule is written in stone. This is true whether the schedule is for projected committee hearings or mark-ups, news conferences at the upper Senate Park or the Cannon Terrace, or bills, amendments and votes expected on the floor. The haphazard nature of deciding when things in Congress get done is encouraged by more permissive legislative rules than are usually found at the state level. And even these permissive rules may be ignored or waived.

Last minute changes often lead to late nights and hectic schedules. This might be expected in the days leading up to a recess (district/state work period) or the end of the session, but it has also been occurring during non-crunch times in the House. In response, the House has seen a number of organized efforts to promote a more regular, family-friendly schedule. However, this has met with limited success. Late night sessions have occurred less frequently in the Senate in the past few years, as there seems to be a purposeful effort to allow Senators to spend evenings with their families.

Many Members simply play it safe and expect the unexpected as standard operating procedure. Accordingly, every Scheduler knows all the options for Thursday and Friday airline flights between the three Washington-area airports and the boss' district or state.

Third, Members are expected to be entrepreneurs. This trend started about 30 years ago when reforms decentralized Congress. This provided a Member with the means and the opportunity to develop an effective personal organization and to pursue personal goals. Under this system, a Member can pursue objectives, seek re-election, advance policy positions, and otherwise be successful within the framework of Congress without relying on the traditional power structures.

To assist in this task each Member has, as part of his enterprise, an office staff and official allowances that provide funds for computers, multiple district and state offices, and frequent travel home. Members also have access to committee staff, the Congressional Research Service, the Library of Congress, and other resources. These resources provide Members with virtually all they need to effectively cultivate constituent relations and to craft a career in Congress.

One popular technique of entrepreneurship has been the use of informal Congressional Member Organizations (CMO's). These caucuses may be regional (e.g., House Mississippi River Delta Caucus), based on industry (e.g., Congressional Soils Caucus) or used to promote a range of issues (e.g., Congressional Sportsmen's Caucus).

Senior Members counsel new Members that this individual behavior is not only appropriate, but expected. Being a loyal foot soldier to the party today, by itself, is not a guarantee that a Member will pass legislation or gain stature. Whereas years ago power bases, or fiefdoms, could be bestowed from above, now they must be won through individual effort and savvy.

Three Congressional Trends: Close Party Ratios, Influx of New Members and Increased Partisanship

Close Party Ratios

Recently, party ratios in each chamber have been very close when compared to historical standards. With thin majorities, both the House and Senate have been exceedingly difficult to manage. Leadership in both parties have had great difficulties imposing discipline because they often can't control factions and guarantee the votes to pass or block legislation. Consequently, leadership have had to constantly negotiate deals and try to hold together shaky alliances, and always remain concerned that virtually any small, organized group of Members has the ability to kill or demand changes to a bill. It is doubtful that this situation will change in the next Congress so long as neither party has sufficient margins to be able to win decisively without resorting to ad hoc coalitions.

In the House, the Blue Dog Democrats, New Democrat Coalition, Republican Study Committee, Congressional Black Caucus, Progressives and Westerners — to name a few — have become power brokers on various issues. The Senate filibuster rule makes even a single Senator capable of holding the chamber hostage, although filibusters themselves are rare. In practical terms, though, any combination of Senate voting blocs — i.e., conservatives upset that a proposal spends too much money, and progressives upset that it spends too little — totaling a mere forty votes can prevent cloture from being invoked on any given measure.

There have even been examples of the leadership itself being split into factions. For instance, one group might rally around a Member of the leadership promoting a position of staying "true" to party principles, while another faction is favoring a stance of seeking out bipartisan compromise. Again, this is the logical result of narrow congressional majorities.

CHAPTER EIGHT   Understanding the Culture of Congress: An Insider's Guide

From the leadership's perspective, trying to maintain party unity is a delicate balancing act: coordinating with factions, but trying not to cede control to them; offering incentives (committee seats, high-profile task force chairs, campaign assistance) to individual Members to stay loyal, but risking that the strategy won't work. While they are not always effective, these leadership efforts have given junior Members opportunities to exert influence on the process far earlier in their careers than is usually the case. As one House Democratic Member told us,

> "We now revere our freshmen. When I came here in 1992, I was told by the party elders, essentially, 'stick around and we'll talk to you in ten years.' Freshmen were viewed as relatively unimportant. These narrow margins [of control] have made every seat critical and given the freshmen much more standing than we ever had."

Still, leadership doesn't have the flexibility it once did. For example, close ratios have made it difficult for leadership to protect its vulnerable Members against unpopular votes. In previous Congresses with larger controlling margins, a Member could receive a "pass" to vote against the leadership position if he (1) made the case that voting with the leadership could significantly damage his prospects of re-election; and (2) gave sufficient notice to the leadership. In the leadership's eyes, losing a few votes this way was a small price to pay so long as it didn't affect the outcome of the vote. In the era of close party ratios, however, such a concession is politically impossible if the leadership intend to win or block a vote. On the majority side, the results, more often than not, have been that controversial bills never make it to the floor to begin with.

The growing power of moderates and other factions is becoming ingrained into the culture of Congress. Consider, for instance, the committee assignment process in the House. Whereas Members used to refer to a "Pennsylvania seat" or a "women's seat" on exclusive committees (Ways and Means, Appropriations, Energy and Commerce), they are now apt to talk about a "Blue Dog" seat or "Republican Study Committee" seat. These coalitions have expanded their reach from coordinating blocs of votes on the floor to extracting representation on key committees. Committee leaders in the House have come to expect challenges to their bills, even in committee.

Thin congressional majorities and changing party control since 1994, on top of divided government, have also shifted greater legislative power to the Executive Branch, especially in critical and high-stakes appropriations matters. Congress' difficulty in overriding the President's veto forced Congress to become more accommodating to the interests of the President.

Infusion of New Members

Another trend in Congress has been the rapid turnover of seats. Half of the members in the House and Senate were first elected within the last 10 years, a switch from past years when the chambers were dominated by "old bulls" who had served for decades.

The cultural shift resulting from this infusion of new Members has been enormous. For one, Members are rising faster into positions of power. Those whose tenure and limited experience would have ranked them as back-benchers barely a decade ago are now ascending to leadership positions or subcommittee chairs. Seniority still plays an important role in each party's hierarchy of power, of course, but the sheer number of new Members has created far more opportunities for quick advancement.

Many of these new Members have brought with them a non-traditional attitude towards their work. They view congressional service as a job, and a temporary one at that, rather than as a career. Some of these Members have limited themselves to a certain number of terms: usually three or six terms for a House Member, and two terms for a Senator. Other Members have not specified how long they'll stay but have openly expressed their intent to pursue other interests or another career at some point in the future.

This is a shift in thinking. For example, former Rep. Dennis Eckart's (D-OH) decision to retire after 12 years in office was met with blank stares and looks of confusion. How could a 43-year-old Representative from a safely Democratic district who had served barely a dozen years call it quits? Rep. Eckart's explanation that he wanted to spend more time with his family didn't make sense at the time to the Capitol Hill crowd. In the last several Congresses, however, it has not been uncommon to see Members leave Washington to enter the business world or run for other office in their home states after serving just a few terms.

> *"In the last several Congresses, it has not been uncommon to see Members leave Washington to enter the business world or run for other office in their home states after serving just a few terms."*

Many recently elected Members are less invested in the long-term success or well-being of Congress than those they replaced. Some new Members, having achieved powerful positions without working and waiting patiently for a number of years under the tutelage of senior Members, do not value tradition and protecting the institution as much as more senior Members do, or their predecessors did. Other new Members, having planned not to make Congress a career, may not consciously think about the long-term effects of their decisions on the operations of the institution.

Rather, these new Members have brought fresh ideas, a willingness to overturn tradition and a belief that it is acceptable to jeopardize the productivity of the institution when Congress is not meeting their needs. Grizzled veterans may carry on the notion that Members exist to serve Congress, but the prevalent view among many of the newer Members is that Congress exists to serve them.

Increased Partisanship and Lack of Civility

There have been a number of ramifications of close party ratios and an increase in the number of Members not planning on long-term congressional service. One that stands out is an increase in partisanship and the resulting lack of civility in the institution. In the past several years, the rhetoric has grown hot as all sides have become frustrated with the difficulty of getting their priorities through the legislative process.

In both chambers, factions or the minority party leadership have occasionally used protest votes and other tactics to shut down the floor for a time. Tensions have run high as leaders lob charges of obstructionism at each other in the media. In the House, vigorous debate has occasionally escalated into instances of name-calling, and in one or two high profile cases, near fistfights. A June 2000 *Washington Post* article described the situation in the Senate in militaristic terms:

> "Three weeks after the partisan warfare threatened a legislative meltdown, the Senate has stepped back from the brink, pulled itself together and worked its way through two virtually glitch-free weeks. But the fundamental problems that caused a virtual shutdown of Senate business before the Memorial Day recess — including policy disputes, personal tensions, power struggles and the pressure-cooker atmosphere of an election year — remain as threatening as ever. They lurk just beneath the surface, ready to explode again when a new provocation occurs."

This lack of civility has coincided with the fact that Members do not socialize with each other as much as they used to, either within their own party or with the opposite party. Bipartisan poker games among colleagues have declined in number and frequency. The Democratic and Republican Clubs don't attract the deal-making regulars they once did. Members with young families no longer seek out evening companionship with other Members. Instead, they return home as soon as a daily session of the chamber is over. Even staff participation in office softball leagues is down. A story in *The Hill* covering a farewell lunch for a retiring House Member summed it up. The story quoted another Member who attended the party and praised his colleague: "Tom has been a friend. This is not a friendly place. This is a lonely place."

It is one thing to disagree on policy; it is quite another when that disagreement turns personal. It is easier to demonize a debate opponent when you don't know him or her individually. Psychologically, it is a much harder process when that other Member enjoys a drink or two with you, or when your spouses and children get together for outings on a regular basis. In these latter cases, you are apt to recognize an opponent's decency and agree to disagree on the policy at hand.

Conclusion

The three trends discussed in this chapter — close party ratios, the large influx of new Members and increased partisanship — have significantly altered the culture of Congress over the past decade. The leadership have faced tremendous challenges in controlling the legislative agenda, and well-organized factions have taken on a more prominent role. Many recently-elected Members have come to the institution with the idea of not making congressional service a career and have risen to positions of power without going through the traditional, multi-term path to which previous generations were accustomed.

The results have often been both leadership and individual Member frustration with the difficulties of passing legislation, and more recently-elected Members' general acceptance that it is okay to risk the day-to-day efficiency and long-term effectiveness of the institution if it will produce short-term gain. These, in turn, have spawned increasingly partisan, and at times uncivil, behavior among Members. At the same time, however, there have been opportunities for more junior Members to exert influence on the policymaking process earlier in their careers than had previously been the case.

These trends are likely to continue at least through the next Congress, especially if neither party in the House or Senate is able to win a large controlling majority of seats. Members who are attuned to cultural shifts will be in a more informed position to make decisions about their careers and daily operations.

Chapter Summary
The DOs and DON'Ts of

Understanding the Culture of Congress: An Insider's Guide

Do...

- **be entrepreneurial.** Getting what you want from Congress requires individual effort and savvy. Courting leadership is not enough.
- **expect partisanship and a lack of civility.** When control of the House and Senate are tenuously held by a political party, and Members are not interested in establishing careers in the institution, partisanship reigns.

Don't...

- **expect quick action on issues.** Policymaking can be slow, partisan and frustrating.
- **think that a congressional schedule is written in stone.** There are often last minute changes that can result in late nights and hectic Member schedules.

CHAPTER NINE

Defining Your Role in Congress

This Chapter Includes...

☆ The importance of defining your role in Congress

☆ The five major roles available to Members

☆ Balancing major and minor roles

☆ Guidance for selecting your role

Many freshman and veteran Members of Congress make the mistake of assuming that their jobs and roles are largely prescribed by the Constitution and political tradition. For much of American history that conclusion may have proven true. However, as the previous chapter explains, over the past 30 years, Congress has evolved into an institution of entrepreneurs who are expected to chart their own course once elected. The most important step in this regard for a freshman or veteran Member is to define the role you want to play in Congress.

Successful Members recognize early in their tenure in Congress that there are many diverging paths to power and figure out which path they should take. Members who do not understand that they cannot do it all, that they cannot pursue all the paths, tend to fail and grow frustrated with their jobs.

Consequently, the goal of this chapter is to help you define what role you choose to play and help you prosper in this entrepreneurial culture.

The Importance of Defining Your Role

As we will detail in the next section, through its extensive work with Members and their staff, CMF has identified five primary roles Representatives or Senators can play in Congress:

1. Legislative Insider
2. Party Insider
3. Ombudsman
4. Statesman
5. Outsider

Generally speaking, Members can "major" in one of these roles and "minor" in another (provided the "minor" role is not incompatible with the "major" role). Members who are able to clearly define their roles in the institution can guide their careers with the aid of this insight.

When opportunities arise or decisions are demanded, these Members can quickly weigh the issue by asking the simple question: "Does this opportunity or decision support the role I am carving out in Congress?" For example, will serving on a leadership task force help me in my effort to become an effective legislative insider or party insider? Will writing an op-ed criticizing the President on an issue help or hurt my image as a statesman?

Having clarity about your role in Congress will make it much easier for you, and your staff, to make wise and consistent decisions on large and small matters. Over time, clear direction—combined with the discipline to stay your course—leads to successful careers within Congress. If you know your role or how you fit within the institution and diligently direct your resources in support of that role, you will greatly minimize inefficiency or the unproductive "tacking" so common in many House and Senate offices.

> *"If you know your role or how you fit within the institution and diligently direct your resources in support of that role, you will greatly minimize inefficiency or the unproductive 'tacking' so common in many House and Senate offices."*

One of the most common and distinguishing characteristics of very successful people is the ability to know what they want and how they can deploy their strengths to achieve it. This clarity about "what" and "how" seems far more correlated with professional success than does talent or hard work. Defining your role in Congress ideally should be the first step in this process because your choice can make it easier to develop your long-term mission statement and your short-term goals. Not all Members, however, will be able to define the right role or fit in Congress early on. Some experience and experimentation may be needed to figure out their role. Members who feel stymied in their attempts to define their fit should give themselves the time they need to make this decision while still making sure they set annual goals for themselves and their office.

While the argument for role clarification may seem obvious, most Members of Congress ignore this step and prefer to operate more opportunistically. They scan the environment on a daily basis looking for issues to take on or needs to address without ever fully recognizing the problems with this approach. These Members and their staffs routinely struggle to adapt to the opportunities they identify by having to constantly learn new skills, develop new expertise and cultivate new relationships. These offices can almost always be characterized as working too hard and accomplishing too little. What they don't recognize amidst their hard work is that this approach is very time-consuming and stressful, and more often than not leads to disappointment. Success in Congress — particularly early success — requires focusing on what you can do successfully, learning how to do those few things very well by developing process or content expertise, and using your skills and expertise repeatedly.

Of course seniority, and its rich benefits such as committee chairmanships, also greatly contribute to success. However, even powerful committee chairmen can and do squander their strength by failing to sufficiently define their role in the institution and by trying to operate in too many arenas. This approach usually leads these Members to engage in activities which dilute their power and expose their weaknesses.

A Discussion of the Five Roles

Most of the public, and many Members and staff in Congress, tend to view the role of Senator or Representative in rather monolithic terms: to pass bills or make public policy. Consequently, only those Members who pass or shape significant legislation affecting a national issue are deemed truly effective. As we said, this analysis may have been true earlier in U.S. history, but it is no longer true. Working behind the scenes to get bills passed into law is the central activity of Congress, but not the only way to be an effective Representative or Senator.

It is the most commonly understood and most often pursued path to power, but the role of "legislative insider" is not well-suited to many Members. Becoming a policy expert, brokering deals, building coalitions, negotiating agreements, back-slapping, horse-trading—the tools of legislating—are not tools all Members are comfortable or capable of using. Many Members lack the intense people skills frequently required of this role: the patience, the attention to detail, or the love of the process—the legislative wheeling and dealing on which the legislative insiders thrive. Does this mean that these elected officials should resign themselves to a mediocre congressional career? Absolutely not. It means these Members need to carve out another role in the institution for making their mark, rather than trying to conform their skills and interests into the legislative insider role. Of course, operating successfully in another role, in most cases, requires keeping your hands in the legislative process so you can periodically work in the trenches on legislation critical to your goals.

Similarly, if you personally like the legislative insider role but are confronted with a marginal seat, you may decide the role of "Washington insider" carries too many political risks. Instead, you may seek out a role that allows you to make a strong, local appeal to your constituents. You may decide to assume the ombudsman role and focus your attention on meeting local and state needs rather than becoming a central player in the health care debate.

Below we outline all five of the roles CMF has defined in detail to help Members find their fit within this complex institution.

Legislative Insider

Members who succeed in this role work effectively through the committee process to pass legislation. They are generally interested in making the process work and receiving national attention for their accomplishments. Some legislative insiders are strongly motivated by ideology. Others are not terribly ideological and seem primarily motivated to use their formidable legislative skills to broker deals. Both types share a pragmatic view of their work: practicing the politics of what is possible. Both immensely enjoy playing insider legislative politics—building close ties with their colleagues, using these personal relationships for political ends, building coalitions, using their expertise to negotiate agreements and cutting deals behind the scenes.

Most committee and subcommittee chairs and ranking minority Members are legislative insiders, but the role is not limited to those who attain these formal seats of power. It also describes Members who thrive in the insider environment and focus on attaining more power to influence legislation. Legislative insiders are motivated to move up the congressional policy ladder and become powerful chairs, or high-ranking Executive Branch appointees. Examples of Members who comfortably fit this role include former Sen. Pete Domenici (R-NM) and Rep. John Dingell (D-MI).

Legislative insiders tend to have the discipline and focus required to develop policy expertise in a few areas. They have excellent interpersonal skills allowing them to comfortably negotiate and make deals. They are good strategists and tacticians and enjoy the intensely political process of passing bills. Legislative insiders primarily rely on the committee structure and coordination with the party leadership in exercising their power. In addition to these vehicles, they also utilize the national press, and alliances with special interests, to generate support for their legislative activities.

> **Legislative Insiders...**
> ...are interested in making the process work and receiving national attention for their accomplishments. ∎

Party Insider

Party insider defines those Members whose primary interest is to promote the power and ideology of their parties. They include, of course, Members who seek and serve in party leadership positions, but they may also include other loyal soldiers who prefer to operate as team players within the party structure. Rep. David Dreier (R-CA) and former Rep. Rahm Emanuel (D-IL) are good models of the party insider role.

Because legislative power is primarily defined by political strength, party insiders tend to devote extensive time not only to legislative politics, but to electoral politics as well. They bring political skills and savvy to their work that apply equally to both the electoral and policy-making processes—organizing, strategizing, executing, building relationships, communicating. They seek out administrative and management duties that most other Members dislike or avoid, such as counting votes, raising party funds and organizing party meetings. Unlike the legislative insiders, however, they are generally less interested in the details and long-term ramifications of specific bills and amendments. Rather, they are more focused on the big picture and achieving their party's desired outcome. They have excellent media and communications skills and excel in "spinning" the party message to the press and the public.

Party insiders primarily exercise power through party leadership positions and the party structure, or the full range of formal and informal party assignments. But they also seek to serve on committees that give them broad powers to be political operators within the institution (i.e., House/Senate Budget, House/Senate Appropriations, House Rules, House Administration/Senate Rules and Administration, House Ways and Means/Senate Finance). Outside of Congress, they use their party service to make their mark both nationally and locally. They pursue their party-oriented goals by working closely with party contributors and activists, local party officials and the media. Like legislative insiders, their career paths focus primarily on moving up the national political ladder, either in Congress or in appointed positions in the Executive Branch.

> **Party Insiders...**
> ...are interested in promoting the power and ideology of their parties. ∎

Ombudsman

Ombudsmen are Members whose primary focus is creating a strong image of themselves and a strong record as champions for local or state interests. They make local rather than national issues their top priority, provide high-quality constituent services, and tend to generate a high local or state profile through these activities. Effective ombudsmen in Congress are Sen. Mary Landrieu (D-LA) and Rep. Frank Wolf (R-VA).

Ombudsmen are sometimes motivated to take on this role because of external factors, such as a marginal seat or overwhelming constituent expectations, which create a constant pressure to service the needs of the folks back home. Others are motivated by personal preferences. They get greater gratification from taking care of tangible and manageable problems of their constituents than they do from engaging in broad and complex policy debates that may take years to resolve. They also may be more interested in advancing their careers within the state than within Congress. To them, becoming governor carries more attraction than becoming a powerful committee chairman.

> **Ombudsmen...**
> ...focus on creating strong images of themselves at home and championing local or state interests. ■

The vehicles ombudsmen use to achieve their ends include: serving on committees that can provide economic development funds or services to their communities and their constituents (i.e., House/Senate Appropriations, Agriculture, Small Business and Veterans' Affairs; House Transportation and Infrastructure/Senate Commerce, Science and Transportation; House Natural Resources/Senate Energy and Natural Resources); obtaining federal grants for their districts or states (which usually requires committing staff resources to this end); joining regional and industry caucuses (e.g., the Border Caucus or the Steel Caucus); working closely with the state delegation on local matters; working with the local or state political parties; and getting their messages out through the local or state media.

Statesman

Statesmen are Members who view themselves as serving in Congress to do "what is right" for the country, rather than what is politically expedient. They may advocate for specific legislative ends, reforming the process or protecting the institution. Their objective is to promote what they view as good public policy without alienating themselves from the legislative and party insiders. Statesmen, after all, seek to rise above the political fray only when they believe it is necessary, rather than operate as an outside critic. They understand that they can exercise both internal and external power so long as they are not viewed by their colleagues as being unreasonable in negotiations or using their rhetoric to damage the insiders. As a result, statesman criticisms, while vocal, are usually not shrill or alienating. This is in contrast to the outsiders, who view their jobs as speaking the truth regardless of the political consequences.

Statesmen sometimes enthusiastically pursue this role because it fits the skeptical way they view the political process and/or the principled role they envision for their political careers. Other Members gravitate over time to this role less by choice than by fit. They don't enjoy the legislative leveraging surrounding them, and/or they are unsuccessful in integrating themselves into the more insider roles. Instead, they work the legislative process when it meets their needs but also assume the role of conscience of the process. This allows them to speak independently, and try to generate a national profile and national attention for their views. Members who fit this role include Sen. Russ Feingold (D-WI), Sen. Richard Lugar (R-IN), and the late Rep. Tom Lantos (D-CA).

Statesmen are frequently characterized as policy "wonks" with views that do not follow party doctrine or ideology. They have excellent oral and written communication skills. They do not enjoy the "schmoozing" and politicking of the legislative insiders and have little interest in controlling party machinery or taking on the organizational tasks of the party insiders. As demonstrated by the names listed above, statesmen can become influential players, even if they are not embraced by their leadership or do not spend extensive time forming close ties with dozens of their colleagues. They use their formidable policy knowledge and communication skills to deliver their message through the national media. This success in reaching a national audience often compels their colleagues in Congress to change direction and address their concerns.

Of course, House freshmen or sophomores cannot quickly assume the statesman role. They lack the stature and credibility amongst their colleagues and the media to be heard. However, junior House Members can aspire to this role and lay the groundwork for it early in their careers. Senators, on the other hand, can assume this role more easily because of their larger profile and greater access to the press. Not surprisingly, statesmen often operate fairly independently of their party and pursue a career path that could lead to being considered for President, Vice President, a cabinet appointment, or to taking on public policy jobs outside of Congress that allow them to communicate their ideas, and ideals, unencumbered by politics.

> **Statesmen...**
>
> ...view themselves as serving in Congress to do "what is right" for the country, rather than what is politically expedient. ∎

Outsider

Outsiders share many of the statesmen's predilections and discomfort with the legislative and political process, but they choose to express themselves more boldly. They define themselves primarily as critics of the system or advocates of a single issue. Consequently, rather than trying to straddle the insider and outsider roles as do the statesmen, they accept and usually embrace being an outsider. Their tactics frequently create resentment within the institution, as they try to influence policymaking by framing the debate through their public rhetoric rather than through the regular legislative process.

Outsiders usually gravitate to the role when they recognize that they do not have the interest or skill to assume the other roles. They tend to be impatient with the pace, tactics and ground rules of the insiders' game, and unwilling to or uncomfortable with forging personal ties with their colleagues or abiding by the ideology or wishes of their party. Outsiders are usually risk-takers who steer away from the safe path and are interested in using their seats as a platform to communicate their ideas, if not to make laws. The critical skill required of this role is the ability to communicate effectively through the media. Outsiders use op-eds, relationships with reporters, and alliances with like-minded Members and advocacy groups outside of Congress to get their message out. They seek to define themselves through independence from the institution, yet utilize their seat as the source of their credibility. Some examples are Rep. Ron Paul (R-TX), Rep. Dennis Kucinich (D-OH) and Sen. Bernard Sanders (I-VT).

Using this role to create a successful career in Congress presents a great many risks. Relying on media interest in what you have to say is far more difficult than relying on good committee assignments. And the conventional rule of thumb used to be that once you blatantly opposed party elders, you were forever condemned to a career as an outsider. However, over the past decade, some Members have used this role to effectively transition to an insider role.

> **Outsiders...**
> ...define themselves as critics of the system or advocates of a single issue. ■

For example, former Rep. Jim Nussle (R-IA) spent his early years in Congress as part of the "Gang of Seven," a group of rebellious Republicans who protested the abuses of the House Bank and Post Office. His position as an outsider seemed cemented when he wore a paper bag over his head during a floor speech to indicate his shame at the scandals. When the Republicans took control of the House, they began instituting some of the internal reforms called for by this group of firebrands, and Nussle was given a leadership position as chair of the House Budget Committee. Later the president tapped him to become director of the Office of Management and Budget. Nussle moved from renegade to a cabinet-level position, from a clear outsider to an inside player.

The successes of Nussle and other Members in using this outsider/maverick role to avoid paying some of the dues of the conventional path, makes this role more attractive and somewhat less risky to Members today than in the recent past. However, the dangers of assuming this primary role in Congress are still significant.

Balancing Major and Minor Roles

Members can choose to "major" in one of the five roles and "minor" in another role. This strategy allows some Members to expand their reach and capability, and modify the political image that selecting only one role creates. For example, a statesman who wants to command national attention to her views, but is concerned that this national profile may create political problems back home, may look to modify this image by taking on the secondary role of ombudsman. Similarly, a legislative insider who spends most of his energy working within his primary committee may decide he should also invest some time in the party insider role, thereby supporting and building helpful ties to the party. In short, developing the right fit often requires balancing the right two roles.

Of course, not all roles are compatible, and developing your role in Congress calls for more than choosing the one or two which are most attractive. It requires choosing two roles that work well together. For example, a legislative insider cannot credibly decide on occasion to assume the outsider role and passionately criticize the institution and its leaders without his legislative work paying a high cost. A party leader who uses the party's machinery to leverage desired outcomes cannot also operate as a statesman, a Member above the political fray. An ombudsman who quietly works with colleagues on Appropriations to obtain funding for projects in his district cannot also spend some of his political capital as an outsider, criticizing the system and the insiders he relies upon in his primary role.

In addition, trying to take on more than two roles—which Members frequently do—can lead to serious problems. Members often want to remain as flexible as possible so they can respond to a wide range of options. They assume, incorrectly, that straddling 3-5 roles actually allows Members to effectively play musical chairs with these different roles: shape a party strategy one week, broker a deal in a committee mark-up the next, speak out boldly against their party's interests soon after and still work with legislative insiders to get funding for a road project in their district when they need it. Obviously, this perception is folly.

> *"Trying to take on more than two roles — which Members frequently do — can lead to serious problems."*

Congress as an institution respects and trusts Members who specialize or who take the time to develop process or substantive expertise. These Members are rewarded with added responsibilities from the legislative and party insiders and the goodwill of their colleagues. These rewards can be parlayed into increasing effectiveness or power. In contrast, Members tend to dismiss colleagues who do not do their homework to develop expertise, yet still seek to operate as insiders. These Members run the sizeable risk of being viewed by their colleagues as "lightweights" or "dilettantes" and rendered ineffectual by the institution.

Selecting Your Role

Sometimes Members consciously choose a role to pursue. More often, though, the Member gravitates towards a role as his or her career progresses. In this latter case, "selecting your role" is probably better understood as simply recognizing which way the forces are taking you, and not standing in the way of your progress. The process of consciously choosing your role or your "fit" requires analyzing and balancing four factors:

1. An understanding of your personal strengths and weaknesses and how they match the activities of Congress.
2. Clarity about your mission or, broadly speaking, what you hope to accomplish through your tenure in Congress (see Chapter 11, "Strategic Planning," for details on developing a mission statement).
3. Clarity about the needs of your district or state.
4. Clarity about your political circumstances (i.e., your electoral strength, constituent expectations, future political plans, and the general political climate).

Analyzing these factors will lead some Members to reach easy conclusions about the role or roles that they want to pursue because their strengths and interests coincide neatly with the needs of their district or state and their political circumstances. For most Members, however, deciding on a role will require balancing competing interests.

A second-term House Member CMF met, for example, wanted to pursue the legislative insider role and was well-suited to excel in this role. However, he recognized that his constituents may not understand or support this focus. The Representative decided that rather than making the legislative insider role his primary role, he would make it his secondary role. Instead, to strengthen his base, he would make the ombudsman role his primary role for another term, and he hoped he would be able to switch these roles in two years.

In another case, district needs and political circumstances suggested that a freshman Member should take on the role of outsider. His very popular predecessor fit that role well and his populist constituents expected he would assume a similar role. The Member, however, expressed concern that he may not possess the communication skills or the temperament of his predecessor to succeed in such an independent role. He decided to focus on the statesman role that would allow him to speak out on issues from time to time, while still relying on the benefits of the legislative process to build a track record of accomplishment.

In most cases, the most telling factor on this list—and the factor that deserves the greatest attention—is understanding your strengths and weaknesses. Socrates' admonition to "know thyself" is as relevant to 21st century U.S. Members of Congress as it was to the young men he taught in ancient Greece over two thousand years ago. Many junior Members have a clear vision of the type of Member they would like to be. They may base this vision on a legislative role model that they admire. The problem with this approach is that they may not have the skills, personality or temperament to play that role.

Coming to grips with how your personal attributes match the congressional workplace is the most difficult step in this process. It may require self-analysis in a way that you have never done before. It may also require confronting some painful realities, such as: you don't have the intellectual bent to play the statesman role; you don't have the people skills to succeed in the legislative insider role; you don't have the political acumen or organizing skills necessary to become an effective party insider; or you don't have the media skills to succeed in the outsider role. But remember, closing some doors allows you to open others that are better suited to you.

To conduct an honest self-assessment of strengths and weaknesses, you should not rely solely on self-judgment. Instead, seek feedback from those who know you well. Good options to turn to are former and present colleagues, your key staff, your spouse and close friends. Better yet, get your kitchen cabinet together over breakfast and ask them what they see as your strengths and weaknesses, and in what role or roles they think you can excel. Do they see you as a strong negotiator, great with managing details, or a visionary thinker? Are you better at analyzing than communicating, at strategizing than implementing? The feedback you receive will help you make choices about the roles you should

> *"Get your kitchen cabinet together over breakfast and ask them what they see as your strengths and weaknesses, and in what role or roles they think you can excel."*

Figure 9-1

Congressional Role Selection Chart

Role	Goals	Vehicles of Power	Personal Attributes
Legislative Insider	• Advocating ideological interests and/or making the legislative process work • Accumulating more legislative power; rising up the committee ladder	• Committee structure; legislative process • Coordinating with the party leadership • National media • Alliances with special interest groups	• Enjoys working the legislative process • Interested in developing legislative expertise • Excellent people skills • Effective negotiator and alliance builder
Party Insider	• Promoting the interests and ideology of his or her party • Attaining more power by moving up through the party structure	• Party leadership positions and assignments • Committees that exercise influence over the institution and the legislative process • National media • Alliances with local/state party officials	• Interested in big picture, rather than details of legislation • Skilled at organizing and strategizing • Interested, skilled in electoral politics • Excellent media/communications skills
Ombudsman	• Promoting the interests of the district/state and providing outstanding constituent services • Receiving high visibility back home	• Committees that can provide aid and services to communities • Federal grants • Regional and industry caucuses • Local and/or state media	• More service-minded than ideologically-minded • Interested in tangible outcomes rather than broad policy questions
Statesman	• Advocating good public policy, doing "what is right" vs. politically expedient • Wanting to be viewed as rising above the political fray when appropriate • Exercising both internal and external power	• Committee structure; legislative process • National media • Alliances with legislative and party insiders	• More interested in big picture ideas than the details of legislation • Doesn't enjoy courting colleagues and engaging in insider politics • Excellent media/communication skills • Enjoys playing with and framing ideas
Outsider	• Influencing the process by influencing debate through rhetoric and criticism • Advocating change or new approaches • Wanting to be viewed as bold and honest, willing to do "what is right" or challenging the status quo	• National media • Joining ideologically-based caucuses • Alliances with advocacy groups	• Comfortable operating independently, rather than as part of a team • Doesn't enjoy courting colleagues and engaging in insider politics • Outspoken and sometimes risk-taking • Excellent media/communications skills

play. Figure 9-1 (see the opposite page) summarizes the previous discussion of the five roles to help you and your kitchen cabinet talk through these options.

Changing Roles
What do you do if, after a couple of years, you decide you are traveling down the wrong path? The answer is, you modify your choices. Finding the right fit in such a complex institution as Congress may take some experimentation and fine-tuning. Assumptions about your skills, your interests, or what you find rewarding may prove to be incorrect. The insight you gain from these decisions and experiences will allow you to modify your role or improve your fit and succeed in Congress. The costliest and most common mistake is not selecting the wrong role, but selecting none at all.

It is also possible that over time you come to realize that you have outgrown the role or roles you previously selected. You can, of course, decide to change roles. But, as in college, the cost of changing "majors" is far greater in your senior year than in your sophomore year. Consequently, instead of making major changes, Members are more inclined to make minor modifications. Generally speaking, most Members who change roles do not take on brand new roles. Rather, they switch their major and minor roles. This is the hope of the second term Representative discussed earlier. If he succeeds in making his seat safe, he will focus greater attention on his legislative duties, and somewhat less attention on his constituent service duties.

Conclusion

In this chapter, we have tried to provide both freshman and veteran Members guidance on how to thrive within the entrepreneurial culture of Congress. A successful career in Congress usually requires Members to seek to fill one or two roles and recognize that they cannot successfully pursue all five available. Congress rewards those who specialize and who follow a path of becoming outstanding at a few aspects of their job, rather than trying to excel at all of them. The difficult challenge facing Members is to decide what specialization best suits them. This task requires that Members take the time to figure out where their skills, interests and needs match the work requirements of Congress. Freshman Members who go through the selection process outlined in this chapter will develop greater clarity about how to plan and develop their careers. Veteran Members should use this analysis to check their past choices, and if it makes sense, develop a new strategy that better suits their needs and goals.

CHAPTER NINE

Chapter Summary
The DOs and DON'Ts of

Defining Your Role in Congress

Do...

- **figure out the right role for you in Congress by analyzing and balancing:**
    1. your personal strengths and weaknesses
    2. your mission in Congress
    3. the needs of your district/state
    4. your political circumstances
- **define your role as one of the following:**
    1. Legislative Insider
    2. Party Insider
    3. Ombudsman
    4. Statesman
    5. Outsider
- **determine if you want to "major" in one role and "minor" in another.**
  Balancing two compatible roles can lead to increased effectiveness and power.

Don't...

- **operate opportunistically without the benefit of defining your role.**
  Members adopting too large a range of issues can work very hard but accomplish little.

CHAPTER TEN

The Member's Role as Leader of the Office

This Chapter Includes...

☆ The Member's role as leader of the office
☆ How to create a positive office culture
☆ How to assess and improve your leadership style
☆ How to address common leadership problems

Most freshman Members of Congress come to their new jobs with minimal management experience. The majority of recently elected Members, for example, served previously as lawyers and state legislators. While they handled significant responsibilities in these jobs, they were not responsible for leading and overseeing an entire organization. Even those who've had previous management experience quickly learn that Congress is a unique institution with its own culture and unique organizational demands.

New Members tend to come to their new jobs believing that the necessary ingredients for success in Congress are the personal talents responsible for their past successes: political savvy, good conceptual skills, excellent interpersonal skills, an abnormally strong work ethic, a drive to succeed, and perseverance. Most come to realize, however, that success in Congress requires a strong organization as much as personal abilities. Consequently, it is critical that Members learn to become effective leaders of their offices. The advice in this chapter is based upon years of experience during which CMF has analyzed dozens of House and Senate personal offices, interviewed hundreds of personal office staff, and worked with dozens of Members and Chiefs of Staff in improving the effectiveness of their offices.

The Member as Leader

Most of the best-managed offices in Congress follow a basic formula: The Member is the *leader* of the office, responsible for setting the course or direction of the office. The senior management staff (e.g., Chief of Staff or AA, Legislative Director, District or State Director) are the *managers* responsible for the office's day-to-day operations and for ensuring that activities supporting the leader's goals are effectively carried out. As the leader of your office, you, the Member, will:

1. Decide where you want to go and set a direction for the office.
2. Articulate and "sell" this direction to the staff so that they are excited about their jobs and have a clear understanding of how to prioritize their work.
3. Help develop the general strategy or plan for how to achieve the goals set out.
4. Create a productive "organizational culture" that permeates the work of the entire office.
5. Make critical decisions and solve critical problems related to the achievement of the office's strategic priorities.
6. Empower the staff, by delegating to them authority and responsibility to execute the plan.

Of course, this is not the sum total of a Member's duties, nor of the functions to which you ought to be devoting the majority of your time. You are also responsible for a wide range of activities that, for the most part, cannot be delegated: learning the issues, casting votes in committee and on the floor, meeting and negotiating with other Members and legislative interests, meeting with constituents and attending district/state events, and speaking with local and national reporters. However, you must recognize that you cannot escape your office leadership responsibilities (though many Members try).

Members will be able to focus on these leadership responsibilities when they delegate to the Chief of Staff and other senior management the following management duties:

1. Implementing the office plans to achieve the stated goals.
2. Supervising the staff, answering the majority of daily questions, and resolving the majority of the regular decisions and problems that arise.
3. Ensuring that the routine functions and systems of the personal office are carried out effectively (i.e., mail, casework, press, scheduling).
4. Apprising the Member of the general activities of the office and involving the Member in the range of issues that require Member input.

For this division of responsibilities to work effectively, three essential conditions must be met:

Members must have or develop good leadership skills. Some Members will bring these skills to the job, while others will need to make concerted efforts to cultivate them.

The Chief of Staff and/or the other senior management staff must have excellent management skills. If the staff responsible for following through on the Member's priorities lack the requisite management skills, the Member will, quite rightly, feel compelled to oversee much of the day-to-day operations.

A high degree of trust must exist between the Member and the Chief of Staff. If this relationship does not work well — if the Member is not confident that his Chief of Staff can effectively implement his plans — the Member once again will feel compelled to take on time-consuming responsibilities that will impair his office's effectiveness.

Organizational Culture

Defining Organizational Culture

Being a truly effective leader requires more than creating a winning vision, making wise decisions, motivating, and empowering the staff. It also requires creating a productive *organizational culture*. Every organization has a culture: A set of rules (formal and informal), values (positive or negative), practices or norms (prescribed and implicit), and taboos that define the organization and the way it works. Some organizational cultures enhance the effectiveness of an organization, while others actually serve to undermine it. It is the leader who determines whether the values and behaviors practiced and reinforced are productive and propel the organization forward.

"Being a truly effective leader requires more than creating a winning vision, making wise decisions, motivating, and empowering the staff. It also requires creating a productive organizational culture."

Most leaders of organizations tend to focus their energies on clarifying and reinforcing the formal rules, the stated principles, and the prescribed practices. They make the mistake of assuming that the most compelling messages are the ones they deliver directly to their staffs in writing or orally. They fail to realize that they communicate more powerful messages to their staffs through indirect means — through their spontaneous comments and actions.

Staff members are very attentive to their boss. They know that "actions speak louder than words." Consequently, they pay greater attention to the daily behavior of their boss than they do to any set of written rules or formal statements uttered at staff meetings. Over time they interpret from this range of experiences and observations — first individually, then collectively — the real ground rules by which they should operate: What angers the boss? What pleases the boss? Which work habits are valued and which are disliked? Which issues excite her and which bore her? How is displeasure expressed and appreciation shown? What personal values are important to the boss? On what basis does she judge others? How does she treat her staff? How does she analyze issues? How does she solve problems, cope with stress, or respond to conflict?

The answers to these and many other little-discussed questions create an organizational culture that reflects the preferences, values, and work style of the leader. The workers then begin conforming their behavior to meet the expectations and rewards of the culture. In this manner, organizational culture, more than established rules, defines how people work. In addition, the culture transmits the informal ground rules to new staff. Cultural values become self-enforcing. This is the power of organizational culture. Once established, the culture tends to continue to shape the behavior of the staff even if management tries to change the way the organization functions.

The Power of Culture in Congressional Offices

There are few organizations in which the leader has a greater opportunity to define the culture of her organization than in a congressional office. Staff understand that they are not working for this large institution called the U.S. Congress, but that they serve as "at-will" employees of their individual Senator or Representative. And most congressional staff like it that way. They seek jobs where they can work for someone in whom they believe, and with like-minded colleagues, rather than working in large bureaucratic organizations where rank and experience are far more important than convictions and initiative. They expect you, the Member, to have your own set of political ideals, personal values, and professional ambitions. They view their job as understanding your psyche — the underlying motivations of your actions or positions — so they can think and act in accordance with your wishes.

In Congress, the Member's political ideals, personal values, and professional ambitions are the basis of the office's culture. Your primary leadership duty is to present your ideals and values in a way that inspires your staff to adopt them, and motivates them to do their best work to achieve the shared ends of the office. If you do this job well, you will find that the range of management issues facing you and your office will get resolved

CHAPTER TEN   The Member's Role as Leader of the Office   145

effectively without your input. Correspondingly, if you fail to create a positive organizational culture, you will find that hiring talented managers and designing effective systems will not protect you from seemingly intractable management problems.

Consequently, it is critical that Members of Congress, especially freshman Members, take time to consciously think about the type of culture they want to create for their offices and how they intend to create it.

Creating a Positive, Motivating Office Culture

We have found through our research, training, and one-on-one work with congressional offices that the most productive offices in Congress tend to have Members who share the following overriding characteristics:

1. The Member has a clear mission and goals, about both what the office should do and how it should do it, which the staff understand and admire.
2. The Member operates day-to-day, in public and private, according to consistent personal values that the staff respect.
3. One of the values to which the Member consistently adheres is treating the staff with trust and respect, clearly conveying that they are the Member's most important asset.

These Member practices almost always create a culture within which staff adopt the Member's values and work style, commit themselves to achieving the Member's goals, and work effectively as a team committed to common ends and common values.

The Importance of Mission and Values

The most effective leaders, in Congress as elsewhere, are those who understand that staff want more than clarity in their work; they seek meaning and value through their work. They want to be committed to something of higher purpose than their own job satisfaction and financial well-being. It doesn't have to be global in nature or grandiose in scope. It just has to give them the feeling that their work is important and has meaning.

> *"The most effective leaders, in Congress as elsewhere, are those who understand that staff want more than clarity in their work; they seek meaning and value through their work."*

In a congressional office, the staff will develop such a sense of purpose when they respect the ambitions of their boss as well as develop a personal respect for the Member's values. When this occurs, a positive organizational culture will develop around the Member. Moreover, for such a positive culture to truly flourish, the Member must actively model the values or goals he espouses. In other words, through the power of example, great leaders provide meaning and purpose to the work of others, and inspire those around them to produce their best work. This holds true in Congress as it does in corporations, government agencies, the military, schools, and sports teams.

In one Senate office, for example, an active and dynamic Member refused to "horse-trade" on any legislative votes, believing that horse-trading, although frequently expedient, pollutes the integrity of the policy-making process. Over time, his steadfast compliance with this value created a devoted staff that took great pride in doing things "above board" and "going the extra mile necessary for winning the votes on the merits."

A bright and energetic House Member preached the value of "innovation." He regularly pushed himself and his staff to look beyond the issues on the front-burner, to "look for new ideas and create new solutions." The office was dynamic, exciting, and unusually creative in their approach to everything from policy initiatives to office leave policy. The office was not without its problems, but the staff loved their work and deeply admired their boss for his intelligence, hard work, and trust in the creative intelligence of young but talented staff.

In another House office, the Representative spoke passionately to her staff about providing exceptional constituent services. She regularly spoke of "caring for our constituents," "treating our constituents with dignity and respect," and "using our considerable resources to make their lives better if we can." Many Members of Congress seek the political benefits of providing excellent constituent services, but this Member exhibited genuine compassion for her constituents, even insisting on getting involved in critical casework matters. Arguably, calling agency officials on behalf of constituents is not an optimal use of a Member's time. However, her advocacy for people in need defined the office and fostered tremendous staff respect for their boss. As a result, her staff provided unsurpassed constituent services in both Washington and the district that aptly reflected the compassion of their boss.

In short, congressional staff will go through fire for Members they admire. They will make significant personal sacrifices if they believe that what they are doing is important. Rarely will they do the same for a boss whose values and goals they do not respect.

Creating a Culture that Values Staff

Congressional staff have to contend with very demanding working conditions: long and unpredictable hours; little to no job security; low pay; frequent underemployment; lack of public recognition; and cramped quarters.

Yet, some of the top graduates of our best colleges, law schools, and graduate schools come to Washington every year seeking that "prestigious" congressional job. Congressional staff tend to be young, well-educated, inexperienced, idealistic, ambitious, assertive, and impatient. In other words, they tend to be talented and green.

The Members who bestow a genuine sense of trust, respect, and appreciation on their staffs enjoy the incalculable benefit of loyal, committed, and motivated staffs. Unfortunately, many Members who do not do this well pay the customary price: high job turnover, loss of office productivity, insufficient institutional memory, lack of office continuity and teamwork, and Member anxiety. Frequently, the Members who lead these offices explain away these problems with the mistaken refrain, "If only I could find the right people."

In the best offices, the Members understand that loyalty is a two-way street. It is not bought simply by providing staff with jobs they seek. It is earned over time and regularly reinforced. In short, these leaders understand that their staffs are their most important resource and treat them accordingly. Specifically, the best offices adhere to the following practices:

Members openly share information with their staffs. Discussing the challenging issues facing you is the most exciting component of the job for many staffers. It creates staff ownership in the office and offers great opportunities to learn the process and how you think, and demonstrates to them that you trust them and value their opinions.

Members seek staff input whenever possible. Such behavior conveys that you value staff ideas and analytic abilities, even from staff whose daily duties do not primarily involve conceptual thinking. It also frequently leads to interesting and worthwhile discussions that improve decision-making and let staff exercise their problem-solving skills. Staff should even be encouraged to criticize or challenge your judgments or those of other staff.

Members provide regular feedback, both positive and negative, to staff. Highly motivated staff want to know when they have succeeded and how they can perform their jobs better. Through constructive, honest feedback, well-managed offices build staff confidence, job satisfaction, and enthusiasm as well as greater understanding of the Member's style and preferences. Be sure to follow the Marine Corps leadership maxim: "Praise in public, condemn in private."

Members take a personal interest in the professional development of staff. Most personal office staff are young and take jobs in Congress soon after graduating from college. They seek to develop their professional skills and to clarify their career interests.

Members empower their staff. They do so by giving staff the authority to solve problems, make decisions, take on difficult assignments, and generate their own projects or initiatives. In this way, staff will be challenged to grow

MANAGEMENT FACT
In recent years, the average tenure of House and Senate staffers in the Washington office is slightly more than 3 years.

in their jobs, expand their skills, and enhance the quality of their work. Empowering staff also means rewarding initiative, as well as remaining silent when initiatives fail or staff will cease taking chances. These practices let staff know that they are responsible for the overall effectiveness of the office, not just the quality of their own work.

Members celebrate and reward accomplishments. Because events move so quickly in Congress, it is difficult to take time out to celebrate and enjoy the successes. But a small party, a nice note, bonus pay, lunch with a staffer, a public acknowledgment of their work, or a personal gift are all small, but important ways that offices show their appreciation of valued staff. It also helps carry staff through the more arduous and frustrating periods when they are struggling to move legislation or to assist needy constituents.

Unproductive Office Cultures

Quite simply put, Members create negative or unproductive cultures by *not* doing those things that create positive organizational cultures.

Failing to display clear, consistent values through action. Over time staff will define the office culture based upon their needs and their experience in coping with the inconsistency or lack of clarity in the office. In one office, for example, a Member insisted his staff meet deadlines but routinely failed to do so himself. This contradictory message created problems. Staff were resentful of a demanding and hypocritical boss who essentially told them to "do as I say and not as I do." Staff responded to their frustrations over time by simply letting deadlines slip. The Member tolerated this situation rather than having to confront the staff and face his own poor work habits. Over several years, the staff's cynicism about deadlines became an entrenched and unproductive cultural value that defined the work of the office.

Promoting mistrust of others, dishonesty or laziness. Putting commitment to personal success ahead of the public good. When confronted with these types of leadership values, staff tend to follow one of two courses. They either learn to treat their work as a job rather than a source of growth, conviction, or meaning in their lives, or get out. Neither option contributes to a dynamic, high quality organization.

Treating staff like expendable parts rather than valued and respected partners. This will certainly reduce staff loyalty, motivation, initiative, morale and enthusiasm.

Members who follow any or all of these three courses essentially forfeit the opportunity to create a positive culture and an effective office. Their staffers are rarely loyal or committed to any higher purpose other than using the job as a stepping stone to something better. The culture does not motivate staff to work to their full potential, and the Member is frequently frustrated with the lack of quality work she receives.

Members who fail to create healthy, productive cultures are left to lead primarily by virtue of their position in the chain of command. But fear of authority does not yield the same result as personal commitment to an admired leader.

Assessing and Understanding Your Leadership Style

Why Is Your Leadership Style Important?
Part of the process of shaping your culture is understanding how you are perceived by the people you supervise and the impact you have on them. The better you understand your own leadership style, the more effective you will be in defining the culture you seek. Lack of awareness of the strengths and weaknesses of your leadership style leads to practices that underutilize office strengths, demoralize staff and seriously impede office productivity.

Assessing and Understanding Your Leadership Style
The first step in the process is to get some honest feedback from colleagues who have worked with you and for you. For veteran Members that's easy. You have a staff of people — most of whom believe they are experts on the subject of your strengths and weaknesses — who can provide valuable comments about your leadership style.

However, it may be difficult for you to get honest feedback from your staff on personal and sensitive issues such as your ability to: communicate with them, remain focused, provide feedback, make decisions, work collaboratively or motivate them. You can't simply ask a couple of staff members into your office one evening while waiting around for votes and ask them to discuss what they think of your leadership style and skills.

Instead, we recommend that you use confidential methods that allow staff to offer their candid views without the risk of punishment or the discomfort of confronting you with potentially disturbing criticism. Here are three methods you should consider:

1. Develop a survey seeking staff evaluation of your leadership skills. Free Web-based survey software is easy to use, allows staff to maintain their anonymity, and automatically tabulates the results. You may also distribute a written survey, instruct staff to return it anonymously, and have a staffer summarize the results. CMF can

work with you to develop the survey so that it assesses appropriate leadership attributes.
2. Have someone, a consultant or an outsider you and your staff trust, run a confidential focus group with four to six staff assessing your leadership strengths and weaknesses. That person can then provide you with a summary of the key issues on which there was general consensus.
3. Another approach — very popular in the corporate world but rarely used by Members of Congress — is to attend a management or leadership training program. These intensive, several-day-long programs provide feedback to the participants through analysis of a range of questionnaires you and your staff complete on your management practices and beliefs. (Offices interested in conducting this feedback process can call CMF at 202-546-0100 for advice and/or assistance.)

Freshman Members will have to be a bit more industrious to get some quality feedback. However, there are a couple of possible approaches to explore. First, if you served as a manager prior to your election to Congress, you can contact your former colleagues or employees and ask for their assessment of your management style and skills, or you could have someone make these contacts on your behalf. Second, you can wait three to six months into your first term and then survey or set up a focus group with your first-term staff. The downside to this approach is that some avoidable damage may occur in the six-month start-up period.

Another strategy for freshmen to consider is establishing a regular monthly meeting with your Chief of Staff or management team at the beginning of your first term to evaluate each other's performance. For this approach to succeed, you will need to overcome the previously mentioned reluctance of staff to speak frankly on this subject at open meetings. This can be accomplished by keeping the regular meeting schedule and by other words and actions that demonstrate your sincerity in wanting and valuing staff feedback.

Using Feedback to Improve Your Leadership Skills
The feedback you receive should serve as a blueprint for improving your leadership skills. The key to improving your leadership abilities is to make sure you fully utilize your strengths and learn to overcome or neutralize your weaknesses.

Some weaknesses are quite easy to address. For example, some problems spring from behavior of which Members are not aware but which are easy to change. In one office with which we worked, the Member rarely praised or criticized the staff. When confronted with this issue, the Member acknowledged

CHAPTER TEN The Member's Role as Leader of the Office

the accuracy of the criticism, explained that he had not realized the importance of such feedback, and was able to quickly begin to provide it.

However, many of the problems that will surface will take more work to ameliorate. They may require developing new skills or changing some of your present leadership inclinations. This can only be accomplished through concerted effort and attention.

One of the best ways to modify your leadership practices is to enlist the assistance of your Chief of Staff (or management team) in regularly scheduled meetings. The feedback presented in the meetings should be as concrete as possible. For example, "When you insisted on writing the speech yourself, you undercut the Press Secretary. It would have been better for the office had you discussed your ideas for the speech and given Sue a chance to provide you a draft rather than taking action that was interpreted as a demonstration of your lack of confidence in Sue." Such meetings create a constructive two-way dialogue that promotes not only the skills of the Member, but also the skills of management staff and the building of a cohesive management team.

Finally, there may be some problems Members simply cannot or will not correct. In these cases, we have found it is necessary for the office, specifically the Chief of Staff and the Member, to construct an alternative strategy for containing the problem. For example, one Member confided that he realized that he was too tough on his staff, ran too tight a ship and, to make matters worse, failed to balance his criticisms with praise even when it was clearly deserving. His staff, not surprisingly, were demoralized and hostile to their very talented but unappreciative boss. After a talk about the significant problems his style was causing in his office, he and his Chief of Staff developed a containment strategy. The Chief of Staff would take on the responsibility of providing all positive and negative verbal feedback to the staff, but would also regularly ask the Member to pen notes of praise to staff when appropriate. Consequently, the Member was relieved of duties he neither performed well nor liked to do. These changes did not make an uncomfortable manager of people into a better leader; but they did make for a better organization by meeting some of the staff's needs and minimizing their discomfort with their boss.

In the above case the Member was fortunate to have a Chief of Staff who had many of the skills her boss lacked. She was able to compensate for a significant leadership weakness of her boss. If Members recognize their weaknesses, they can hire management staff who bring to the office the skills and strengths they lack. More often than not, however, Members tend to hire Chiefs of Staff and other key staff who share their strengths and skills rather than compensate for their weaknesses. Part of being a good leader is recognizing what you do well and what you do not do well and finding others to fill the holes in the organization.

How to Address the Two Common Leadership Problems

In this next section, we will discuss the two primary pitfalls Members of Congress face that impede the development of highly productive offices: the inability to make trade-offs and the urge to micromanage.

Problems in Making the Hard Trade-offs

The most common problem we encounter in our work in Congress is the inability of Members to set priorities and balance their reach with their resources. Bound by campaign promises to the district/state, the needs of individual constituent groups, or the desire to pursue areas of personal interest or national concern, many Members find it difficult to choose just a few on which to focus their energy.

The problem is that neither Senators nor Representatives have the resources to keep an active hand in more than a few issues. Many Members, unfortunately, deny the limits of their energy and their staff. They generate new initiatives and new ideas almost daily and do not take kindly to staff suggestions that the office lacks the resources to take on new projects. Consequently, they overburden themselves and their staffs, wreak havoc on the systems and morale of the office, forfeit their leadership responsibilities to make the hard trade-offs, and find that for all of their Herculean efforts they have accomplished very little because they are spread so thin.

"The most common problem we encounter in our work in Congress is the inability of Members to set priorities and balance their reach with their resources."

To be an effective Member and run an effective office, you must make strategic choices about what you and your staff will and will not do. This approach can frequently mean bypassing attractive press events, forgoing issues that excite you personally, angering valued constituents, and disappointing your staff. You can't do it all any more than the federal budget can support all the important and worthwhile needs of the country.

This process starts with clarifying your broad long-term priorities on paper (one page or less), then developing specific one or two-year goals for the office. With clarity of purpose, and *only through clarity of purpose*, the challenge of making difficult trade-offs becomes easier. Specifically, when you are clear about what you are trying to achieve — your goals — you can quickly assess if new initiatives will support, distract or undermine your efforts.

CHAPTER TEN The Member's Role as Leader of the Office

It's hard for many Members to find the discipline to clarify their offices' goals and then measure all new opportunities against those goals. But the advantages are profound. What your office does do will be done effectively; what goals are set will have a much better chance of being accomplished. (For an in-depth discussion of this topic, see Chapter 11, "Strategic Planning," in Part III of this book.)

The Member as Micromanager

One of the most pervasive and troubling management problems facing first- and second-term Members is that they spend too much time managing the day-to-day details that usually can be competently managed by other staff, and too little time focusing on their primary responsibilities. Consequently, many Members spend an inordinate amount of their time editing every document that leaves the office regardless of its relative importance, serving as the decision-maker on virtually all office and policy matters, personally overseeing all the major work of their staffs, and becoming the primary coordinator of the office's work.

These relentless management tasks simply crowd out the more important responsibilities that only the Member can perform: setting the direction of the office, creating a productive organizational culture, studying the issues, learning legislative procedure, and meeting with other colleagues. They also limit the time the Member can devote to the essential legislative

Remember The "Vasa"

A Lesson in Micromanagement and Too Many Priorities

For those Members of Congress who micromanage their office operations or keep adding new initiatives to the office agenda — we encourage you to consider the tale of the Vasa.

In the early 17th century, the new King of Sweden, Gustavus Adolphus, wanted to create the mightiest of warships ever built, the "Vasa." He hired the best ship makers and laid before them his grandiose portrait of his magnificent vessel. Once informed of their leader's directions, the ship builders went about their business and began designing and then constructing an amazing ship. The king took an unusual interest in construction, examining every detail. He directed the builders to double the number of guns and to change the basic engineering of the ship to make room for articles of vanity like statues.

Finally, the day came when the Vasa was completed and was to set sail on its maiden voyage. King Adolphus stood proudly, marveling at the wondrous creation standing before him in the harbor. The Vasa pulled away and fired a mighty shot from its imposing gun deck. But then, suddenly, the ship began to rock back and forth unstably. The crew ran from side to side to try and balance out the weight, but they could not prevent disaster. The overweight and imperfectly designed ship sank within minutes.

The moral of this 17th century story applied to a 21st century Congress? First, hire the best staff you can, provide them clear direction, but then let them manage the day-to-day activities of the office. Second, you cannot continually add new priorities and new initiatives to your agenda without making conscious and difficult trade-offs. If you do, your boat won't sail well or may even sink — regardless of your good intentions. ■

and representational tasks of the job (e.g., attending hearings, developing initiatives, and meeting with key constituents).

The end result of offices where the Member is involved in all management aspects of the office is almost always an office that is *over-managed* and *under-led*. The office manages the day-to-day work well, but the staff, and frequently the Member, are sapped of their strength to get beyond simply reacting to the daily demands of the job. The Members are worn down by 14-hour work days in which little of significance is accomplished. Over time, unless this pattern changes, the Member becomes disillusioned and begins asking if the sacrifices required by the job are worth it. Correspondingly, the staff begin losing their commitment because they lack a sense of purpose and ownership in their work. They cannot answer the critical questions: What are we trying to accomplish? How are we going to make it happen? And, what is my role in this undertaking?

Transitioning from Manager to Leader

There are a number of logical reasons why Members, especially freshman Members, are prone to focus on the management responsibilities of the job ahead of the leadership responsibilities. They initially lack trust in the abilities of new staff. They feel it is important early-on to understand all of the operations of their enterprises. Many Members understandably attribute their past professional successes to their ability to manage details effectively.

All of these reasons make sense. Freshman Members should take time to learn and measure the capabilities of their staffs and understand the general office operations. However, a major first-term management challenge is to delegate the day-to-day operations to management staff once these ends have been achieved. We also are not arguing that Members should have no involvement in overseeing the work of the office. Rather, Members must be very selective about which details are worth their attention and which are best left to staff to scrutinize. After all, the more time they spend sweating the details, the less time they have to devote to their primary roles: national policy-makers, representatives of their constituents, and leaders of their congressional enterprises.

We have found that the key to making this successful transition from manager to leader of the office is the quality of the Member/Chief of Staff relationship. In offices where the Member develops a strong sense of trust in his Chief of Staff, the Member usually is comfortable delegating management responsibilities. The ongoing tension between the Member's need to ensure that his thinking and style are reflected in all the work of the office and his need to focus on the big picture is comfortably balanced. In contrast, when a trusting and comfortable partnership does *not* exist,

Members are resistant to letting someone else make decisions or oversee the work that leaves the office.

Good Member/Chief of Staff relationships are not just, however, a matter of fit. They also require a good deal of discussion and continuing negotiation about roles and expectations: What are the Member's management duties and which fall to the Chief of Staff? What is the Member's role in making personnel, budget, or policy decisions and when can the Chief of Staff act without the Member's approval? Neglecting to engage in these important conversations contributes to misunderstandings that can undermine trust on both sides. Consequently, we recommend that Members and their Chiefs of Staff, especially in freshman offices, discuss their roles thoroughly at the outset and then continue to meet regularly throughout the first term to modify their roles. Such discussions will allow the Member to make a comfortable and orderly transition from manager to leader.

Conclusion

Your effectiveness in Congress will be significantly determined by your leadership abilities — your ability to build an organization that effectively supports you and allows both you and your staff to produce your best work. For virtually all Members of Congress, learning to become an excellent leader is a difficult task that requires the development of new skills and capabilities. Many Members, unfortunately, shy away from this challenge and instead expect their Chiefs of Staff and other staff to create outstanding offices on their own. They are almost always disappointed with the results. Outstanding organizations, in business or Congress, require effective leaders.

Regardless of the leadership or management experience you bring to your job, you can learn to become an effective leader. Leadership, like most other skills, requires a willingness to experiment, grow, and, most importantly, work. It cannot be learned simply by reading good management books or talking with wise and successful leaders. Cultivating your leadership talents will require effort and practice. We encourage you to focus some of your energy on this task from the beginning of your career in Congress. It will pay immense dividends down the road in the quality of your office as well as the quality of your working life in Congress.

Chapter Summary
The DOs and DON'Ts of

The Member's Role as Leader of the Office

Do...

- **understand that you are the leader —** not the day-to-day manager — of your office.

- **assess and understand your leadership style.** Request honest feedback to help you analyze your leadership strengths and weaknesses.

- **hire a Chief of Staff whom you can trust** to manage the office with broad guidance you provide. If you lack confidence in your Chief of Staff, you will feel compelled to micromanage the office.

- **take the time to assess the capabilities of your staff** so you can feel confident in delegating work. This will allow you to focus the leadership responsibilities of the office.

- **create a positive office culture by:** having a clear mission and goals; operating according to personal values that will result in staff respect; and treating staff with trust and respect.

Don't...

- **create a negative culture by:** failing to adhere to clear, consistent values; promoting the mistrust of others; making staff feel that they are expendable.

- **deny that every office has resource limitations.** Members who constantly generate new initiatives and projects without making strategic trade-offs in priorities overburden themselves and their staff and accomplish little for their efforts.

- **neglect the Member/Chief of Staff relationship.** To work well, this relationship requires a good deal of discussion and negotiation about roles and expectations.

Part III:
Managing Your Congressional Office

Chapter Eleven:	Strategic Planning in Your Office........................159
Chapter Twelve:	Budgeting and Financial Management...............179
Chapter Thirteen:	A Process for Managing Staff..........................197
Chapter Fourteen:	Managing Constituent Communications...........215
Chapter Fifteen:	Strategic Scheduling 239
Chapter Sixteen:	Managing Ethics 267

☆ ☆ ☆ ☆ **SETTING COURSE**

Icons Used in Setting Course

Notes a series of questions. Your unique answers can help you make decisions about managing an office and a career.

Alerts you to a situation which Hill offices have found to be problematic. Proceed with caution and pay close attention.

Notes a concept or recommendation that CMF has determined, through its research with congressional offices, to be helpful.

Identifies an office or organization which you may wish to contact for further information on the topic.

Notes a process or steps you can use in the operations of your office.

CHAPTER ELEVEN

Strategic Planning in Your Office

This Chapter Includes...

☆ The value of planning
☆ The steps of the planning process
☆ Tips for conducting a planning session

Planning should be no stranger to you. To win your congressional campaign, you developed and executed a clear plan that reflected your personal strengths and interests, the concerns of your constituents, the political climate, and the resources available to you. In our research and consulting work, we have found that the most successful Members are those who succeed in transferring good election planning skills to their congressional offices.

This chapter will help you develop a strategic plan for your office and enjoy the political and managerial benefits that accompany good planning.

The Value of Planning

It is natural that many elected officials wish to be all things to all people. Despite the negative connotations of this sentiment, it also harbors an admirable quality. Elected officials at every level want to satisfy their audiences by serving them well. Whether the crowd is a committee room full of congressional colleagues, a school auditorium filled with parents, past campaign contributors, county workers or a group of reporters, most Members seek some way to satisfy the audience — to meet the needs of those who ask for assistance.

This tendency is summarized in the old political adage about government bureaucrats and politicians. Bureaucrats, it is said, are people who hate to say "yes." Politicians are people who hate to say "no." Planning, and the practice of setting goals and priorities, is the process of learning how to *strategically* say "no" — of accepting that there is no Santa Claus, no free lunch, and no way elected officials can do everything they want to do in Congress.

Planning for congressional offices is the process of establishing a sensible, flexible set of overall goals and priorities that provides purpose and direction to the office. It permits the elected official to be a proactive leader on issues and service programs of choice, and be reactive when desirable, not just when political circumstances force a reaction. This means the successful plan will reflect not only what one hopes to accomplish, but also what is to be avoided.

The benefits of planning are most obvious for freshman Members, who must address a host of critical questions in the first few months after an election: what committee assignments to seek; what, if any, legislative issues should receive priority attention; how much time to spend on party or leadership matters; how many staff to hire and whether to base them in Washington or the district/state; whether to hire a highly-skilled and well-paid Communications Director or use those resources to get a top notch Legislative Director; how many district/state offices to open and where to locate them; how much time to spend back home and what groups deserve the most attention.

All of these freshman questions can be addressed systematically if you first develop a clear sense of priorities, but you can't begin to answer them in a coherent fashion until you've first articulated a strategic plan for your office. And only after you've communicated that strategic plan to your staff can your office develop a sensible first-year budget, legislative agenda, district/state scheduling objectives, an annual press plan, or even office job descriptions, consistent with the office's overall goals.

This advice is as relevant for veteran Members as it is for Members-elect. Congress is cluttered with offices that have very little sense of direction,

CHAPTER ELEVEN   Strategic Planning in Your Office

and the results are predictable. These offices usually work very hard, but because of inadequate planning, they do not work very smart. They tend to spend too much time shifting priorities and pursuing non-essential objectives. They inadequately coordinate the differing office functions and activities. They are overly reactive and never have enough time to follow-up on their own initiatives. Both the Member and the staff tend to be frustrated, if not downright disillusioned.

CMF's research and consulting work has shown us that the general benefits of strategic planning for all offices are substantial. They include:

- Setting clear priorities and making thoughtful trade-offs in light of those priorities.
- Forcing both Members and staff to look at the "big picture," rather than constantly making decisions on the parts.
- Allowing offices to be proactive and forward-thinking, instead of reacting to daily events.
- Allowing offices to develop clear strategies for accomplishing defined goals.
- Generating a clear sense of purpose that directs and motivates the Member and staff.
- Creating a process for rationally allocating the office's resources (i.e., the Member and staff's time, the office budget).
- Expediting decision-making by establishing clear criteria to follow.
- Improving the coordination of the full range of office functions (i.e., legislation, press, scheduling, casework, projects, mail and administration).
- Reducing the potential for Member and staff frustration and burnout by focusing the office's energies on a manageable plan rather than a potpourri of initiatives.
- Providing an instrument for measuring the overall effectiveness of the office.

Strategic planning forces offices to think more analytically before setting new goals or agreeing that last year's activities, with minor changes, should be pursued again in the coming year. It requires anticipation of the events that will shape the agenda (e.g., political, economic, international, national, local), which allows the Member and staff to analytically and logically determine how to take advantage of opportunities and guard against the events or trends that can impede effectiveness or threaten viability.

Veteran Members and their staffs frequently are reluctant to engage in this type of analysis because they believe it will inhibit their ability both to react quickly to changes in the policy and political environment and to complete their necessary routine functions. The planning CMF recommends, however,

MANAGEMENT FACT
70 to 80% of office time is spent on routine but essential functions and reacting to events.

assumes that 70 to 80 percent of a congressional office's time is spent completing the routine, but essential, office functions and reacting to events. How the other 20 to 30 percent is utilized becomes the essential question. If no plan is in place for guiding this "discretionary" time, the time tends to be used ineffectively — exploring a changing array of initiatives, continuing to simply react to events, or staying focused on the office routines. The strategic planning process outlined in this chapter will help all offices manage discretionary time more effectively by incorporating vision, strategy, teamwork, and discipline into the office.

The Planning Process

What should be included in a strategic plan? What process should you follow in developing your plan? How can you keep the plan from becoming obsolete? There is no one best way to answer these questions. Management literature abounds with a seemingly endless variety of planning models. What we present here are general planning concepts and practices that CMF has found work effectively in congressional offices. You should adopt or modify our recommendations as appropriate for your office.

In general, a planning process should incorporate an assessment of the following:

1. The Member's personal goals and interests.
2. The needs and interests of the Member's constituents.
3. Office strengths and weaknesses.
4. Opportunities and threats.

These decisions are best made collectively, with the input of the Member, staff, and — sometimes — a few people from the Member's kitchen cabinet. The planning process benefits from the staff's insight and expertise, and staff members receive a sense of "ownership," which increases their dedication and commitment to making the plan work.

The Planning Time Frame

Most congressional offices that conduct a formal planning process meet annually to produce a one-year plan. There is, however, a compelling reason for developing a two-year plan simply because Congress operates on a two-year calendar. Also, staff usually take longer than a year to accomplish key goals, such as passing legislation. Furthermore, most House Members already plan their political activities on a two-year basis because of the election cycle. Though the two-year horizon can make planning more difficult, the longer time frame can also lead to broader, more creative thinking.

CHAPTER ELEVEN   Strategic Planning in Your Office   163

If you choose to develop a two-year plan, however, you must also hold at least one interim planning session to review the plan. Congress is a dynamic environment and, unless the office modifies its plan to incorporate unexpected political changes and new information, the plan soon will be outdated and ignored. CMF suggests that offices informally review and reassess their plans every six months.

Whatever time frame you choose, CMF also recommends that the planning session take place between November and March. Doing so will allow you and your staff both to take advantage of the usual legislative break at this time of year and to incorporate the entire annual legislative cycle into your plan.

> **Additional Information**
>
> The CMF publication, *Keeping It Local: A Guide for Managing Congressional District & State Offices,* includes a thorough discussion on the importance of establishing a coordinated agenda between the DC and district/state offices, and the most common planning methods.
> Visit www.cmfweb.org or contact CMF at 202-546-0100 for more information. ■

The Mission Statement

Congressional office planning often centers on the task of surveying the political landscape for opportunities to serve constituent needs, meet the Member's political objectives and affect public policy. Though seizing such opportunities is important, it alone does not constitute effective planning. The plan must also reflect the Member's values, political ambitions and personal interests. It should inspire, motivate and reinforce the aspirations of the Member or else it is unlikely to be followed. If the Member has no clear sense of mission, short-term objectives are less likely to contribute to any long-term accomplishments. Productivity in diverse areas over many years doesn't necessarily add up to any clear sense of solid achievement.

> *"If the Member has no clear sense of mission, short-term objectives are less likely to contribute to any long-term accomplishments."*

For example, during a planning session that CMF facilitated, a third-term House Member realized that the primary reason that he decided to run for Congress had been neglected in his office's activities during his six years in Congress. Why? *Because he had never articulated it to his staff, to his constituents, or to his colleagues in Congress.* Six years of responding to the exigencies of the political moment had led the Member away from the central goal, the reason he ran for Congress in the first place. When the Member finally told his staff what his broad mission was, the priorities and work of his staff changed dramatically to support the mission. It also gave both the Member and his staff a clearer sense of purpose and commitment to their work.

Conducting an Effective Planning Session

1 The Member should not dominate the session. Almost nothing stifles creative and original thinking more than having the boss answer all of the questions raised by the process before staff analysis and discussion. Consequently, Members must understand that their role is as much to listen to the ideas and analysis of staff as it is to present ideas.

2 Make the session as participatory as possible. The planning session can be exciting and exhilarating, but it can also be slow and arduous. Staff participation is critical to making it energized and productive. If a large number of staff is involved, break up into small groups to do some analysis and report those findings back to the full group.

3 Hold the meeting outside of the congressional office. In the office, the Member and staff will be distracted and feel like it's business as usual. Changing the environment helps staff approach the assignment with some energy and excitement. There are limits on how the office may use official funds, so consult the Committee on House Administration or the Senate Rules and Administration Committee before proceeding.

4 Give staff time to prepare. With a 1-2 day session, it must be as productive as possible. Explain the objectives ahead of time and get staff thinking strategically beforehand by giving them questions to ponder or answer. Without adequate preparation time, it will be hard for staff to shift gears from routine, day-to-day activities to strategically analyzing the next two years.

5 Encourage creativity and original thinking through informality. Encourage staff and the Member to dress casually and operate informally. Promote debate, spontaneous speaking and humor.

6 If possible, use an outside facilitator. A facilitator can assist in shaping the planning process and ensure that issues raised are resolved fairly and expediently. If the Chief of Staff runs the session, it can impede its effectiveness by limiting their own participation or by giving staff the impression that the process is rigged to gain consensus for predetermined views. One option is to rotate the facilitator role among staff so that one person does not control the entire process and other staff can develop facilitating skills. CMF, which produced this book, assists congressional offices with the development and execution of strategic planning sessions. Contact CMF at 202-546-0100 for more information. ■

CHAPTER ELEVEN Strategic Planning in Your Office

To maximize the chances of making significant long-term accomplishments, we recommend that the Member kick off the planning process by preparing a written mission statement. The mission statement should clearly define broad yet distinctive goals that the Member hopes to accomplish while in Congress. Many Members, when pushed to write a mission statement, offer up such platitudes as: "To make a difference;" "To get re-elected;" "To give my constituents the best representation possible." These are noble aspirations, but they offer the staff little guidance as to what vision drives the Member (and should drive the staff), or how this mission differs from those of virtually every other Member of Congress.

An effective mission statement should present a broad, but concrete, vision. The themes addressed in a mission statement can focus on broad legislative goals, constituent service goals, or political goals. Examples of workable mission statement themes include:

- To become a leading advocate of educational reform in Congress.
- To play a lead role in my state's economic development.
- To get elected to the Senate in this decade.

In facilitating office planning processes, CMF has found that many Members operate intuitively. The challenge of the mission statement is getting the Member to clarify and articulate the values, ambitions, and experiences that comprise this intuition. Discussing the following questions should help provide some clarity:

- Why did you run for Congress? What specifically did you hope to achieve if elected?
- What would you like to be remembered for at the end of your tenure in Congress?
- What Members of Congress do you most respect and why?
- What is your vision of America's future?
- What values or characteristics should define the way your staff works and the office operates?

The mission statement should embody no more than four main themes, but preferably just one or two. The more focused the mission statement, the more direction it provides the entire staff. If a mission statement has more than four themes, the Member has yet to make the hard choices the process demands. An office can't successfully pursue more than a few long-term goals at any one time without spreading its resources too thinly. A quick review of the most effective Members of Congress should demonstrate that they developed early in their careers a clear, long-term focus — and adhered to it steadfastly.

Finally, the mission statement does not need to be revised every year or two. Rather, it should be used as the starting point of the planning process. The planning team should then review the mission statement at the start of each Congress to make sure it still reflects the Member's long-term vision and goals. Usually, the mission statement needs only minor alterations. However, sometimes a Member's mission changes significantly. The Member decides, for example, that he or she no longer wants to pursue the goal of becoming a leader in energy policy. Instead, he or she wants to become an influential leader within the party. In that case, a new mission statement needs to clearly embody this new direction and the rationale for pursuing it.

Developing Goals

Once the office has a broad mission statement that spells out the Member's long-term vision, short-term vehicles should be developed for pursuing these broad themes. These goals should relate directly to the mission statement and should be concrete, realistic, meaningful and achievable. Here is an example of how a Member's mission statement can be used to develop short-term goals.

A Representative CMF worked with several years ago developed a mission statement that had three themes. One of the themes was to take a prominent and national leadership role to ensure that the budget surpluses projected for the next decade were managed wisely. Based upon that long-term theme, the office developed a one-year goal of "raising the Member's knowledge, visibility and credibility on the issue, locally and nationally." During the planning session, the office then brainstormed options for what the Member and office could do over the next 12 months to meet this goal. A number of Washington office activities were selected to pursue, including organizing lunches with the Member and some economics and federal budget experts, introducing legislation, commissioning a GAO study, and working to get a seat on the Budget Committee in the next Congress. Corresponding district activities were also developed including: conducting town hall meetings on the topic of managing the surplus, writing an op-ed for the major daily newspaper, and routinely advocating policies for retiring the national debt in speeches when back home.

Staff should prepare for the goal-setting process by answering the following questions individually, in small groups, or in one large group. Write down the answers on large flip chart paper and then post them around the room for easy referral.

1. What are the main themes of the Member's mission statement?
2. What key issues is Congress likely to deal with in the next two years?
3. What possible national and international issues or trends — economic, political, demographic, technological or scientific — might emerge in the next two years and command congressional attention?

CHAPTER ELEVEN   Strategic Planning in Your Office   167

4. Which, if any, key issues or trends would interest the Member or would significantly affect constituents?
5. What issues are likely to dominate the district's or state's political/economic agenda in the next two years?
6. Which district/state issues or trends might deserve special attention from the Member or staff in the next two years?
7. Which issues do constituents currently feel most strongly about?
8. What campaign promises did the Member make that constituents now expect to see fulfilled?
9. What kind of image does the Member want to project, and how should the office reflect this image?
10. What political problems or weaknesses should the office be sensitive to in the next two years (e.g., criticism of a vote, impact of an anti-incumbency movement)?

Armed with all of this analysis, staffers should have a good sense of the important factors, events and trends necessary in developing office goals, and the office should now be ready to begin the process of defining the goals through a brainstorming exercise. As the planning team calls out possible goals, one of the team members writes them down immediately on a flip chart that the whole group can see. Participants should resist the temptation to evaluate ideas during the brainstorming session. Doing so inhibits the creative process. Staff will be reticent to toss out ideas spontaneously if they see their ideas being critiqued immediately.

Evaluating Potential Goals

A good brainstorming session should generate an impressive list of potential goals. As with mission statement themes, an office should keep its list of short-term goals to a minimum. CMF recommends no more than six, but preferably only three to five, short-term goals. Again, the purpose is to single out the goals that are most important, most feasible and most consistent with the office's mission statement — not to make a shopping list of enticing possibilities. To facilitate this goal evaluation process, the following organizational tools may be helpful.

The first of these is a simple device to help assess goals. Pictured in Figure 11-1 is a grid that relates the two factors of "impact" and "ability to achieve." To use it, place each potential goal in the quadrant that most closely characterizes it. The grid is most helpful when there is difficulty agreeing on how to select and rank goals.

For example, you may decide that championing legislation to legalize cocaine, if passed, would significantly reduce cocaine usage and the street violence associated with the illicit drug trade (as well as raise your political

Figure 11-1

Impact Achievability Grid

Ability to Achieve

	High	Low
Impact High	1st Priority	3rd Priority
Impact Low	2nd Priority	4th Priority

stock). You may also decide that the chances of gaining passage of such a bill are extremely low. Consequently, you would probably decide to rate it as a third priority.

However, you may believe that a solid waste disposal bill would have a very positive impact on your state and that its likelihood of passage is good. You may then give it first priority status in your office.

Another, more precise method is to weigh potential goals against a set of criteria. The following list of questions provides some examples an office might use to develop criteria to select its goals:

1. Is the goal consistent with the Member's overall mission?
2. What is the likelihood of achieving this goal in the next two years?
3. Does the goal interest the Member?
4. Will the goal positively or negatively affect the Member's constituents?
5. Will accomplishing the goal provide the Member with substantial benefits?
6. What resources will be required to complete this goal?
7. Will pursuit of the goal place excessive demands on the Member's time or on the staff's time?
8. Will the work involved utilize the office's strengths (e.g., the skills and expertise of the Member and staff and the Member's committee assignments)?
9. Can the expertise developed in pursuing the goal be applied effectively to other future office goals (i.e., the reusability of information and expertise)?

In Figure 11-2 we have simply placed these questions into a "criteria scorecard," providing a way to measure competing goals against a formalized set of standards. This figure proposes generic criteria that should be modified

CHAPTER ELEVEN Strategic Planning in Your Office

Figure 11-2

Scorecard for Goal Evaluation

	POTENTIAL GOALS					
	Goal	Goal	Goal	Goal	Goal	Goal
Consistent with Mission						
Likely to be Achieved						
Fits with Member's Personal Interests						
Consistent with Constituent Needs						
Success Provides Substantial Benefits						
Not an Excessive Drain on Member's Time						
Not an Excessive Drain on Staff's Time						
Uses Office's Strengths						
Develops Reusable Expertise						
Other:						
Other:						
Total Score:						
Scorecard Ranking:						

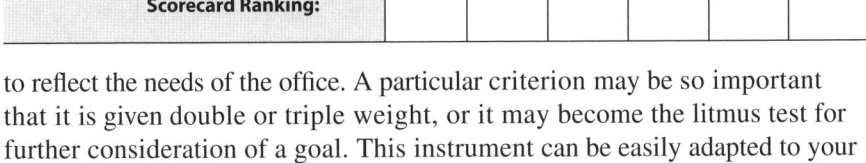

to reflect the needs of the office. A particular criterion may be so important that it is given double or triple weight, or it may become the litmus test for further consideration of a goal. This instrument can be easily adapted to your needs.

To use it, write each proposed goal across the top. Then, score how strongly the goal meets each criterion on a 0 to 3 scale, with 3 being the highest rating. To obtain each goal's total score, add the goal's scores for all of the criteria. The goals can then be ranked from best to worst according to their total scores.

Developing Action Plans

After establishing your one-year or two-year goals, the next step is to devise action plans for accomplishing each goal. The action plan lists the specific actions and tasks that must be taken to achieve a goal. Some goals might require just a few steps, while others might require as many as 20. To be effective, the action plan should also list the person(s) — including the Member — responsible for each task and the deadline for completing each action.

Assigning responsibilities in the action plan pulls together the staff as a team. It also prevents task redundancy and provides an opportunity for staff to use their specific skills and talents. Knowing the agreed-upon deadlines improves the likelihood that staff will accomplish tasks on time and can lead to increased accountability among the team. Without them, staff may not understand which tasks are most important.

By formulating an action plan, an office gets a written document that coordinates the activities of different staff (even those working out of separate offices); creates a clear strategy instead of an unrelated series of steps; and increases Member and staff accountability by ensuring that everyone is aware of his or her responsibilities and when work should be finished.

This action-planning process also has the benefit of giving the office one last chance to determine whether it really makes sense to pursue a goal. Frequently, offices for which CMF has facilitated planning sessions revised one of their goals at this stage. After listing the tasks necessary to achieve the goal, they came to realize that it would be harder to achieve and/or would take more of the Member's and staff's time than they had imagined. It's much better to discover this problem in the planning session than after six months of hard work.

For example, while reviewing action plans, one Senate office discovered an important issue: one LA was primarily responsible for three of the office's five major legislative initiatives for the year. Everyone quickly recognized that this LA would be buried by this plan. The planning team then developed three options for dealing with this projected train wreck: drop one of the goals and replace it with another issue, hire another LA on a short-term basis to handle one of the three legislative initiatives, or recruit an experienced and skilled congressional fellow to take on one of the issues with coaching from the LA and LD. After a failed attempt to find a suitable fellow, the office decided to hire a former LA on a short-term basis to manage one of the issues.

The action plan in Figure 11-3 shows how a complex or formidable initiative can be broken down into orderly, easy-to-follow action items and measure progress toward the goal. Breaking large tasks into smaller ones, and putting assigned responsibilities in writing for all to see, makes it more likely that the

CHAPTER ELEVEN   Strategic Planning in Your Office   171

Figure 11-3

Sample Goal-Oriented Action Plan

PROJECT TITLE: Pre-Natal Care Legislation

OBJECTIVE: Increase utilization of available pre-natal care services by low-income women by introducing and obtaining passage of legislation this year

Actions	Staffers Responsible	Start Date	End Date	Status
1. Identify federal agencies providing educational outreach to low-income women	LA	2/1	2/15	Completed
2. Meet with agency staff, review present programs, discuss legislative ideas for improving services	LA, LD	2/15	3/15	In progress
3. Identify/interview pre-natal care specialists to discuss ideas for increasing utilization	LA	2/15	3/15	
4. Work with Legislative Counsel to draft legislation	LA, LD	3/15	3/25	
5. Identify revenue sources and obtain CBO cost estimates	LA, LD	3/26	4/4	
6. Send out draft for comment to interested parties in district	LA, Mail Mgr	4/5	5/15	
7. Find Senator to introduce and push companion bill in Senate	Member, LA, LD		5/15	
8. Member meets with committee chair and staff on bill introduction and field hearing	Member, LD, LA		5/15	
9. Finalize legislation	Member, LA, LD, Chief of Staff		6/15	
10. Develop local and national press strategy	Press Sec., LD, Chief of Staff		6/15	
11. Introduce legislation	Member		6/18	
12. Hold field hearing (see separate action plan)	Member, DD, LA, Chief of Staff		6/25	
13. Hold mark-up at full committee	Member, LA		9/10	
14. Vote bill out of committee	Member		9/20	
15. House floor vote	Member		10/1	
16. Support Senate passage (see separate action plan)	Member, LA, LD		10/5	

DUE DATE: Pass House by 10/1, Senate by 10/5

whole job will be done properly and on time. The office should prepare an action plan similar to this one for every significant or long-term project the office undertakes — from a large conference in the district/state to introducing a piece of legislation. Most offices underutilize this valuable, highly versatile planning and monitoring tool.

This sample action plan is organized around a strategic *goal*. However, many offices organize their plans around office *functions* (e.g., legislative, administrative, press, scheduling, constituent services). For example, the Communications Director writes an action plan that incorporates the press objectives developed by the planning team, while the Legislative Director devises an action plan to meet the legislative goals.

Both goal-oriented and functionally-oriented planning are workable so long as they are driven by agreed-upon, office-wide goals. What should be avoided at all costs is structuring a planning process in which goals are independently developed for each functional division. Such a process, while not uncommon, encourages each staff member to determine independently what the Member's priorities ought to be. The result may be a press plan, devised by the Communications Director, that pursues priorities that are different from or even in competition with those set forth in the legislative plan generated by the Legislative Director and Legislative Assistants. And both the press and legislative plans may conflict with the priorities outlined in the scheduling plan devised by the Chief of Staff, District/State Director and Scheduler.

In short, a functional planning process can encourage the development of clear office goals by forcing the Member and staff to discuss and resolve their differences.

Implementing the Plan

The culmination of all the effort described in this chapter will be a written plan distributed to the whole office. The plan should summarize the office's strategy for the next two years and outline the steps that will be necessary for that strategy to be effective. It will contain all of the elements discussed so far: the Member's mission statement; the supporting short-term goals and why they were selected; and the action plan needed to accomplish each goal.

However, the planning process does not end with the distribution of a written plan. For a plan to continue to be effective, it must be updated and fine-tuned regularly. If not, your plan, like many others, has a good likelihood of ending up gathering dust on a shelf. Why? Because even if the planning process generated great ideas and enthusiasm, it's natural for staff to revert to an old and comfortable routine. It's understandable, too, that staff attend to the matters immediately at hand, and chronically feel they can't afford the time to begin the new initiatives described in the strategic plan. Thus,

CHAPTER ELEVEN Strategic Planning in Your Office

along with the planning process itself must come the method of monitoring the plan's implementation.

Probably the biggest challenge offices have in implementing the plan is keeping the Member and the staff focused and regularly working on it. In particular, offices will almost always find that attractive new issues and possible initiatives arise. Too often, offices, at the encouragement of the Member, will begin pursuing these new issues with virtually no consideration of the impact of this new work on the goals enthusiastically agreed upon in the strategic plan. Consequently, the new issues slowly and methodically crowd out the old ones.

The problem is that frequently the new issues do not warrant the attention they receive. They are not more important, more advantageous to the Member or more achievable than the goals in the plan they replace. It's just that there is no management mechanism in place to ask the critical questions that ensure offices weigh these new ideas as critically as they did the initiatives included in their plan. Specifically, Members and staff alike need to collectively ask two questions before embarking on any new and major initiatives:

1. Is this initiative sufficiently attractive that it warrants supplanting another strategic goal or action item in our plan?
2. If so, which goal or actions will be sacrificed to make room for working on this new initiative?

Sometimes offices will find that the new idea does have more merit than one or more of the goals listed in their strategic plan. In that case, it can be substituted for an existing goal and a new action plan should be developed. However, more often than not, offices will find that when subjected to scrutiny, the exciting new initiative of the day does not warrant the bumping of a previously established goal.

How can offices maintain the discipline necessary to effectively follow through on their strategic plan? We recommend that you adopt some of the following, simple methods.

Frequent ad hoc planning meetings. Consider organizing ad hoc meetings to address specific problems or opportunities that arise (e.g. breaking events or general office problems). The key is to convene the meeting with the appropriate staff, set aside the necessary time and don't try to squeeze problem-solving meetings into the weekly staff meeting. The issues will be addressed more efficiently if only those who need to participate are there; they have ample preparation time and the necessary information to think about the problem or opportunity; and are not forced to reach decisions prematurely with too little time for consideration.

If, for example, the Member wants to pursue a new initiative, then a meeting should be scheduled that includes the Member and the relevant staff affected by the initiative to evaluate its merits and consider the two questions raised previously. Possible outcomes of such a meeting include: deciding to include a new goal in the plan and drop an old goal; deciding not to pursue the new idea; deciding to conduct some further preliminary research before making a decision. Over time, such meetings will create office discipline and enhance office follow-through while further fostering strategic thinking.

Functional meetings. Rather than trying to do most of your coordination and oversight in a single weekly staff meeting, organize other meetings by office function. For example, schedule regular (weekly, bimonthly or monthly) meetings to discuss legislation, scheduling and constituent mail.

Weekly or monthly progress reports. Weekly updates from staff to the Member and Chief of Staff or District/State Director can keep management well informed of the staff's progress. To ensure this reporting does not become simply a rundown of what staff are working on, CMF recommends that offices apply the following rule: require staffers to begin each update by reporting on their progress on activities that relate directly to the office's strategic plan rather than on the most recent events. This practice reminds staff that their first and foremost responsibility is to meet the plan-related activities and not just to handle the daily, routine work and react to events. The format and process is less important for these updates than the documenting and sharing of information among staff. The focus should be on the outcomes — the staff's progress — not the updates themselves.

Monthly strategic planning meetings. Chiefs of Staff should hold all-staff meetings at the beginning of each month to review progress on the strategic goals. The Member should *not* be present at these sessions, but the Chief of Staff must know the status of the Member's progress prior to the meeting. The Member, like the staff, must remain accountable to the agreed-upon goals.

The primary purpose of the meeting is to determine if the action items listed for completion in the previous month were, in fact, completed. Such regularly scheduled meetings clearly communicate the office's commitment to meet its goals and not simply fall into the old routines. Another important purpose is to discuss problems staff may be having with meeting their deadlines. The action plan may underestimate the amount of time it takes to get a piece of legislation drafted by the Legislative Counsel's office. Or maybe a staff person became distracted by another assignment he thought deserved to become an overriding short-term priority. These meetings are a good opportunity to identify and discuss problems and to make the regular and necessary adjustments required.

Quarterly senior management meetings. Similar to private-sector quarterly board meetings, these meetings are another effective tool for reviewing progress and maintaining coordination. The Member, Chief of Staff, District/State

CHAPTER ELEVEN Strategic Planning in Your Office

Director, Legislative Director, Communications Director and any other senior management staff should meet to review progress towards office goals. The team should examine underlying assumptions of the overall office plan and assess the relevance of new information or events that have transpired since the plan was drafted to determine whether the goals warrant revision.

Individual meetings. Clear action plans and regular oversight are critical components of an effective management system. These tools need to be reinforced by a management practice of holding all staff accountable. The Chief of Staff should make clear that staffers who turn out high-quality work on time will be recognized, while staff who fail to meet their deadlines or whose work products are inconsistent or substandard will

> *"The Chief of Staff should make clear that staffers who turn out high-quality work on time will be recognized, while staff who fail to meet their deadlines or whose work products are inconsistent or substandard will not be rewarded and may face consequences."*

not be rewarded and may face consequences. In too many congressional offices, management fails to properly acknowledge outstanding workers and address the unacceptable work performance of others. Over time, this management failure tends to demoralize the best performers and discourage the average or substandard staff from making the effort to address their performance problems.

As discussed in greater detail in Chapter 13, "A Process for Managing Staff," the best practices for building an office culture that promotes excellence is to engage in ongoing dialogue with all staff about their performance. Supervisors should meet with individual staff either quarterly, monthly or weekly to review action plans; determine if individual goals are still appropriate; the status of goals, projects and tasks; what resources are needed to accomplish them; and review performance issues, if any. Be clear about what is expected of them, what they do well and where they need improvement. Then, inform them when their work product meets or exceeds expectations and when it falls short. Recognize outstanding work with bonus pay, raises, office-wide praise and, of course, public and private words of appreciation from the boss. Staffers who consistently do not meet deadlines should be counseled regarding their performance and its subsequent impact on the office and potentially be placed on a Performance Improvement Plan (PIP) by their manager. Do not wait until the end of the year to discuss a staffer's performance, whether positive or negative. Meet with the staffer regularly to review expectations and performance, which serves both the interest of the staffer and office.

Timelines. Some Chiefs of Staff hang a large timeline on their walls that chart the office's goals and the primary "milestones" or timeframes when significant actions are to be completed. Such a visual display will catch people's attention, let them know that their duties will not be allowed to slip through the cracks, and create an easy reference status report on which to base further discussion or meetings.

In short, the plan must be a living document. If the plan is regularly reviewed and revised when necessary, it will provide a way to rationally integrate shifts in the Member's interests and the policy terrain. It will also keep the office focused on its priorities while allowing for intelligent trade-offs based on a strategic view of your options.

Measuring Office Performance

In addition to guiding offices, plans are useful tools for evaluating your office's performance by answering the following questions:

- Did we meet the goals laid out in our plan?
- Where did we succeed, and where did we fail?
- When we succeeded, what were the variables that contributed to our success?
- When we failed, what were the variables that contributed to our failure?
- Given this analysis, what changes should we make in our operation this year to improve performance?

Asking these questions does more than simply make the office accountable. Such evaluation also creates a process for promoting organizational growth. The best offices in Congress, like the best businesses, have a strong capacity for improvement. They regularly identify and address problems. They learn from their mistakes and they turn shortcomings into growth and success. Through this learning process good offices become great offices.

A Senate office conducted this end-of-year review with the entire DC staff and analyzed its successes and failures. They reached the disheartening conclusion that even though the office accomplished most of its goals, they had failed repeatedly to receive sufficient credit back home for all that they had accomplished. This insight led the office to engage in a very animated, no-fault discussion of how the office conducted its media outreach in the state. Based on this analysis and out-of-the-box thinking from non-press staff, the office developed more aggressive and creative strategies for raising the Senator's visibility and helping reporters understand the newsworthiness of the Senator's work. These new strategies were then incorporated in the action plans for the coming year.

Conclusion

Whether in your first term or your twelfth year, your effectiveness will be greatly enhanced by the ability to set clear goals that reflect your constituent needs and your personal interests, and to balance these goals with the national policy and political environment in which you operate. It takes concerted effort and can be difficult to begin. But it's a crucial first step toward conveying a sense of purpose to your staff and charting a clear direction for your congressional career.

CHAPTER ELEVEN

Chapter Summary
The DOs and DON'Ts of
Strategic Planning in Your Office

Do...

- **engage in strategic planning — especially if you're a freshman —** to set goals and priorities for the Member and staff, allocate resources and enable your office to be more proactive and effective.

- **consider developing a two-year strategic plan,** rather than just one-year, to take advantage of the full legislative cycle and to encourage comprehensive thinking for the entire congressional session.

- **balance four perspectives in your planning:** the Member's personal goals and interests; constituent needs; office strengths and weakness; and opportunities and threats.

- **develop a system for evaluating potential goals** that considers the overall office mission, the resources needed to pursue the goal, and the likelihood of its success.

- **monitor progress on goals** through written action plans; weekly, monthly and quarterly meetings; and regular progress reports.

- **hold all staff accountable** by recognizing outstanding performers and addressing the sub-par work product of others.

- **measure office performance at the end of the year.** Create a process and a checklist of questions. Where did we succeed, where did we fail, and why?

Don't...

- **operate without a clearly defined long-term vision** of what the Member seeks to accomplish in Congress.

- **write a mission statement that is too broad or establishes too many themes.** The more focused it is, the more direction it provides to staff.

- **hold major planning meetings in the office or make them too formal.** Go offsite to encourage enthusiasm, creativity and original thinking.

- **develop more than 3-5 short-term goals.** Single out what's most important, most feasible and most consistent with the office's mission statement.

- **undertake a major project without first drafting a comprehensive action plan.** Deadlines and clearly defined responsibilities are essential to keeping everyone accountable and focused on the plan.

- **pursue a new initiative without scrutinizing how it would affect the strategic plan, goals and office resources.**

CHAPTER TWELVE

Budgeting and Financial Management

This Chapter Includes...

☆ The strategic importance of budgeting

☆ A process for budgeting toward your goals, year after year

☆ Suggestions for establishing office accounting procedures

☆ Cost-saving and budgeting tips recommended by veteran offices

A congressional office, like a small business, requires two things in order to operate: (1) a mission or purpose (a reason for existing), and (2) resources to support that mission. In Congress, you are largely responsible for developing your mission — your reason for coming to Washington — and for deciding what you want to accomplish and contribute while here. Your resources, on the other hand, are given to you by Congress and paid for by the American taxpayer.

This chapter is designed to help each congressional office use its budget as a strategic tool to achieve its office goals. The message is simple: spent wisely, your resources can greatly boost your chances of success and achievement in Congress; spent foolishly, they can lead to ineffectiveness and even public embarrassment.

This chapter should be read by freshman offices looking ahead to their second year and veterans who wish to ensure their budgeting is in sync with their priorities. (Freshman offices should also read Chapter 3, which contains an introduction to House and Senate budgeting rules, a discussion of the Member's role in budgeting, and guidance for creating a first-year budget.)

The Strategic Importance of Budgeting

Meeting Your Goals

There are many strategic budget choices associated with running an office. Each Representative has approximately $1.5 million per year for official uses. Each Senator has between $3.1 million and $4.9 million (depending upon state population), as well as a number of smaller accounts. From these sums, the office must decide:

- How many staff to hire;
- What staff positions to fill;
- How much to pay each staffer;
- How many district/state offices to maintain;
- What types of computer, software, and telecommunications systems to buy;
- How often to travel between the district/state and Washington (Member *and* staff);
- Whether to send any unsolicited mailings to constituents;
- Whether to pay for professional training for staff; and *many* additional smaller items.

What are the best choices? That depends upon your circumstances. No two districts or states are the same, in geography, population or economy. And no two Representatives or Senators are the same, whether comparing missions, styles or strengths.

The Members who make smart budget decisions are the ones who continually keep the big picture in mind — why *they* came to Congress and what *they* hope to accomplish. These Members use their strategic plans as blueprints for making budget choices. Once goals have been established, they devote financial resources to achieving them.

These Members tend to be the most successful. They are the ones who become national or local leaders on an issue, subcommittee or committee chairs, or national leaders in their party. Why? Because their offices have the structures in place that enable them to recognize and respond quickly to opportunities to advance their goals.

MANAGEMENT FACT

Each Representative is annually allocated about $1.5 million and each Senator is allocated between $3.1 and $4.9 million for office expenses.

Specialized Software

Both the House and the Senate have software programs specifically designed to help Member offices create customized budgets, monitor expenditures, generate reports, and produce vouchers. House offices use PeopleSoft, FinMart, and the Congressional Accounting and Personnel System (CAPS). Senate offices use the Financial Management Information System (FMIS). Training for each is available from the respective chambers. ■

For example, if one of your goals is to be a leader in agriculture policy, you may want to: spend extra to hire a skilled agriculture attorney for your Washington office; pay to train some of your other staff in agriculture issues; frequently send your Washington legislative staff to your district/state to meet with agribusiness leaders there; or subscribe to agriculture journals.

If, on the other hand, one of your goals is outreach to new constituencies in your far-flung district or state, you may spend funds to: open more district/state offices than did your predecessor; locate a large percentage of your staff in the district/state; travel to the district/state every available weekend; or send targeted "outreach" e-mails to these groups.

One Senate staffer told us that his boss saw himself as a world statesman and wanted to be recognized as such by the media and public. The office consequently paid more for travel, cell phone expenses and subscriptions relating to national and international affairs so the Senator and staff could remain subject matter experts. The Office Manager explained the decisions this way: "[We spend on] travel because he wants to be everywhere, and on communications because if he can't be there, he wants to talk with you wherever you are."

> *"[We spend on] travel because he wants to be everywhere, and on communications because if he can't be there, he wants to talk with you wherever you are."*

Your visible, financial commitment to your goals will also pay dividends in increased staff morale. Your staff will be especially focused when they see that goals are not merely buzzwords for the office, but define the basic choices that you make.

Maintaining a focus on your goals also makes budget trade-offs clearer. Expenditures in one area often mean you will need to economize in other areas. If you buy the best computer system, you may not to be able to afford extra Legislative Correspondents to respond rapidly to constituents. The trade-off is clear, although the choice might not be easy. One House Chief of Staff explained why her fiscally conservative boss decided to spend all of his MRA rather than turn back part of his budget: "When you return money, you maybe get one story in the local press. Most constituents won't read it or care. But constituents will care if you don't answer their letters. The money is better used to hire staff to respond to constituents promptly." Perhaps another Member would draw a different conclusion and make a different choice.

Avoiding Problems

In some ways, your budget is a double-edged sword. Your official funds can help you meet your legislative and representational goals. If mismanaged, however, they can constrain your office's activities and even lead to public embarrassment.

There are three budget problems you may encounter:

1. **Spending on the wrong things (non-priorities).** Many offices lose sight of their goals in the rush of normal legislative business. They often make major spending decisions (e.g., hiring a new staffer, sending out a mass mailing to constituents) to solve short-term problems, without considering how the decision will affect their long-term agenda. Such decisions (e.g., hiring the wrong type of staffer), can be difficult to undo, and take resources away from achieving the Member's strategic plan. The best way to avoid this problem is simply by asking, "How does this investment affect my long-term goals?" whenever you consider a major expenditure.

2. **Overspending.** There are two types of "overspending." Members learn fast that if an office overspends its *official allocation of funds*, the Member is personally liable for the excess expenditures. No Chief of Staff wants to be the bearer of this bad news, and the House Finance and Senate Disbursing Offices can detect many potential problems early. But there is another far more frequent type of overspending — overspending *your budget* early in the year, in one category or many, forcing the office to forgo items that were in the budget for later in the year (e.g., to cancel some Member travel, eliminate an important mailing to your constituents, or put off hiring another Legislative Assistant). Financial planning can also help prevent this mid-year ad hoc rearranging of priorities.

3. **Media scrutiny of your expenditures.** The media (and the public) have access not only to information about your total allocations, but also to a detailed summary of your office's expenditures (twice a year in the Senate, four times a year in the House). Many reporters and bloggers will plumb the depths of your expenses for a story on your "fiscal mismanagement" or "political corruption." The media views two types of spending as inherently suspect: (1) dealings with a Member's family, business associates, or campaign contributors, and (2) expenditures that are out of line with the norms of other Member. The Member and staff need to be aware of these considerations when authorizing major expenditures such as district/state office rent, a computer system, or a printing and mailing job. Keep the taxpayers in mind before making *any* purchasing decisions.

Even small expenses can cause trouble if the public and press deem them extravagant or symbolic of misplaced priorities. One Office Manager told us of a senior state staffer who "tested out" a new

MANAGEMENT FACT
Members are personally liable for excess expenditures.

restaurant for the Senator, to the tune of a $45 tab. The Office Manager brought it to the attention of the Chief of Staff, and both decided to cut the reimbursement to the state staffer by half. They could not justify paying that much for a meal with official funds. Perhaps more important, though, they reasoned that this small expenditure, if it became public, could undermine large efforts by the office to fashion an image of fiscal responsibility and public trust.

If you have any questions about the propriety of an expenditure, you should use the many resources available to you. The *Members' Congressional Handbook*, or the *Senate Manual*, provide guidelines on what you can and cannot do with your official funds. House offices should also consult with the Committee on House Administration, the Committee on Standards of Official Conduct, and the Finance Office. Senate offices should consult the Senate Rules and Administration Committee, the Ethics Committee, and the Disbursing Office. Developing relationships and checking with staff in all three offices is highly recommended. And for questions on the political (or management) implications of an expenditure, a veteran Chief of Staff in a trusted office can also be a good resource.

Budgeting Toward Your Goals, Year After Year

Creating a first-year congressional budget differs in one obvious way from the second year and beyond: after the first year, an office can look at its *own* spending patterns to develop the budget for the following year. This information becomes more valuable when it is used to evaluate whether a budget truly reflects an office's priorities.

Consider the analogy that updating a budget is a lot like editing a speech that you gave last year. There are two general approaches you could take. First, you could polish the speech by asking: Are there any inaccuracies or obvious mistakes in grammar or spelling? Can outdated references be freshened with more recent cases? If legislative work or sponsored bills are mentioned, are there new examples to include?

Alternatively, you could start by asking more fundamental questions: What are the objectives of this speech? Does the speech meet those objectives? Could the objectives be accomplished more effectively through another format or focus (shorter/longer, more/fewer jokes, a demonstration rather than a speech)? You could even start with questions about the direction of the office itself: What are my office goals? Have they changed since last term? Does the speech advance one or more of those goals?

Congressional budgeting offers the same two choices. Chiefs of Staff, Administrative Directors/Office Managers and other members of the financial team, can take last year's budget and make the obvious changes, adjusting for inflation, staff turnover, and increased/decreased allotments. Or they can take the more demanding, but ultimately rewarding, route of evaluating whether their budget spends in a way that reflects their priorities. Many offices resist taking this route, though it has much to offer. One reason is that it takes work, energy, analysis and time, all of which are in limited supply for busy offices. In addition, offices that spent a significant amount of time developing last year's budget might rationalize that there's no need to go through it again. Also, it is difficult to predict how much revision a budget might need. Indeed, sometimes very little is required. After thoughtful review, an office might draw the conclusion that the budget is basically sound, and only in need of minor changes. Uncertainty and complacency encourage offices to take the path of least resistance without exploring the underlying assumptions of expenditures.

CMF does not advocate an annual reinvention of the wheel, but Members and senior staff will be best served if they keep in mind the strategic potential of a budget. Below we offer an approach to updating your current budget to ensure that this important management exercise becomes an effective, strategic instrument rather than a rote process. Our advice is that even though your budget may not change significantly from year to year, at the very least you should still look at it carefully each year and ask: Have our priorities shifted this year and, if so, how should those changes be reflected in a reconceptualized budget?

Step 1: Note any changes to your strategic plan or office priorities.

There is a natural tendency to start the budget update process with your existing budget, but it makes more sense to look first at your goals and update them if needed. Money may be one of the most important tools you have, but it is only a tool. Your goals drive your budget. So ask yourself: Do I want to continue to be a leader on education policy? Is constituent outreach still a major concern? Have I passed that tax bill I've been pushing for three years, and if not, should I push harder next year or put it aside? Have I decided to run for another office or a congressional leadership post in a few years? The answers to these types of questions will provide a solid basis for allocating resources and making the required budgeting trade-offs.

Step 2: Brainstorm what resources it will take to accomplish the revised priorities.

Be as specific as you can, and feel free to list a couple of options rather than limiting yourself to one course of action. Be forewarned: this step might highlight glaring inconsistencies between your goals and your budget allocations.

CHAPTER TWELVE   Budgeting and Financial Management

For example, while offices have sought to increase constituent services with new and ever more complicated computer and Internet technologies, some still hire for the Systems Administrator position based on qualifications from a decade ago: 22-year-old, just out of school, willing to take on LC duties, willing to work for an entry-level salary. These offices should not be shocked when their systems go down regularly. Instead, they should seriously evaluate how much it will cost to hire a qualified SysAdmin, shared employee, or contractor who can perform the job they need done.

Another example: a Member with little seniority in the House decides to concentrate on constituent services. Fast forward a couple of terms, and she's moving up the committee roster and being talked about for an open deputy whip post. At the same time, Washington-based legislative projects have become her top priority. Or so her office says. A look at the budget shows that she's still spending heavily on outreach, with four fully-staffed district offices, a mobile office, two annual newsletters and flights home every weekend. Meanwhile, two Legislative Assistant slots in Washington remain vacant, perhaps for lack of funds. She shouldn't be surprised when the office can't fully exploit legislative opportunities. Now is the time to figure out what it will really take to become a legislative player.

Step 3: Look at last year's budget with an eye toward surprises.

It is important to note not only how you *intended* to spend your money, but what you *actually* spent it on. These are your *de facto* priorities. Was more or less spent on office supplies, franking or salaries than originally planned? What caused these discrepancies? What were the effects on reaching your goals?

A House Chief of Staff told us that she likes to keep an eye on staff travel because it's something that can "escalate surprisingly in some years." Similarly, Office Managers have noted Senators' travel costs can be four or five times what was anticipated if there was an unexpected increase in the use of charter flights. In both cases the office should ask whether the costs were justified. The answers will make travel budgets for the following year more realistic.

Step 4: Take note of rules changes and other factors that could affect budgeting.

Here you are looking for changed circumstances that could affect how much money and other resources you will get, and where your costs might increase. A 10 percent increase in your allowance or skyrocketing utilities in your district office would affect your budget.

Has maximum per diem or mileage reimbursement changed? This could affect travel costs. Is your new computer system paid off, leaving only the costs of the maintenance contract? Have postage rates increased? This could affect your franking expenses. Is there inflation in the economy generally?

Senate offices need also to remember the effect that a cost of living adjustment (COLA) might have on a fiscal year budget. If a Senator passes on a COLA to staff, it will probably take effect in January. But since Senate office budgets run on a fiscal year, from October through September, the office will need to calculate the fiscal year impact of this change. A staffer's fiscal year salary will include three months at the lower salary (October–December) plus nine months at the higher salary (January–September).

Step 5: Determine which expenses are flexible and which are longer-term commitments.

While in theory, *all* spending is flexible, in actuality some decisions and commitments are harder to undo than others without incurring financial or political costs. Don't be deterred. At this point, focus on gathering information about the degree of flexibility of your expenditures, and on the costs and timeframe required to make changes in spending.

A high-end computer system with multi-year payments and maintenance contracts is an obvious long-term commitment. But there are others. If you fire hard-working staff because they are experts in "yesterday's" issues, you risk damaging the morale of those remaining who see you as heartless. Close a district office and the message to the city or neighborhood is "I don't care" about the constituents who need the office's services, or about the city.

Sometimes longevity itself can produce budget pressures. One House Chief of Staff noted the irony that keeping a good, loyal staff around for a number of years — usually desirable — can lead to staff salaries taking up an ever increasing percentage of your budget through COLA's and pay raises.

It may be tempting to view "routine" office functions such as answering phones, conducting legislative research and answering constituent correspondence as nonnegotiable "must-do's" for every office. But remember, while they need to get done, there can be a great deal of flexibility in how they are performed and by whom. The variety of office setups testifies to that truth.

Step 6: Critically review and update the major allocations in your current budget.

So far you've thought about your goals and how they've changed, what resources it would take to reach those goals, how actual spending differs from intended spending, the rules changes and other factors which need to be taken into account and what commitments you've made.

Now ask yourself, "Can each major allocation in our current budget be justified and linked to accomplishing one or more of our revised office goals?

Are there alternative ways to spend the money to better accomplish those goals?"

Some of the spending changes you might wish to make may be viewed by your staff, constituents or other "stakeholders" as negatively impacting their own interests. You'll have to consider whether the political fallout is manageable. Maybe you can help them see how the changes will in fact meet their needs in ways they haven't explored. Or perhaps you will opt to take the hit, put it behind you, and get on with the new vision.

Step 7: Build a new month-by-month budget reflecting your changes.

Allocating your new budget monthly will allow you to review it regularly as the year progresses and determine whether your spending to date is where you expect it to be. Some expenses will be fixed items appearing each month. Others will be one-time or seasonal expenses. Your office should estimate, as best it can, when an expenditure is likely to occur.

Establishing Financial Procedures for Your Office

Written Office Policies

Once the office has a clear financial plan, establish policies and procedures to ensure that the money is spent the way it was intended, and that the financial regulations of the Committee on House Administration and the Senate Rules and Administration Committee are met. These procedures must also promote the fiscal philosophy and financial management practices that you want. There are numerous practical questions that must be addressed concerning how funds are to be handled in your office. Your office manual should expressly address these financial matters, such as spending authority, reimbursements, out-of-pocket expenses, and record keeping.

The particular method that your office uses to meet the accounting and record keeping requirements for a congressional office should also be established in writing. Although the requirements are explained in the *Member's Congressional Handbook* and *Senate Manual*, there are a variety of methods that can be adopted to meet these specifications. Making a considered decision is far superior to developing accounting practices by default, something that occurs in many offices. Often your computerized budgeting and financial accounting program will guide those decisions.

The Accounting System

The budget that the financial team has created represents what you *intend* to spend and is the monitoring tool for your overall financial plan. Tracking what you *actually* spend is the practical side of the financial management process.

By regularly comparing expenditures with budget projections and year-to-date position, you can decide whether your office is about where it is expected to be, or if it is overspending or developing a surplus. The House Finance and Senate Disbursing Offices will also be doing projections for you, primarily in the interest of making sure you don't overspend. Your office must take responsibility for ensuring the spending is wise and in accordance with your budget.

Below are some general guidelines to help you develop an accounting system. The House Learning Center (202-226-3800) and the Senate Office of Education and Training (202-224-7628) offer classes for staff who will be part of your system.

Record Keeping. The House and Senate may one day make congressional budgeting fully paperless, linking up each individual Member's office with the House Finance or Senate Disbursing Office. They aren't there yet, but they're getting closer each day. Each chamber's intranet offers financial advice, forms and (with the proper clearances) access to your accounts. The House Finance Office also offers FinMart, an online system that allows you to see up-to-date reports on your office's finances. Still, paper vouchers must be submitted with *original* signatures and receipts. You will need a system for keeping track of this paperwork.

Payment Processing. The scrutiny that congressional offices endure is part of day-to-day life on the Hill. You can easily avoid embarrassment by asking in advance whether or not an expenditure will be allowed. Make sure that all of your staff understand (1) who in the office can approve expenditures (typically only a few members of your financial team), and (2) office rules on travel spending (e.g., per diem amounts, reimbursement policies).

You also should be sensitive to how your *allowable* expenditures will be listed in the House's Statement of Disbursements or the Secretary of the Senate's Report. Offices should learn the standard budget categories and common expenditure language to avoid using language that may give the "appearance of impropriety." For example, one freshman House Member opened a district office and served cookies and punch. He submitted a voucher describing the expense as "new office celebration." A House Finance Office employee commented that it "sounded like the staff getting together for beer and pizza." She suggested alternative language that highlighted the constituent benefits of the expense and didn't raise any unnecessary red flags.

This example also highlights the importance of establishing a good working relationship with the Finance and Disbursing Offices staff. In addition to providing advice on budget categories and expenditure language, they can be valuable resources in explaining the requirements of the system, estimating the "turnaround time" for vouchers, suggesting fine-tuning procedures, and resolving discrepancies.

Finally, it is important for your financial team to establish a standard operating procedure for staffers to follow when they are requesting reimbursement or submitting a bill for payment. Staff should know in advance what supporting documentation is required, what the deadlines for submission are, what form their requests should take, and any other procedures they may need to follow. The *Member's Congressional Handbook* and *Senate Manual* can supply the details of how to prepare the vouchers accurately, but the financial team must establish the office routine and policy.

Reconciliation. Every month, the House Finance and Senate Disbursing Offices will send your office a financial statement, to help you make sure that your numbers match the official numbers. In some ways, though, monthly reports are an anachronism, as both chambers' intranets post the status of vouchers overnight so that you could reconcile daily if you wanted to. Your office will have to decide how often to perform the task of reconciliation.

The monthly statements will have a detailed listing of expenditures made the prior month, sorted by category, expenditures to date, and balance available. The statements have also begun to include funds which have been committed, but have not yet been paid (i.e., dollars committed to district rent, payroll, franking, etc.). Vouchers which arrive at the Finance or Disbursing Office too late in the month to be processed in time for

> **Sharing an Office Financial Specialist**
>
> More than 100 House offices and a few Senate offices have turned to part-time, specialized employees to take care of routine office expense processing. Often one part-time staffer will be shared among several offices.
>
> Some of these offices have found that since current budgeters tend to have other titles and duties as well (Office Manager, Systems Administrator and Scheduler), using part-time help frees up full-time staff to concentrate on these other tasks. The part-timers also require virtually no training and often have excellent contacts in the House Finance or Senate Disbursing Offices. They may also be able to suggest spending alternatives or creative options to stretch the dollars a little further. And of all the typical office functions, bookkeeping can be considered the most apolitical. In fact, some part-timers have been known to work for Members of both parties over their careers.
>
> If utilizing a shared employee, confirm that they are complying with the regulations of your chamber and are filing any necessary disclosure forms. ∎

inclusion on the current month's statement will obviously not appear that month.

Auditing. A number of audits are already built into the congressional system. For example, the House Finance Office processes each voucher under the guidance of the Committee on House Administration, while in the Senate, the Disbursing Office and the Senate Rules and Administration Committee ensure each voucher meets that chamber's regulations.

Your financial team could also create a system that provides for periodic checks on your office accounting system to ensure that all regulations are being met, your financial wishes are being respected, and the system is not being abused by the record keeper or any other staff member. Some guidelines for conducting your internal audit are:

1. Have someone other than the record keeper perform it.
2. Do not announce in advance when you are going to conduct the audit (the best way to get a true picture of the system).
3. Perform it at a time of month that would not interfere with your normal voucher and payroll processing.
4. Look only at a random sample of transactions (e.g., audit every 20th transaction).
5. Do not give the perception that the audit is any reflection of the record keeper's work. It is a good business practice to audit the books, regardless of the experience of your record keeper.

Monthly Financial Review

Drafting a budget is one thing; sticking to it is another, and requires the dedicated efforts of the Member, Chief of Staff, and the Administrative Director/Office Manager. But like all plans, budgets are living documents. They can only support your efforts if they are subjected to an ongoing evaluation process. If prepared correctly, they will provide the necessary flexibility to respond to changes in priorities, workload, or political climate. To maximize this feature, a financial plan needs to be reviewed regularly, and may need to be adjusted to keep pace with the roller coaster nature of constituents' concerns. Periodic review will also ensure that you have stayed within your allowances and that resources are available to meet new challenges. We recommend that you conduct such a financial review monthly.

Earlier in this chapter we emphasized the importance of re-examining your goals and strategies as part of your annual budgeting process. Now we are further urging you to compare your goals and your spending activities regularly throughout the year. In this way, you will be able to determine whether your strategies and goals are being achieved. Regular financial review provides an opportunity to decide if the staff needs to devote more energy towards meeting that goal or whether another priority has superseded it.

Your financial team can determine when this review should be conducted. Requests for new expenditures or funding for projects to address new or existing goals can be discussed during these sessions. The Member should be advised of any major variances between the projected financial position and the actual position. Incorporate options for adjustments into your financial plans. Revise the plan and the budget as necessary over the year, keeping accurate records of the changes and the decisions underlying them. These records will prove valuable when producing next year's budget.

Tips for House and Senate Offices

Your staff can adopt cost-saving measures and prudent financial policies to maximize your limited resources, and allow your office greater flexibility in matching your resources to your goals. We compiled the following tips from congressional offices, but always make sure your actions fall within House or Senate regulations. The applicability of any given suggestion in this section will depend largely on the style, mission, goals, and systems of each office.

Equipment, Supplies, and Services
- Weigh the expense of leasing against the possible early obsolescence of purchased equipment.
- Select the technology and services that will best meet staff needs and skills. The most advanced tools are a waste of money if they are unused. If you lack staff expertise, invest in training or consider canceling the service.
- Design your work spaces to minimize duplicate equipment items (i.e., share printers), and design the work day to allow the maximum use of computers (i.e., have interns work different shifts and share workstations).
- Ask the House and Senate technical support offices to conduct a free technology consultation before purchasing a new computer system, or upgrading the equipment you have.
- House offices are not required to buy maintenance contracts for their computer system or other equipment, but they should weigh the cost savings of forgoing a contract against potentially large repair costs in the future.
- In the Senate, try to use the Senator's main account rather than the Economic Allocation Fund for computer equipment purchases in the first

few years of the term. Save these funds for later years when other office expenses put pressure on the main account.
- Regularly maintain your office's CMS/CSS database. You will save yourself a lot of time if it contains standardized addresses and no duplicate records.
- In the House, develop a good working relationship with CAO Office Services.
- Have staff keep a list of potential end-of-year purchases to review and evaluate against your goals for the next year.
- Set aside money for an end-of-year move in DC (after the election).
- In the House, buy stationery and internal office supplies in small quantities. There is little cost advantage to large orders. Office relocations and committee reassignments are common, so you may need to update letterhead accordingly. Regularly organize your supply closet and gather extra supplies from staff desks — you might be surprised at how much you have on hand.
- At the end of the year, consider "paying down" equipment payment plans or purchasing frequently used office supplies in bulk with unexpended office funds.

Communications
- Respond to incoming constituent e-mails with e-mail. Cost savings are increased if you reply via e-mail to any communications that come from someone whose e-mail address you have on record.
- Franking-approved e-mails are considerably less expensive than direct mail in the long run and have the potential to reach more constituents.
- Only respond to mail that originates in your district/state and refer non-constituent mail to the proper Member.
- Take every opportunity to gather constituent e-mail addresses. The more you communicate electronically, the more time you save.
- Desktop publishing has sufficient capabilities to produce a newsletter for most needs, provided one of your staffers knows how to use it.
- Always obtain several bids on print jobs.
- Postal patron mailings cost less per recipient than other types of outreach mailings and also avoid the cost of entering and maintaining extensive mailing lists, although they sacrifice personalization.
- Be persistent in obtaining accurate postal patron counts from the Postal Service, which could save thousands of dollars in unnecessary printing costs.
- Consider substitutes to mass mailings for outreach to your constituents. Inserts in your local Sunday newspaper, radio spots, e-mail, or posting information on your website can be cheaper than large mailings. However, often the content of these outreach methods, just as with mass mailings,

must follow franking regulations (see Chapter 14, "Managing Constituent Communications," for a discussion of the pros and cons of outreach communications).

Telecommunications
- Telephone bills are a month behind so be sure to set aside money for the last month of the year.
- Conference calling and videoconferencing may reduce the number of trips a Member must make to the district/state.
- Always check for special government rates when installing or purchasing new products or services.
- Check into alternative and cheaper calling plans for your office cell phones.
- Use the blast fax system to cut down on the need for modem lines or additional fax machines, not to mention paper and toner.

Travel
- Consider longer and less frequent Member trips to the district/state.
- Always check for government discount rates for air travel, car rental, and lodging; often the savings can be substantial. (In some cases, though, the excursion rate is even cheaper.)
- Use airline frequent flyer programs to accumulate credits toward future official travel.
- Having staff stay over a Saturday night almost always reduces airfare.
- Staff who volunteer to stay with family or friends in the district/state can save the office hotel room costs.
- For district/state travel, a single long-term car lease may be cheaper than repeatedly renting cars every time the Member or staff need to travel.
- In some cases, a daily car rental with unlimited miles may be less expensive than reimbursing staff for mileage in their own cars.
- Careful coordination of trips and errands will reduce the amount of mileage expense that must be reimbursed.
- Establish a maximum per diem meal allowance for staff on official travel.

Publications and Subscriptions
- Monitor subscriptions for duplication, value, and use. Consider online subscriptions.
- Compare the relative cost of receiving several publications with the cost of using a clipping service.
- Use the CRS reading room for periodicals.

Personnel
- Use part-time employees as appropriate.
- Hire fewer employees overall. This allows you to pay top-notch staff higher salaries and still reduce overall salary expenses.

- If you are fortunate to have access to leadership or committee funds, use those resources wisely to complement rather than duplicate the strengths and weaknesses of your personal office.
- Shared employees can provide more expertise and be more cost-effective than hiring a permanent staffer.

District Offices (for House Offices)
- Private space may be cheaper than federal space and can be more accessible on weekends.
- Moving a district office can cost a significant amount, so be sure to set aside enough money to cover all relocation costs.
- Sharing space with state and local officials can save rent and supply costs.

State Offices (for Senate Offices)
- If you want cable TV, the Senate Sergeant at Arms will pay for this service if written into your lease. However, if it is not part of the lease, your office will be responsible for payment out of your budget. Contact the Sergeant at Arms' State Office Liaison (202-224-5409) for more details.

Conclusion

Every Member of Congress can, and indeed will, spend official resources with or without a formal budget. Members will employ staff; run district/state offices; buy equipment, furniture and office supplies; visit their district/state and correspond with their constituents. But offices that budget wisely make spending choices that not only keep their offices functioning, but that also contribute to achieving their office goals.

These Members allocate their resources strategically, and track their outlays during the year to catch troubling spending patterns before they have a negative impact. When they prepare next year's budget, these Members do not simply update and tweak current spending, but they examine the underlying rationale for it, asking themselves whether circumstances or office priorities have changed, and whether spending priorities should change as well. These are the Members who substantially increase their chances of having successful congressional careers.

Chapter Summary
The DOs and DON'Ts of
Budgeting and Financial Management

Do...

- **use your strategic plan as a blueprint for making budget choices.** Make financial decisions and allocate resources with your strategic goals in mind.

- **follow the seven-step approach to updating your budget:**
  1. note any changes to your strategic plan.
  2. brainstorm to identify what resources it will take to accomplish priorities.
  3. analyze how you actually spent last year's budget.
  4. note any rule changes affecting the budget.
  5. identify expenses that are flexible or long-term commitments.
  6. review and justify major allocations in your current budget.
  7. create a new month-by-month budget.

Don't...

- **succumb to common budgeting pitfalls by:** spending on non-priorities; overspending; spending taxpayer's money in a way that invites media scrutiny.

- **overlook the importance of developing an accounting system** to track what you actually spend. The House Learning Center and Senate Office of Education and Training offer classes to help staff develop this system.

- **fail to write down established budget policies and procedures.** Your office policy manual should address spending authority, reimbursements, out-of-pocket expenditures and record keeping.

CHAPTER THIRTEEN

A Process for Managing Staff

This Chapter Includes...

- ☆ Why a performance management system makes sense for congressional offices
- ☆ Five steps towards an effective performance management system
- ☆ Handling staff with different needs
- ☆ Evaluating your system

Of all the skills required for running a congressional office, managing staff has proven to be the biggest challenge for most. When staff are not well managed, inefficient operations, missed opportunities, added stress and debilitating rates of employee turnover result. At its worst, poor staff management could lead to a lawsuit under the Congressional Accountability Act.

One Chief of Staff claims that he can spend five minutes in a congressional office and be able to determine how many terms the Member has served by the order within the office and the confidence with which the staff goes about their business. He listens for the sustained hum of a staff focused on action, in contrast to the intermittent sirens of a staff rushing to the latest emergency.

Naturally, it takes time for a freshman office to smooth out its operation, put policies in place, and let the staff grow their "sea legs." But some offices continue to operate like a freshman office year after year, taking a toll on both Member and staff. The reason frequently lies in a lack of a system or process for managing staff. Unfortunately, the blame often lies with the Member and/or Chief of Staff who confuses frenzied activity with accomplishment, and who views high turnover as an acceptable cost of doing business.

This chapter will lay out a coherent process for managing all the staff in your office. If you follow this process, you will find that, in short order, staff productivity and morale will improve, as will the overall effectiveness of your office.

Rationale for a Performance Management System

Have you ever seen someone doing something right, waited to mention it and then not done so? Have you ever seen a staffer doing something wrong, but not taken the time to give him guidance on how to correct it? And then, did you wait until the situation deteriorated so that when he did a small task wrong, you ambushed him with criticism?

This is the antithesis of performance management.

A performance management system is an annual, ongoing process for continually improving the performance of your staff. It is built on some very simple notions that rarely get practiced on the Hill. First, staff should understand precisely what is expected of them — clarity of purpose. Second, staff progress should be monitored throughout the year to help them meet office expectations. Where necessary, senior management should work collaboratively with staff to help them achieve their goals. Third, staff should be held accountable for achieving the goals established at the start of the year. Finally, staff who meet or exceed expectations should be recognized, and senior management should figure out how to best address the performance of staff who fall short of their goals.

In other words, performance management is based on the premise that by investing wholeheartedly in the development of staff, managers can create more productive, effective and loyal employees and build a better office. Yes, this approach requires discipline and takes time, but research suggests it also pays large dividends to organizations that employ it.

In contrast to this process, most Hill offices use a much more haphazard approach to managing staff. Managers tend to intervene only when performance problems arise. Little is done proactively to reduce staff performance problems, to help turn good staff into great staff, or to ensure that great staff don't become bored and look for new growth opportunities elsewhere.

Some offices employ elements of the performance management process, such as conducting staff performance evaluations or developing job descriptions, but lack a sustained commitment to "growing" better staff. Consequently, the results tend to be minimal. Employing all of the steps of a

Aspects of a Model Performance Management System

- Staff should understand what is expected of them.
- Staff progress should be monitored throughout the year.
- Staff should be accountable for achieving goals.
- Staff who meet or exceed expectations should be rewarded; senior management must address how to deal with staff who fall short of expectations. ■

performance management process may seem far too labor-intensive to most managers in Congress. However, this proactive process will take far less time than many offices spend on the range of personnel problems that routinely crop up throughout the year, such as dealing with under-performing or disenchanted staff, or with high turnover.

Implementing a Performance Management System

Figure 13-1 shows the five steps of a performance management system. It's a circular process and, for the best results, ideally should be conducted annually for each staffer. This section will explore each step in-depth.

Figure 13-1

Five Steps of Performance Management

STEP 1: ESTABLISH PERFORMANCE GOALS FOR EACH STAFFER

STEP 2: MONITOR PROGRESS AND PROVIDE FEEDBACK THROUGHOUT THE YEAR

STEP 3: CONDUCT FORMAL EVALUATIONS

STEP 4: FOLLOW UP TO PREPARE EACH STAFFER FOR UPCOMING YEAR

STEP 5: RECOGNIZE HIGH PERFORMING STAFF

Step 1: Establish performance goals for each staff person.

The first step in establishing a performance management system requires each manager to sit down with each staff person he or she supervises to set goals and expectations for the year. People perform best when they understand what is expected of them and how their performance will be evaluated. All too often, congressional offices are reluctant to take the time to clarify what is expected of staff individually.

Some Hill managers argue that setting goals is too confining and rigid for a fluid workplace; others contend that it is unnecessary because staff almost

> **Congressional Accountability Act**
>
> Though House and Senate staff are "at-will" employees, they are still guaranteed certain protections under the Congressional Accountability Act (CAA). Members of Congress and staff responsible for managing personnel should familiarize themselves with the 12 civil rights, labor, and workplace safety and health laws applicable to the Legislative Branch.
>
> The CAA also created the Office of Compliance (OOC), which educates congressional offices and employees about their rights and responsibilities and investigates alleged violations. More information on CAA and OOC is available at www.compliance.gov.
>
> The Office of House Employment Counsel (202-225-7075) and the Senate Chief Counsel for Employment (202-224-5424) provide legal guidance on personnel policies and practices and represent employers in litigation arising under CAA. ∎

always know what their priorities are, and where they should be focusing their energies. Both arguments are easily rebutted. First, individual staff goals, like overall office goals, can be modified during the year should office priorities, or the duties of the staff person, change. Second, CMF's experience in working with many House and Senate offices annually is that staffers often do not understand what their priorities should be. The result is a workforce that lacks direction, and workers who tend to work very hard but who do not improve their skills as quickly as they should.

Some staff, for example, may not recognize that their writing skills, which were well-suited for college, are not up to par for the demanding congressional environment. Some may ignore the hints and comments of their supervisors, or pass off heavy editing as the obsessive tendencies of the Member. Clarifying in a meeting that a Press Secretary's writing skills do not meet the requirements of the job, and that he or she must "learn to write more crisply, so press releases require less editing and op-eds get published more often," is more likely to yield improvements.

Similarly, you may have an industrious LA who devotes a lot of time to an issue, and makes passing legislation on that issue a top priority. Yet, the issue shows up nowhere in the office's strategic plan. A meeting with the LD that establishes, in writing, the goals for that LA will help him or her understand what exactly is expected and how performance will be evaluated.

An excellent starting place for this goal-setting process is developing job descriptions. Committing to paper both primary and secondary responsibilities will help the staff and their supervisors understand individual responsibilities and determine annual performance goals. In addition, it is very important that these individual goals reflect the overall strategic goals of the office. Consequently, a staffer and his or her supervisor should also review the office's strategic plan and determine which goals require that staffer's involvement, and what specifically he or she should be doing to accomplish these goals.

Staff performance goals can also address an individual's personal goals. For example, a State Director may choose to focus on becoming a better public speaker; a Legislative Assistant may want to learn negotiations skills; or a Scheduler may want to take a course on event planning. All performance goals should be viewed by staff as reasonable and attainable. The purpose of this exercise is neither to create undue staff anxiety, nor force staff to become overachieving workaholics.

Regardless of how these goals and expectations are established, they should be in writing so both staff and supervisors can refer to them throughout the year. The staff must understand that these goals will be the basis for how they are judged and recognized during and at the end of the year.

Step 2: Monitor progress and provide feedback on staff performance throughout the year.

After setting the goals and expectations for each staff person, it is important to determine how best to support that person in meeting his or her goals. At a minimum, managers should monitor staff progress periodically throughout the year. For staff who remain focused, this may simply mean asking how their work is going every once in a while or checking in with them over lunch. When staff have a tendency to lose sight of their goals, this may mean meeting monthly to review progress, or having those staff develop action plans outlining, step-by-step, how they intend to accomplish their goals. Even well-intentioned, highly motivated staff can lose sight of their goals, especially when they take on too much work.

Feedback is the act of evaluating performance with the intention of influencing an employee's behavior. Feedback can be positive or negative. Acknowledging good performance and letting staff know when they have met office expectations is as important as critiquing performance. The key to effective feedback is to provide it soon after an activity is completed, in an objective manner that clearly identifies the specific behavior you seek to reinforce or improve. The closer the feedback is given to when the activity or behavior occurred, the more likely the staffer will incorporate the feedback into their performance.

All too often managers assume that someone given clear critique of his or her performance will be able to improve it. In some cases, this assumption is not accurate, and staff need additional specific guidance in *how* to improve. The job of the manager is to then figure out why someone is failing to successfully incorporate feedback into his or her work, and to help that person do so.

When staff lack the skills or knowledge necessary to improve, sending them to training programs to improve their skills is an option. Other professional

MANAGEMENT FACT
The Office of the House Employment Counsel and the Senate Chief Counsel for Employment are available to assist with the performance management process, including developing job descriptions and evaluation forms.

development options include having them read relevant materials or reviewing memos or speeches that exhibit the kind of work product sought.

A more labor-intensive, but often more successful approach is to provide the staff person with one-on-one coaching. That is, someone works with the staff person on a regular basis to address a problem or support a skill enhancement effort. Coaching is appropriate when a manager decides that the staff person needs ongoing guidance to improve, or to improve more quickly, and feedback by itself will be insufficient. A coach may be the supervisor or someone designated by the supervisor.

Coaches therefore need to determine what is needed of them to help staff improve. Do they need to teach skills such as how to manage time better or communicate effectively with the Member? Do they need to address attitude problems? Once the rationale for coaching is clear, the coach works with the staff on an ongoing basis to bring about the desired change. Coaching may require a series of ad hoc meetings over several weeks or regularly scheduled meetings lasting for a year or more.

The first challenge managers face in providing useful feedback or coaching is to create a climate of trust between them and the staff they supervise. Staff must be confident that their supervisors are committed to helping them grow and flourish in their jobs. If they do not have this confidence — i.e., if they suspect that their supervisor doesn't really care about their growth, or is interested in taking credit for staff successes — they are unlikely to enter into a constructive coaching process. In a trusting relationship, staff will feel comfortable admitting that they need to improve a skill or change an attitude. They will be able to candidly discuss the anxieties they feel when asked to change their behavior. If this type of frank discussion cannot take place, neither feedback nor coaching is likely to succeed.

While this monitoring, feedback, training and coaching work can happen on an informal basis, managers should not forget to record these activities in a personnel file. It is only fair to make sure there is some record that reflects the staffer's overall performance over the course of the year. This data about how well a staff person did or did not do in pursuing performance goals, or responding to feedback and coaching, is critical in determining performance goals for next year and salary increases. Alternatively,

> **tip!**
>
> **Establishing a Trusting Relationship with Staff**
>
> - Be honest and sincere; don't seek to manipulate.
> - Be fair, evenhanded and consistent.
> - Do the things you say you will do.
> - Really listen to your staff.
> - Ask your staff for input; if you don't incorporate their suggestions, explain your reasoning.
> - When you disagree with staff, explain your reasoning. ■

documentation is vital should you need to take steps to improve performance or begin disciplinary action.

Step 3: Conduct formal staff evaluations.

Formal evaluations are the linchpin of the performance management system. They are the primary vehicles through which staff will be held accountable for their performance and should be conducted once or twice a year. Most congressional offices conduct staff reviews in December or January, when there is time to engage in thoughtful discussions, and when offices are focusing on goals for the new year.

Evaluations require preparation on the parts of both supervisors and the staff they oversee. These six steps should help managers prepare for staff reviews:

1. **Require staffers to review their own performance goals and fill out a job appraisal form, so they're prepared for the review.** Staff should be asked to submit written self-evaluations (see Figure 13-2) to their supervisors a few days before evaluation meetings are held. In these self-appraisals, staff should be expected to address specific questions regarding how well they've met their goals. These job appraisals can then form the basis for an open exchange between supervisor and staff during the evaluation sessions.
2. **Decide who is the best person(s) to deliver the evaluation.** Usually, the staffer's supervisor should handle the review process. But if senior managers (such as the Chief of Staff or District/State Director) have views to share, they should also be included. Alternatively, the supervisor can interview other managers about their views of the staffer's performance, and incorporate those views in the evaluation. The Member can make a brief appearance to reinforce the evaluation of outstanding staff, but he or she should not sit through the whole review, nor conduct it, unless the staffer is principally supervised by the Member (e.g., Chief of Staff, District/State Director).
3. **Review the written self-evaluations.** Carefully reviewing the self-evaluation will help managers determine where they agree and disagree with staff perceptions. They should write down reactions and questions to raise and discuss in the meeting.
4. **Review documentation in the staffer's personnel file.** As discussed in Step 2, supervisors should be keeping a record of the staff's performance throughout the year to ensure the performance review is not just a product of recent memory. Based on these notes, supervisors can then develop other questions or issues they wish to raise.
5. **Choose your core message.** What are the key points the staffer should take away from the meeting? The more messages included in

the session, the more difficult it is to ensure you are understood. A core message for a star performer could sound like this: "You have met or exceeded all of your goals and are doing a fabulous job. How can we make sure you are challenged and fulfilled in your job in the coming year?" Whereas, a core message for an underperforming Mail Manager might be: "You've shown growth in how you're handling our incoming mail volume this year. One area, however, where we should discuss improvement is being more proactive during recess periods, so we can take most advantage of responding to backlogs during that time. How can I help you tackle this problem more successfully this year?"

6. **Generate examples that support your core message.** Even the brightest staffer is not telepathic. Clear examples from the course of the year or the review period will provide a more precise understanding of achievements or shortcomings. If a Chief of Staff offers a vague comment such as, "You need to coordinate more with the district office," without spelling out exactly what that coordination entails, the staffer will be less likely to act on this recommendation. Additionally, such a vague comment is open to the staffer's interpretation of what "more co-

Figure 13-2

Sample Staff Self-Evaluation Form

1. What were your performance goals for the past year?
2. How successful were you in meeting each of these goals?
3. What obstacles or problems hindered your success in meeting these goals?
4. What could you have done better over the past year to meet or come closer to your performance goals?
5. What could the office have done better to support your efforts to meet these priorities?
6. Beyond these individual goal-related activities, what else did you do this year to help the office achieve its goals?
7. What actions did you take that go beyond the expectations of your job?
8. What ideas or projects did you propose and/or initiate over the past year?
9. What were your greatest disappointments or sources of dissatisfaction over the past year?
10. What are your weaknesses, or in what areas would you like to improve or develop over the coming year?
11. What support do you need from this office (the Member, Chief of Staff, other staff, or other resources) to assist you in improving your performance in these areas?
12. How can this office promote your overall professional development in the coming year?

ordination" means. Examples are the best tools managers have to help staff understand why change is necessary and in their interests.

The principal purpose of the evaluation session is to help staff improve performance in the future, not simply review the past. Everything, from the topics selected to the tone of the meeting, should support that forward-looking goal. If there is a climate of trust and regular staff feedback throughout the year, the review will be like a checkup and should take only 30-45 minutes. If there has been little or no feedback throughout the year, the performance evaluation will be more like a complete physical, taking a couple of hours. Since staff should have been receiving feedback all along, the review should not hold any surprises. An evaluation that surprises staff is an indication of a failure to provide adequate feedback and coaching throughout the year. It means that managers have deprived staff of valuable information that could have helped them perform better during the year.

> *"The principal purpose of the evaluation session is to help staff improve performance in the future, not simply review the past. Everything, from the topics selected to the tone of the meeting, should support that forward-looking goal."*

To begin, the manager should set a positive tone for a discussion and state the purpose and structure of the meeting. Ask the staffer where he or she wants to begin and let them do much of the work. This review should be an opportunity to nurture their growth and learning, not a chance for the manager to demand or dictate change. It should be a dialogue, not a top-down lecture. Let the staff person grapple with the hard questions, such as why he or she did not meet performance goals. The manager should facilitate useful discussion, clearly state the core message, and focus constructively on how to use this review to improve performance in the future. For underperforming staff, the manager might identify areas of weakness, explore factors that might be inhibiting the staffer's productivity, and discuss ways the staffer might improve in these areas. For the solid and star performers, the manager might identify their strengths, cite specific contributions they have made to the office, express appreciation for their efforts and encourage staff to continue to leverage their strengths for successful outcomes.

The session should end with the manager repeating his or her message and developing an understanding on the next steps for the coming months. For star performers who want to expand their skills and responsibilities, ideas on development opportunities and new duties should be discussed. If the employee is not meeting expectations, the manager needs to discuss why and how the employee should improve. The manager should draft a Performance Improvement Plan (PIP) that describes the specific steps the staffer will take

How to Run Successful Staff Performance Meetings

1 **Focus on performance, not personality.** Discuss what has or has not been accomplished, and use specific examples whenever possible to support your points.

2 **Listen carefully and patiently.** Staff may have data or perceptions that you did not consider, which could reshape your assessment of their performance.

3 **Strive for insight, not indictment.** Work to solve problems, rather than focusing on assigning blame.

4 **Strive for understanding, not agreement.** When there is disagreement, it is important to realize that one goal of these sessions is to reach understanding of each other's point of view. However, it is not necessary for staff to agree with the assessments of their supervisors in order to improve performance.

5 **Focus on staff development, not staff discipline.** The goal is to improve performance in the future, not to punish past transgressions.

6 **Start with low-risk items and build towards more difficult issues.** If you can get agreement on the smaller items first, it makes it easier to tackle the larger problems later.

7 **Clearly state your core message.** Make sure that employees walk out of the meetings with an unambiguous picture of how their work is seen and what they should work on in the future to improve their performance and contribution to the Member.

8 **Thank the staff for their time and candor.** These meetings can be difficult and a source of anxiety for staff. Make sure you thank staff for their efforts.

9 **Promptly write up a meeting summary for the file.** Record what was discussed and agreed to. These memos will form the basis of future performance goals and activities and serve as important legal documents in cases of termination.

10 **Evaluate the session and your performance.** Conducting these sessions requires skill and practice and the best way to improve them is to take a few minutes to evaluate, in writing, the meetings you lead: what went well; what did not; and what you would do differently. ∎

to remedy the problems identified, as well as the steps the office will take to assist the employee in his or her efforts. A PIP should include performance goals, how the supervisor will measure progress, and dates for formally assessing progress (i.e., weekly, monthly).

In cases where an employee's performance jeopardizes his or her employment, the employee must clearly be told what must be done to improve performance or face termination. He or she must also be told, however, that the supervisor and the office are committed to helping them improve, so dismissal can be avoided. Staff, especially underachieving staff, need to know the score and be given a fair chance to improve their work. By and large, firing an employee should be an office's last resort and an action taken only after other remedies have proven unsuccessful. This is both a good management practice and a prudent legal practice. Offices that fire staff without ample warning run a greater risk that charges will be filed against them for unfair treatment.

There is one forbidden subject during this discussion — money. Obviously, most offices link pay to office performance. However, if staff believe that an objective of the meeting is to determine how large a salary increase or what level of bonus pay they should receive, they will, understandably, be reluctant to reflect openly on how they can improve. Instead, they will probably focus on how they can make the best case for the most money. Consequently, offices must de-link these meetings from actual compensation decisions. Offices can do this by making it clear that salary and bonus decisions will be made weeks, if not months, after the session. They could even decide and announce compensation decisions before the staff evaluation meetings.

Step 4: Follow through on the evaluation and prepare for the upcoming year.

After the session, managers need to make sure that the process that has been initiated does not get placed on the backburner and forgotten. No task is more important to managers than devoting time to improving staff performance and enhancing their contribution to the office. Supervisors and staff should develop specific written products as a follow-up to the performance evaluation session within a few days to a few weeks after the meeting. If the follow-through steps are not in writing, they are far less likely to occur.

Staff who received good or great evaluations should be asked to draft a new set of performance goals for the coming year. Those who received poor evaluations should be given a Performance Improvement Plan (PIP) by their manager.

In both cases, managers should ensure that these documents are consistent with what was discussed at the evaluation meeting. In some cases, a short follow-up meeting may be necessary to clarify, or even renegotiate, goals, timelines, or the actions expected from staff or the office.

Step 5: Recognize high-performing staff.

Just as under-performing staff need to be made aware of how they are falling short, good and great staff who meet or exceed the office's expectations need to be made aware that the caliber of their work is recognized and appreciated. CMF recommends that offices reward staff who achieve their goals through a combination of monetary (i.e., salary increases and bonuses) and non-monetary means.

In an effective performance management system, pay is tied to performance. The staff who best achieve their established performance goals are most highly compensated. Ideally, offices should use a combination of both permanent salary increases and bonus pay (or temporary salary increases). Salary increases are generally more appreciated, but frequently offices make salary decisions at the end of the year. This means that it is often months before a staffer is rewarded monetarily for outstanding work. A one-time bonus, made soon after a project is completed, is a far more effective staff motivator and morale builder than a payment made later. In addition, bonus payments, given throughout the year or at the end of the year, afford managers greater budgetary flexibility. Salary increases are automatically built into the baseline budget in subsequent years, while bonuses will not impact the following years' budgets.

Non-monetary rewards for high-performing staff might include providing opportunities to work more closely with the Member; expanding their job responsibilities or providing more development opportunities; or providing time off or a more flexible work schedule. Congressional offices too often neglect these non-monetary rewards and the value staff place upon them. The non-monetary rewards can be discussed and selected in a job evaluation session because they are part of the "next steps." But, as we mentioned earlier, money should never be discussed during the performance review.

MANAGEMENT FACT
Average lump sum bonus in a House office in 2009:
$3,521

Average lump sum bonus in a Senate office in 2006:
$2,792

Handling Staff with Different Needs

All offices face very real constraints on the amount of time they can devote to managing and developing staff. The central question is, if an office invests in a comprehensive, year-round manner in staff development, will the benefits outweigh the costs? Will the dividend of better thinking, better writing, greater staff focus, increased productivity and improved office morale justify the time required of the managers and staff? CMF believes the return far exceeds the investment.

Nevertheless, managers need to recognize that the question of how much time they devote to this process and, specifically, how much time a manager decides to devote to each staffer he or she supervises is an important question to consider. Performance management ensures that all employees experience all five steps of the process, but some staff get more attention than others. Managers must decide where their limited time is most profitably spent, and which staff development strategies provide the greatest benefit to the Member and the office.

For example, in an office where media coverage is of paramount importance to the Member, devoting considerable time and resources to quickly turning an inexperienced, but promising, Press Secretary into an outstanding performer makes a great deal of sense. In contrast, devoting the same amount of attention in an office that does not see the media as critical to their success would be imprudent. Most managers make the mistake of devoting the most time to their weakest employees or the sub-par performers, and tend to ignore the solid and star performers. Avoid this mistake. Performance management is primarily a staff development, not a remedial, process.

What follows is a discussion of how managers can adapt the performance management tools outlined above to develop staffers at different levels.

Motivating Star Performers

Star performers are an office's best producers. They are usually integral to the office's success. So, for starters, tell these stars through formal and informal feedback how valuable they are, and how much they are appreciated. Your main challenge in working with your stars is to keep them motivated and committed to their jobs and the office. How will you do this? Work jointly with these staff to develop strategies for keeping them happy and enthusiastic about their work. Talented, hard-working, driven people tend to get bored easily. Some key questions to consider in developing a strategy include:

- What rewards do you believe will be most appreciated by the staffer? This question should be part of a discussion with the staff person. If the answer is more money, make sure she gets a significant raise and/or bonus, not just slightly more money than everyone else receives. If it is spending more time with the Member, make sure you schedule some lunches for her with the boss on slow days.
- What aspects of the job could a star employee improve upon, or how could she better capitalize on her strengths? Jointly devise a development plan that may include training, coaching, attending conferences, etc. that might promote further skill development.
- What does she like to do and do well? How can your office make greater use of these skills and abilities?

- Do you have a career path for your highest achievers? Future plans for these staffers could include added responsibilities, the development of new skills, or an understanding that the office will promote a star LA to LD when the LD leaves.

Working with Solid Performers

In some ways these people are the backbone of your staff. Typically they work hard, are good at what they do and enjoy what they are doing. Day in and day out they are reliable and turn out solid work. They do not require a great deal of attention, so what strategy makes sense with these staff? Generally, the best strategy is to help them improve incrementally. However, sometimes a manager may realize that an inexperienced, but talented, staff person is capable of elevating his game and becoming a star performer. These staff probably deserve some extra management attention to fully tap their capabilities. To improve the performance of your solid performers:

- Tell them how well they are doing. Give them plenty of positive feedback.
- Ask them to take on more work in the areas at which they excel.
- See if they are interested in growing and trying to develop new skills to enhance their work for the office.
- Help them become better learners, to grow faster in improving their present skills and knowledge, and acquiring new skills.

Addressing the Problems of Sub-Par Performers

Sub-par performers are those staff, usually a small minority in congressional offices, who are falling short of office expectations. These staff present very real problems to Member offices: inadequate work products; drain on managers responsible for managing and editing their work, and on other staff asked to pick up the slack; Member frustration; and declining staff morale if they perceive the problems of the sub-par staffers going unattended.

So what should good managers do to address these problems? When a supervisor notices performance issues with an employee, it is important to use a consistent and straightforward process that may include the following components.

Observation. Look for patterns or changes in the employee's productivity or behavior, such as attendance, performance, behavioral and physical changes. Questions you may want to answer include:

- Do they understand their goals and what is expected of them?
- Are they floundering due to a lack of coaching and guidance on how to achieve their goals?

- Do they lack skills which can be learned, or do they lack skills or abilities required for their jobs that cannot be easily taught?
- Is it an attitude problem or maturity issue?

Documentation. Maintain consistent documentation of the employee's performance, both positive and negative, to provide an objective view of his or her performance and evidence as to how it has declined. Document factually and define the specifics of the performance problem without judgment. Describe the problem, but do not evaluate it.

Consultation. If the supervisor suspects that the decline in performance is because of an outside personal issue, he or she may wish to contact their chamber's employee assistance service. These offices can help managers prepare for a performance intervention meeting with the employee, explain their resources available to employees and discuss how to make a performance-based referral to the employee assistance service. The House Office of Employee Assistance is available at 202-225-2400 and the Senate Employee Assistance Program is at 202-224-3902.

Performance intervention. The supervisor should approach the problem through the office's existing performance management procedures, including the formal staff evaluation and providing ongoing feedback to staff. In this discussion, the supervisor should clearly define the process for improvement, expectations for ongoing performance and a timeframe for improvement, as well as the consequences if the employee fails to improve. As discussed earlier, the manager should draft a Performance Improvement Plan (PIP) for the employee that includes this information and creates a vision for the staffer of what it would look like if they were to successfully perform their jobs. After the discussion, the supervisor must document details of any immediate or future actions, and monitor them to ensure the employee stays on track.

When the employee's performance is possibly impacted by an outside personal issue, the discussion must constructively confront the performance problem while providing an avenue for effectively intervening in the outside issue without actually discussing the specific personal problem. The goal is to provide a deliberate and proactive process that enables the supervisor to help an employee recognize and address poor job performance and to access the appropriate resources to assist in improvement.

For example, a supervisor might say, "I've noticed a distinct change in your performance over the past six weeks. Since you are a valuable part of our staff, I want to do everything I can to assist you in getting your performance back to the level that you've performed in the past. In addition to discussing a plan to help us both stay focused on correcting these performance issues, I want to also make sure that you are aware of the resources at your disposal, should there be anything of a personal nature contributing to these recent performance difficulties. The Senate Employee Assistance Program/House Office of Employee Assistance offer confidential services for staff. Here's the contact number for their office, should you want to discuss anything with them. If they can assist you with anything that will support you in getting your performance back on track, they are an appropriate resource to help. That way, you and I can keep our focus on your performance itself."

Referral. If the employee's performance does not improve after taking these corrective measures, a referral to the chamber's employee assistance service might be appropriate. This should be conveyed as an additional performance management tool to help the employee deal with a performance issue, not as a disciplinary action.

A referral to the employee assistance service can be formal or informal. An informal referral might be appropriate when an employee informs the supervisor of a personal problem, but there is no impact on the employee's job performance thus far. A formal referral is more appropriate when the employee's personal or behavioral problem, or mental health or addiction issue, directly surfaces on the job and a pattern of deteriorating performance is apparent, or when previous attempts by the supervisor to correct the employee's performance have had no corrective or lasting results. In either case, the supervisor should emphasize the confidential nature of the service and encourage the use of the service to help the employee address problems and improve performance.

Follow-up. Finally, the supervisor must ensure the corrective actions are being taken. With a formal referral to the employee assistance service, the supervisor should follow up with the employee and the service to assure that they are continuing to make use of the resources available to support their performance on-the-job.

Evaluating Your System

As the Chief of Staff or simply a manager in the office, you are responsible for making sure that this staff management process achieves the desired results. It will be difficult to launch a flawless system. Supervisors will need time to improve their coaching and feedback skills. The staff self-assessment form may need some refining. Staff may initially be resistant to developing annual performance goals. Therefore, it is necessary that offices periodically take the time to evaluate how well the system is working and what can be improved, and then to use this data to fine-tune their process.

There are a number of approaches offices can take to evaluate their systems. The views of the staff can be elicited on a private, one-on-one basis. Either the Chief of Staff or, alternatively, a trustworthy staff person (without the manager present) can lead a discussion about what the staff like and dislike about the process. Staff can also anonymously answer a short survey on how well the process has served the office. A less subjective approach would be to look at a number of office performance indicators. For example, what percent of the goals set by staff were actually attained this year and how did it compare to last year's percentage? Has the office become more successful in achieving its strategic goals? Is staff turnover declining? Is the office retaining its "best and brightest" staff? Is management addressing a declining number of personnel problems or firings?

When properly used, a performance management system is a very powerful tool for improving organizational effectiveness. You need to make sure you adapt this process intelligently to your office culture and then get the kinks out of the system. Initially, offices should devote time to evaluating the first round of job evaluations, or drafting development plans at the end of the year. Thereafter, offices can simply issue a survey once a year, or ask a group of staff to assess the system and recommend modifications every couple of years.

Conclusion

Virtually all Members of Congress want staff who are focused on what is important, highly motivated, and loyal, and who stay with the office for a long time. They want managers who will take the time to turn inexperienced but promising staff into valued assets. And they want clear lines of accountability they can trust. This chapter provides offices a process for managing staff that will create this type of staff and office. The five-step performance management process we discussed will allow offices to grow talent rather than leaving that to chance. Any of these steps taken individually should improve staff and office performance to some degree. But, incorporating all five of these steps into an annual process should provide a huge payoff to those offices willing to do so.

Chapter Summary
The DOs and DON'Ts of
A Process for Managing Staff

Do...

- **reap the benefits of improved staff performance and work product by following the five-step performance management system:**
    1. establish performance goals for each staff person.
    2. monitor progress and provide feedback on staff performance throughout the year.
    3. conduct formal staff evaluations.
    4. follow through on the evaluations and prepare for the upcoming year.
    5. recognize high-performing staff.
- **develop a core message for each employee.** Addressing too many issues in the performance review will dilute your key points and reduce understanding of the most important goals.
- **adapt the performance management tools to develop staff at different levels.** Such a strategy keeps star performers motivated, helps solid performers improve, and addresses the problems of sub-par performers.
- **use a consistent and straightforward process to manage an employee's performance problem.** Focus on ways to objectively identify issues and help the employee improve.

Don't...

- **wait until an employee's performance deteriorates** to address the problem. Set expectations early in his or her tenure.
- **assess the employee's performance without first gaining his or her input.** Use job appraisal or performance review forms to allow the employee to create an initial self-evaluation.
- **use the formal performance evaluation as opportunity to indict staff.** Strive for understanding instead.
- **discuss money in performance reviews.** The purpose is to reflect on past performance and identify areas for future improvement, not make the case for a bonus or salary increase.
- **overlook the value of non-monetary rewards for high-performing staff,** which also serve as a motivator and morale booster.
- **devote the most management time to the weakest employee** while ignoring the solid and star performers.

CHAPTER FOURTEEN

Managing Constituent Communications

> *This Chapter Includes...*
>
> ☆ The growth of constituent communications, particularly e-mail
> ☆ Determining the priority of constituent mail and outreach mail
> ☆ How to establish constituent mail policies
> ☆ CMF Mail System, which incorporates the best practices of other Hill offices
> ☆ How to improve the processing of e-mail

One of the omnipresent facts of congressional life is hearing from constituents by letter, e-mail, or increasingly through social media tools like Facebook, Twitter, and YouTube. For many Americans, writing to Congress is as essential to democracy as voting. It is a way of expressing their ideas of what their government should be doing — and a Member of Congress would do well to pay attention, no matter what other demands are placed on your time.

For nearly a decade, CMF has been working to improve communications between citizens and Members of Congress. While the Internet has made it easier to contact Congress, technological developments have been so rapid that neither the senders nor the receivers have learned to use these tools in ways that facilitate truly effective communications. Through our *Communicating with Congress* Project, and CMF's management engagements with individual House and Senate offices, we have identified best practices to manage constituent communications. This chapter is structured to help you handle the mail responsibly and efficiently using these best practices so you can then turn your focus to the many other duties of a congressional office.

Note: This chapter uses the terms "e-mail" and "postal mail" to distinguish between electronic and paper communications. It uses the terms "mail," "correspondence," or "communications" to refer to both types.

The Growth of Constituent Communications

The increase in the number of contacts a Member of Congress receives from constituents is due first and foremost to the growth of e-mail. Since the introduction of e-mail to Capitol Hill in 1994, the volume of incoming postal mail has been greatly surpassed by the volume of e-mail, with congressional offices now reporting that up to 85 percent of their constituent correspondence is e-mail. Keep in mind that staffing levels have remained virtually unchanged during this same timeframe. E-mail's dominance has tilted the playing field, and congressional offices are currently struggling to find ways to keep up.

The growth of communications to Capitol Hill has a number of causes. The obvious ease with which constituents can e-mail encouraged its rapid growth. Environmental factors spurring volume include interest groups both in Washington and at home growing increasingly sophisticated in motivating constituents to write. In addition, when a new administration comes to town or there's a new majority in Congress, a whole new set of initiatives receives attention, thereby generating more mail. "Hot button" issues can also move constituents who haven't written in years — if ever — to hit the send button or affix a stamp.

In 1911 — the year the number of representatives in the House was set at 435 — districts averaged around 75,000 people. Today the average congressional district has grown to 650,000. CMF's recent survey of citizens regarding their perceptions of their interactions with Members of Congress revealed that 44 percent of Americans surveyed had contacted their U.S. Senator or Representative in the last five years.

Additional Information

For more information about the *Communicating with Congress* Project, including research on the views of citizens and congressional staff, review the CMF resources outlined in Chapter 6 or visit CMF's *Partnership For A More Perfect Union* website at www.pmpu.org. ∎

All of this leaves a House or Senate office at a crossroads. Answering postal mail had many offices stretched thin before e-mail burst upon the scene. Some House offices were devoting between 30-70 percent of their aggregate Washington staff time responding to postal letters and phone calls prior to the emergence of e-mail. Now they have to find a way to eke out additional resources to respond to this ever-growing volume. Being unable to manage communication flows may mean that the Member misses an opportunity to communicate effectively with constituents, especially e-mailers.

The Difference Between E-Mailers and Postal Mailers

To respond effectively, offices must understand how e-mailers are unique. Congressional offices have traditionally prided themselves on their capability to provide a well-researched reply with the Member's inked signature responding to a constituent's thoughtful letter. This modus operandi has served Members well for most of the past century. But e-mailers have changed the nature of constituent communications to such an extent that offices need to rethink how to be responsive.

E-mailers are writing more on impulse than postal mailers because the medium of the Internet enables them to. However, most of them are just as committed to their issues and fully expect that their e-mail will be considered as seriously as offices regard postal mail. E-mailers expect a prompt reply and in a culture that wants its responses fast and short, not long and loquacious, offices should seek to meet this constituent expectation.

Some offices still send several pages of what they think the constituent should hear, and they send it in the form that makes offices comfortable: postal mail. This ignores the constituents' needs and expectations. It also adds time and cost to the communication. Congressional offices have the technological tools to process and respond to constituent e-mail in a relatively efficient manner, but sometimes lack the management authority or training to make it happen, resulting in lost opportunities to connect with constituents online. We will discuss the importance of fully utilizing e-mail to respond to constituent communications later in this chapter.

Importance of Being Proactive

Managing constituent communications means more than just answering the mail. In fact, sending a mail reply should be the last option in keeping your constituents informed on the issues that matter to them. Instead, you should use a proactive strategy that reduces the volume of incoming mail, offers superior customer service and frees up staff for other duties. Such a communications plan should include:

- A comprehensive and user-friendly website that provides answers on the hot topics most important to your constituents and allows them to self-serve their information needs. To learn more about website strategies, how to build an effective congressional site, and the best websites on Capitol Hill, visit CMF's *Gold Mouse Project* at pmpu.org.
- A regular (weekly, biweekly or monthly) e-newsletter that keeps constituents informed of timely issues and your legislative work, not just press releases. Many offices also engage constituents through topic-specific newsletters, such as a quarterly update on environmental issues, and through social media, like Facebook and Twitter.

- An ability to satisfy many constituent inquiries at the point of contact when they call in. This tactic includes ensuring that those who answer the telephone have access to the Member's library of form letters, are provided with scripted talking points on "hot" or high-volume issues (especially when the callers agree with your position), and are familiar with the information on your website so they can answer a constituent's question while on the phone.

If you only view mail as something to react to, you will become a content provider instead of legislating, doing constituent outreach, nurturing district/ state projects to completion and generally meeting the larger needs of your constituents.

Assessing the Priority of Mail in Your Office

As we emphasize throughout *Setting Course*, operating effectively in Congress is a balancing act that requires trade-offs. There is no Member who is great at everything — every issue, every press opportunity, every legislative effort, every speech, every piece of mail that must be answered. As with budgeting and personnel issues, your decisions about mail should be guided by your strategic plan.

It is counterproductive to assign mail a high priority and then fail to provide the equipment and staff resources to run a top-quality mail operation. And a good mail program will take resources: Member's time, staff's time, a computer system with the latest mail management software. Ask yourself: What won't you be able to do or buy because you've made mail a priority? Are the resources better spent another way? Maybe the mail is exactly where you should invest your time, energy, and money, but only if you've made this decision strategically and with your goals in mind.

In assessing the priority of mail, you should think not only about *incoming* constituent mail, but also *outreach* mail (addressed in the last section of this chapter). Most Members consider three broad criteria in determining their approach to mail:

View of representative government. Some Members feel it is important to establish and carry on an effective dialogue with their constituents. Under this perspective, the people who sent you to Washington should be an integral part of your work. You should respond to their questions, provide information they may not have requested, and actively seek their advice. Other Members believe they have been sent to represent the district/state as they see best. They will

CHAPTER FOURTEEN   Managing Constituent Communications

listen to their constituents' views and explain their positions, but feel that an active outreach mail program would tap resources that could be put to better use for the district/state.

Definition of your job. Some Members view their job as one that requires them to be an ombudsman for constituents, cutting through red tape, providing casework services, and facilitating the acquisition of federal grants. Others view their job as legislating. All Members do both, but the emphasis can vary dramatically, affecting the amount of resources devoted to mail.

Electoral situation. Some Members are from politically marginal districts/states. They may be to the left or the right of their constituents' leanings. These Members often find that they need to be highly responsive to communications from their constituents, who may not be certain that their interests are being represented. Other Members' future electoral prospects are more evident. They may be ideologically close to their constituents or a known entity that the district/state has come to trust. They may choose to be highly responsive to constituent communications but find that it is not critical to their continued careers in Congress.

Whatever priority you give the mail, it needs to be reflected in the way you manage your office. Otherwise, the conflicting signals sent to your staff and your constituents may hinder your efforts on mail and other priorities and, ultimately, reduce your effectiveness as a Member. Frequently, Members say one thing about mail and mean another. Your actions and attitudes may contradict your stated policies — when, for example, you tell staff that you want all mail responded to within two weeks despite the fact that mail regularly sits in your own inbox waiting for your approval well beyond that target turnaround time. Staffers are good at sensing what you mean and following your lead.

Members also tend to talk about mail as a higher priority than they are actually willing to commit resources to. You will frequently hear Members say to LAs or Press Secretaries: "Great job on corralling those votes for that amendment," or "Terrific headlines in the weeklies back home." However, it is rare for a Member who ostensibly regards mail as a top priority to say, "Great, you answered 300 letters this week!" Be honest with yourself and your staff about the mail. Having too many top priorities means it is unlikely you will achieve any of them because your resources will be spread too thin.

Once you are clear where mail fits within your list of priorities, communicate this perspective clearly and directly to staffers. Like most things, it is easier to establish priorities, standards, and accountability from the beginning than it is to regain control when the backlog of letters has reached 60 days, 90 days, or even 120 days (and, unfortunately, such backups frequently occur on the Hill).

Establishing Mail Policies

Using proactive strategies effectively should help reduce the volume of incoming mail, but you cannot stop its flow. You can, however, control how you will respond. When establishing your office's mail policies, consider the following:

Desired turnaround. Will you attempt to respond within two weeks of receiving each letter or e-mail? Perhaps four weeks will satisfy you? In CMF's experience, many Members promote a particular turnaround goal and are shocked to find many letters (and e-mail) go unanswered for three months, six months, or even longer. For most offices, acceptable and achievable average turnaround goals are less than one week for constituent mail answered with pre-approved form letters and two to four weeks for mail requiring that new text be drafted and approved.

Quality of replies. Can you respond substantively in one page? Can you feel responsive enough with a short "thank you for your views"? How do your quality requirements affect your turnaround times? In our "on demand" society, most constituents would rather receive a one-page letter promptly than wait six to eight weeks for a long, detailed letter.

Which mail you will answer. You can reduce the mail load by deciding to answer only certain letters. Most Members answer only those from their districts or states. Perhaps you'll also respond to out-of-district/state letters that address topics within your committee jurisdiction. What about postcards and petitions? How about a batch of letters from school children? Will they get the same attention as other letters, or perhaps more? Which categories of mail should be answered in the DC office and which in the district/state office? How will phone calls be handled?

Degree of Member involvement. Your involvement may have a positive effect on quality, but it may dramatically reduce turnaround times. In addition, extensive involvement in the mail may distract you from the functions only a Member can perform. In CMF's experience, many freshmen feel a moral obligation to personally see and answer every letter and review each for legislative accuracy, tone, and grammar. This sentiment is easy to understand, but is simply not pragmatic. A major staff complaint is that a Member's desk can eventually become a "black hole" for letters awaiting approval as that Member becomes busier with other congressional duties. It is a better use of your time to get involved only at critical times, such as determining the response for a particularly sensitive issue or high priority topic, and leave the proofreading to others.

Correspondence format standards. You should establish a sensible letter length: one page is usually sufficient and if responding via e-mail, even shorter is preferred. Use a consistent, standard salutation and closing. Create a standard layout (indentation, spacing, margins, etc.) and adhere to it. In addition, the speed of your replies can be increased if you develop a clear and replicable formula for crafting responses to various types of constituent letters. Responses discussing specific legislation might include a brief status update on the legislation and whether the Member is a cosponsor while responses on general issues might include one or two examples of legislative action the Member has taken in those areas. The goal is to develop reusable templates to the greatest extent possible.

How letters are signed. In the House and Senate, most offices use signature fonts, which allow a digital representation of the Member's signature to be printed along with the letter. Other ways of getting the job done include having the Member (though we strongly discourage this practice) or the staff do the honors; and a few offices still use auto-pens.

CMF Model Mail System

Developing a systematic approach to congressional mail is essential. If your office has only one function governed by strict standard operating procedures, it should be the mail. The diverse nature of Congress assures that every office's mail system will be slightly different, but there are some basic concepts that can serve as a model:

1. **Timeliness is of the utmost importance to constituents.** It has been our experience that a quick response matters most to your constituents in this e-commerce age; far more complaints are lodged regarding the length of time it took to receive a reply than the actual content of the response. Seriously consider eliminating any steps in your system that do not directly contribute to responsiveness or accuracy.

2. **Establish a goal of answering 85 percent of the mail with form responses.** Some new Members feel as though they are somehow cheating constituents if they send them computer-generated form letters. Consider, however, that if your response is sufficient for one person, then it is good enough for others. With the average House Member representing 650,000 people and state populations varying widely, it would not be possible to answer every letter with an original response.

   The other 15 percent represents mail on new issues. Write the responses more general in nature so they can be used again, without alteration, the next time a message is received on that subject. In other words, every response is a potential form response. This practice saves enormous amounts of time for both those writing text and those approving the text. Thereafter, all responses on that subject can be answered by the Mail Manager without needing further attention from a legislative staffer, *until new developments occur on that issue.*

3. **The system should be as simple as possible.** It should minimize detours and duplications, with mail passing through as few hands as possible. This principle must be strenuously applied at three key points:

- Never write a new response when an existing one will do. It makes no sense to write two — or 10 or 20 — unique responses to constituents who ask nearly identical questions.

- Always route any constituent message for which a pre-approved response exists directly to a single staffer who can produce responses without further review by additional staff. These replies can often be sent within a day or two of receipt of the constituent contact.

- Limit the number of people involved in approving new text to one or two. Quality control is important, but so is timeliness. The more people involved, the longer the process. Therefore, it is important to clarify why each reviewer in the system is reading the mail; is he or she editing for political sensitivity, content, grammar, or VIP personalization? Don't waste staff resources by asking multiple staffers to all be looking for the same things. Obviously, the most efficient system would have only one person reviewing the mail who is well-versed in all of the above.

4. **Paper filing should be dramatically minimized.** Do not keep or file paper copies of outgoing letters that are generated through your CMS/CSS. You can reproduce one at will from your system. Nor should you save the original constituent letters indefinitely. If you feel the need to do so, only stockpile them in your office for three months. Staff members rarely return to these files and the time, energy, and physical space that it takes to archive them is prohibitive. Occasionally an angry constituent will call or write, saying you did not respond to their letter or your response did not address their concerns. Few successful politicians see merit in spending countless hours going to the files to pull out the original constituent letter, staple it to the response, and triumphantly proclaim, "I did respond, and my answer's right on target." Instead, apologize and ask the constituent to repeat their request. They will like the extra attention, you will look good, and no one will have to retrieve the original constituent letter. And, hours of unnecessary filing will be avoided. Please note that there are important exceptions to this

CHAPTER FOURTEEN   Managing Constituent Communications

filing rule, including mail that has historical value, such as letters from VIPs, government entities, state and local officials, and representatives of local interest groups.

5. **Correspondence backlogs are an office problem, not an individual staffer's problem.** Establish turnaround goals for each point of the process. For example, LAs may be allowed five days to research and draft responses for mail that cannot be answered with existing form letters. However, if an LA who usually answers mail in a timely fashion is too swamped with work because he or she has to move a hot piece of legislation through committee, the rest of the office should help answer that mail. Why? Because it is the Member's reputation at stake, not the LA's. Most House and Senate offices have LCs whose primary job is to handle the mail. These offices do not have as many problems with other priorities taking over and delaying the mail because they have a dedicated resource to manage the mail. It is important to note here, however, that gone are the days when one staffer — heroic as they may be — is able to manage the entire mail process alone. At the very minimum, there will need to be reviewers that approve outgoing responses, but offices that want a functioning mail process will need to bring in other resources to help various aspects of the mail. Finally, every office must develop contingency plans for how they will deal with surges in volume.

> *"Correspondence backlogs are an office problem, not an individual staffer's problem."*

How the Model Mail System Works

The CMF Mail System is a two-track affair that permits the mature office to answer 85 percent of its mail with pre-approved form letters in less than one week. The remaining 15 percent is assigned to an LC or LA and usually can be answered in one to two weeks, depending upon the priority the office assigns to mail, the amount of research required, and whether unusual events are generating higher than average mail volume.

The Mail Manager is the hub of this system. The person performing this duty is essentially the traffic cop who keeps the system functioning. The individual serving as Mail Manager may serve dual roles, particularly in House offices. He or she could be a Legislative Correspondent, the Systems Administrator or perhaps the Staff Assistant. Senate offices may have an exclusive Mail Manager or Correspondence Director. The Member and the Chief of Staff must ensure that this staffer has the ability and the authority to make the system work.

Mail Managers — ideally a combination of Systems Administrator expertise and LA/LC experience — are given the clout to monitor and enforce the mailflow process. They are asked to think, analyze, and make decisions. They are, in short, in a position of both responsibility and authority. A good Mail Manager takes a tremendous load off the Member and the rest of the staff.

The mail management function can also be performed by a group with a team leader (either the Mail Manager, a Legislative Director, or a Systems Administrator). In this scenario, there is a higher degree of teamwork and strict group accountability for the turnaround times and mail quality. This collaborative model is recommended for the Senate, where more coordination between the technical and administrative staff and the LCs is needed to get the mail out the door.

LAs and LCs love the CMF system. Why? Because all the mail that already has a form response (85 percent in a mature office) bypasses them. It goes to the Mail Manager, and then out the door. LAs and LCs need only keep their response texts current and accurate. They act on only 15 percent of the total mail volume, enabling them to focus on drafting better and more timely responses, rather than on managing the mail.

The CMF system also works for e-mail. We recommend that you automate e-mail processing as much as possible to effectively meet your constituents' expectations and to minimize staff time spent on data entry. CMS/CSS software is designed to reduce labor for congressional staff and to maximize staff productivity, and it is imperative that your office learn and take advantage of its full functionality. Mail filter functions and rules can automatically sort e-mail before a staffer opens a message, and e-mails can be routed much easier than opening and putting a postal letter in a mail bin or staff inbox. Finally, if responding via e-mail, the "printing, folding, and mailing" process is omitted, saving the office time and both human and financial resources. More details on handling e-mail, including why you should respond via e-mail, follows the next section.

CMF Mail System Flow Chart

Step 1: Open, Sort, and Date Stamp (Postal mail only). A Staff Assistant (in the House), mailroom staff (in the Senate), and possibly interns open and sort the postal mail. This is a sorting action, not a reading action. It is the process of scanning the incoming messages to identify constituent communications from all of the other communications an office receives daily. Sort mail into the following categories:

- **Material that is for informational purposes only and requires no response.** This mail is distributed to the staff member who can best use it. It might include whip notices, magazine subscriptions,

trade and research publications, and other such items.
- **Material that is of no use to anyone in the office under any circumstances.** Contained in this category are commercial junk mail or any mail that does not pertain to the work of the office. E-mail that is not from your district/state and spam would also fall into this category.
- **Material that requires a response.** Mail that requires a response must be scanned by someone generally familiar with the issues involved and with the pre-approved responses that exist for letters and e-mails on these issues and sorted accordingly.

Once the mail that needs a response is identified, it should receive a date stamp to track its incoming date, unless the office is able to consistently log in each day's mail on the day it arrives.

Step 2: Log into CMS/CSS. To give offices an accurate accounting of their mail program, all communications — both hardcopy and electronic — should be put into the office's CMS/CSS system within 24 to 48 hours of receipt. You will find that a large volume of mail comes in so rapidly that neglecting to stay on top of this input can cause mail to pile up quickly. Great care should be taken by the data entry staff inputting postal mail and phone calls to ensure that names, addresses, and constituent views are put into the system carefully and consistently. An incorrect prefix or marking someone as being in support of a bill rather than in opposition can prove to be very embarrassing when that constituent receives a response. This is less of a problem for e-mail, because in most cases the original text can be easily accessed.

At this point the office should ensure that each communication entered into the database receives the appropriate issue/topic and affiliation/personal codes, both of which help to ensure that messages and constituents are tracked in your database effectively. Each code is described below:

- **Issue/Topic Codes.** Correctly assigning the issue/topic codes allows very specific issues to be grouped together under broad topics, such as grouping letters about air quality standards and recycling under the larger topic of "environment." This coding ensures the proper routing to the appropriate staffer in the office, and allows the office to report on the broad issue areas that interest your constituents the most.
- **Affiliation/Personal Codes.** Offices often track the interests of certain subsets of their constituencies through the strategic use of affiliation/personal codes. For instance, if you would like to hold a town hall meeting in your district/state on education reform next

year, you can tag the records of constituents that identify themselves as teachers. Then, when it comes time to send invitations to the town hall, you have a ready-made invite list.

Step 3: Determine Track. Mail that requires a response should be given to the Mail Manager or appropriate mailroom staff, who reads and divides the mail into two tracks: pre-approved form track, or "fast track", and the "original draft track." Fast track mail is the incoming mail that the office already has a prepared and approved response available in the letter library. Original draft track mail is the mail that does not have an approved response and requires new text to be written. At this point the office should also identify and handle separately any messages from district/state VIPs or those that are personal enough in nature that the sender should not receive a prepared form letter response.

Step 4a: Fast Track – Assign Response. Fast track mail is assigned the appropriate pre-approved response letter and properly batched for printing or e-mailing. As you can see, it is called the fast track for a reason. With diligence, an established office with an up-to-date letter library can — and should — respond to approximately 85 percent of their mail within just a few days of receiving the incoming message. *(Fast Track Mail bypasses Steps 5 – 7)*

Step 4b: Original Draft Track – Assign Staff. Constituent mail destined for the original draft track is batched with similar responses and assigned to the Legislative Correspondent (LC) or Legislative Assistant (LA) who will write the first draft response.

Step 5: Draft Response. First draft responses are written, with research conducted by staff, or gathered from organizations or sources such as the Congressional Research Service (CRS) and the Legislative Information System (LIS). Obviously, great care should be taken to ensure that all responses are consistent with your legislative record and conform to the standards set by the office.

Step 6: Edit & Review. Completed drafts are submitted for proofing, alterations, and editing. The proofing team often consists of various combinations of the LA, the LD, the Chief of Staff, and/or the Member. It is easier and more efficient if proofing is done online, rather than on paper. Proofreaders can write questions or make wholesale changes to the draft using the "Track Changes" function in Microsoft Word or through the editing and workflow features of your CMS/CSS product. Then, staff can easily make the changes without having to retype them and they receive the benefit of learning from the changes so they can avoid them next time. Just be certain that sufficient safeguards are in place to prevent the marked up draft from being sent to constituents by mistake.

MANAGEMENT FACT
Model offices answer 85% of constituent communications with form responses.

CHAPTER FOURTEEN   Managing Constituent Communications

Figure 14-1

CMF Mail System Flow Chart

- E-mail In
- Postal Mail In
- 1. Open, Sort, and Date Stamp
- 2. Log Into CMS/CSS
- 3. Determine Track

FAST TRACK
- 4a. Assign Response
- 8a. Send E-mail
- 8b. Print Postal Mail
- 9. Fold, Stuff, and Send Postal Mail

ORIGINAL DRAFT TRACK
- 4b. Assign Staff
- 5. Draft Response
- 6. Edit and Review
- 7. Approval
- 8a. Send E-mail

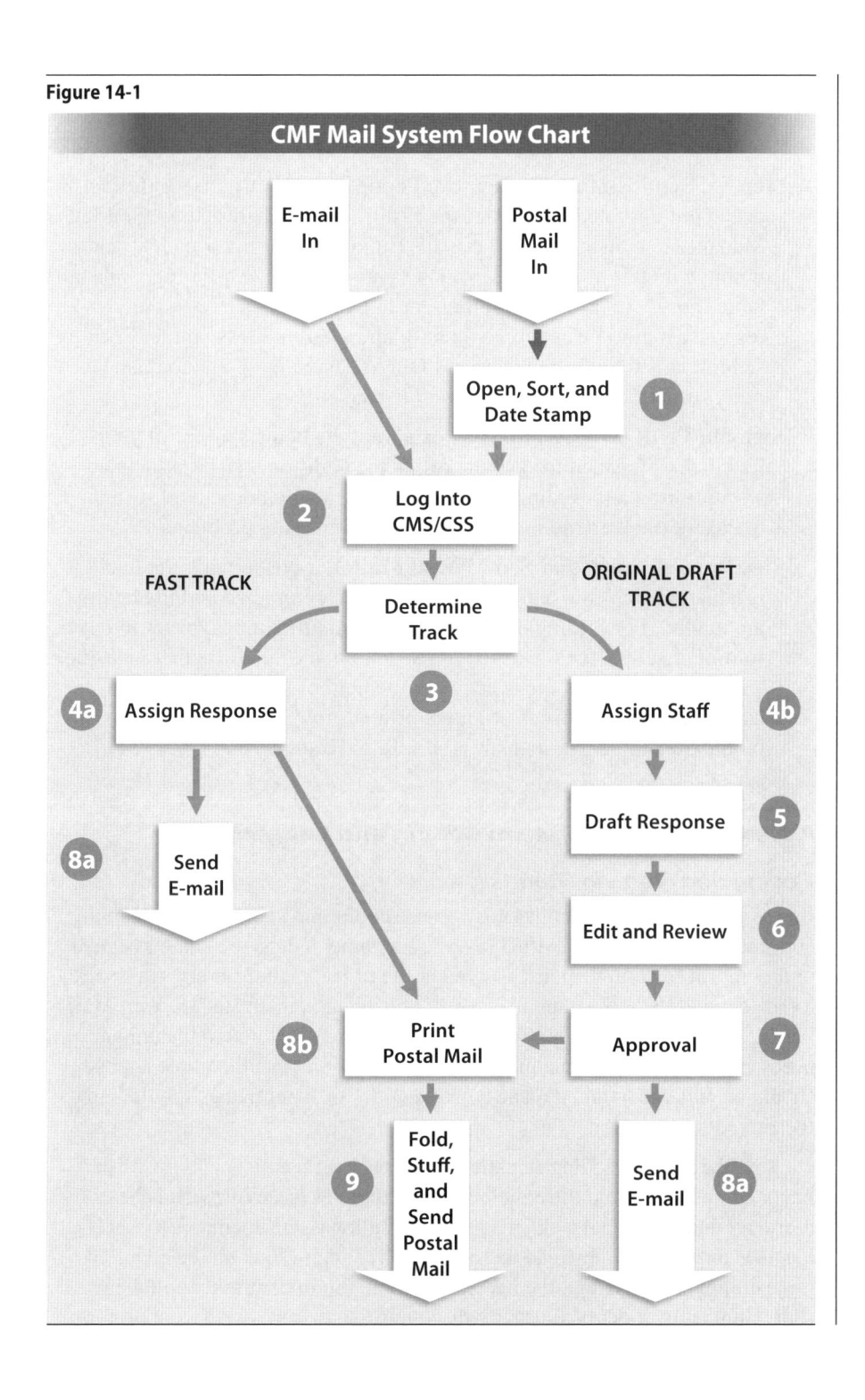

Step 7: Approval. Once the letter is approved for sending, it should be activated in the letter library and regularly reviewed to ensure that it remains accurate and up-to-date.

Step 8a: Send E-mail. The approved drafts (for the original draft track) or the pre-assigned letters (for the fast track) are then sent by the Mail Manager to constituents via e-mail. Hundreds of e-mails can be sent within a matter of moments, which saves on postage, printing, and staff labor. For this reason, it is important to embrace e-mail as a preferred response method whenever you have an e-mail address on file. Prior to sending a batch of e-mails, scan them to ensure there are no mistakes or other formatting problems. *(E-mail bypasses Step 9)*

Step 8b: Print Postal Mail. If a postal reply is being sent, print your letters double-sided to save the office the additional costs associated with printing and folding. Prior to printing a batch of letters, scan them to ensure there are no mistakes or other formatting problems.

Step 9: Fold, Stuff, and Send Postal Mail. For postal mail, the final production steps of folding and stuffing are completed and the letters are mailed. For folding large quantities of mail, you may want to buy a folding machine for the office or use an outside vendor; otherwise, the work can be done in the office with the help of interns. Senate offices can have large quantities of letters printed, folded and mailed off-site by the Senate Sergeant at Arms' Printing, Graphics and Direct Mail service.

Keys to CMF Mail System: Coding and Logging

Coding and Naming Standards

It is essential that you establish easy-to-use codes and standard letter naming conventions within your CMS/CSS. A letter name/code is the name assigned to pre-approved form responses stored in the office's letter library. An issue/topic code indicates the general issue a constituent is interested in. Your Mail Manager or letter-writing staff can develop a system tailored to the unique needs of your office. The naming/coding conventions that the office adopts should be adhered to and anyone creating codes or letter names should know the agreed-upon format.

Any hierarchical coding scheme will do, as long as it lets you establish major subject areas and differentiate within them as issues arise. It is best to use an intuitive, plain English system that allows staff members to easily identify codes when they read them without having to look up the code. The more complex the system, the harder it is to maintain continuity with new staff. Confusing codes also usually discourage staff from using existing form letters. Staff who cannot identify an existing letter from its text code will draft a new letter — and assign it a new code! Now you have two letters on the same subject with different text codes. Even worse, the second letter will have to be approved, wasting valuable time. Eventually, your computer will be clogged with letters no one can identify or use.

One of the worst uses of staff time is to spend an inordinate amount of time looking for pre-approved text in the letter library, or worse still, recreating the wheel by writing text that already exists in another letter but cannot be found. Here are a couple suggested letter naming formats that work for many offices, given that each letter in the library should already be tagged with the broader issue code (e.g., "Science and Technology"):

Net Neutrality – Oppose HR 196 – Keep the Internet Equitable Act – Oct 2011
Net Neutrality – S 196 – Keep the Internet Equitable Act – Con – 112th

If all letters utilized such a format, you would be able to search by the keyword(s) at the beginning, the bill number, or keywords from the short title. The date reference helps ensure that staff don't send out old letters. Non-bill-specific letters would have a similar format, keeping the beginning keyword(s) and the "date stamp," but contain a more general statement like "Join the Congressional Internet Caucus."

Logging and Tracking

Having the Mail Manager log incoming constituent communication into the system enables you to generate mail status reports to track the movement of mail through your office. These reports can tell you the volume of mail you receive on a given subject, the type of contact (i.e., fax, e-mail, postal mail, phone call), and the number of form letters/original responses sent out. Mail status reports can also quantify how much mail is answered in how many days and the volume of the current backlog, which will ensure staff accountability.

Without this accountability, turnaround times will suffer and a backlog can quickly develop. A good tracking system produces a mail report that will raise red flags so problems can be fixed before your constituents notice. The report will reflect which LA/LC is lagging, which one produces the most mail, and how long constituents wait to receive a form letter or an original response.

Proper logging also allows you to consolidate constituent information into one record and ultimately, provide better constituent services. The constituent record typically contains: name, address, e-mail; contact history; issue/topic codes; letters sent in response; and possibly an affiliation/personal code (e.g., DR for doctor, VIP, etc.).

Frequently Asked Questions About the Model Mail System

Q: *What happens when mail volume is so high that we accumulate a backlog?*

A: Establish a backlog alert. It is the responsibility of the Mail Manager to determine when a problem exists. When an LA/LC figures out she will not meet her turnaround deadline, she consults with the Mail Manager who must work with the Chief of Staff and/or the Legislative Director to determine a plan for resolving the backlog. They may assign it to another LA/LC, decide to delay the response until the original staffer is free the next week, or ask the entire staff to stay late one night and help. It is important that everyone knows that mail is an office-wide responsibility, and backlogs are not just an individual's problem. It's not the staffer who will be voted out of office by dissatisfied constituents.

The key to the backlog alert is to invest your Mail Manager with enough clout to prevent your LAs and LCs from abusing it as an easy way to avoid mail. The first time an LC's or LA's backlog reaches critical proportions, pinpoint the cause. Was it other priorities, heavier-than-usual mail on a controversial issue, a larger workload than other staffers, or other issues more complex and time-consuming to write about? Was he or she ill or on vacation? If the staffer was diverted to other higher priorities, or bedridden, the back-up plan is implemented. Otherwise, perhaps the staffer's workload needs to be re-examined and redistributed to less burdened colleagues.

Q: *How do we deal with "frequent flyers" who write us multiple times?*

A: Respond to them every third or fourth time they write. You can group responses to their many questions in one reply or only provide answers to three of the 17 questions they have posed. Focus on responding to the issues that have pre-approved text ready.

Q: *How do you prevent the Member from being a mail logjam, carrying the mail around in his briefcase for weeks, or keeping it buried under another pile on his desk before granting approval?*

A: When a Member says, "Mail is the most important thing in my office, and I want one-week turnaround," he makes a commitment to the staff to review mail quickly. When a Member regularly fails to approve mail in a timely manner, he signals to staff that what he says and what he really means are two different things. Ways to solve this problem are for the Member to take seriously the commitment he makes to the staff; allow staff to schedule mail-review "appointments"; rethink the priority of speedy mail turnaround; or gracefully recuse himself from the process to keep the turnaround time reasonable. Since only 15 percent of the mail should require new drafts in a mature office (with the other 85 percent already in the system and approved), the amount of mail requiring approval at any given time should be relatively small.

Q: How can we handle VIPs so the Member can personalize their letters?

A: A list of VIPs should be developed, tracked within the CMS/CSS, and periodically updated. Code VIPs in the database so this information is readily available to any staff member who accesses the constituent record. It is not uncommon for new staff to take many months to learn the VIPs in a district or state and this enables them to learn as they go. Many times District/State Directors or other outreach staff can be invaluable in identifying constituents who should be tracked in some additional way. In fact, when appropriate and useful, you should use your CMS/CSS to "flag" a constituent name with additional affiliation or interest codes (such as occupation, interest group associations, etc.).

Q: Are there other ways to answer incoming postal mail?

A: For many reasons, you should respond to constituents via e-mail if you have their e-mail address in their constituent record in the CMS/CSS. Also, a phone call from an LC or LA to explain an obscure and particularly complex issue to a thoughtful constituent may be a quicker and more user-friendly way to handle a complicated question than trying to explain the issue in a letter.

Q: How can we keep form letters updated so we don't send out old information?

A: The integrity of the mail system suffers if LAs/LCs do not keep an eye on updating pre-approved letters. It is embarrassing if a Member is telling a constituent in a letter that an issue is "under consideration" when it was voted on the week before.

Establish a system for reviewing form letters. The Mail Manager can make inquiries about what changes need to be made to reflect the previous week's floor action or pass around a list questions about currently approved texts for LA/LC review after the weekly staff meeting. Another approach: the Systems Administrator could check the date a form letter was first produced and if it was months ago, or if he knows there was action on the bill, he could ask the relevant LA if the letter needs updating before he generates a large volume of outgoing letters. Of course, the bill numbers and references to "this year" in all form letters must be changed every year and at the beginning of a new Congress. One approach is to inactivate all form letters at the end of each Congress, reactivating each one only after it has been revised and verified as up-to-date.

Improving the Processing of E-Mail

The CMF Mail System can streamline in-office handling of e-mail to a great extent. Further improvements can come from your choice and use of constituent database software, how you set up your web form, responding via e-mail, and determining your communications policies. For more information on effectively handling e-mail, the Congressional Management Foundation (202-546-0100, www.cmfweb.org) offers over-the-phone advice, in-office consultations and one-day workshops, all designed to help offices identify and leverage best practices.

Choosing Your Constituent Database Software

Your choice of CMS/CSS package is an important decision. If set up and used properly, this software can help you more quickly log-in, code and respond to e-mail communications. Before you choose to invest in any CMS/CSS, ask the vendor for references and talk with several offices that use the software to determine how well it can work for you. (More advice on making technology purchases can be found in Chapter 6.) These technologies are sophisticated and customized to the congressional environment. To take advantage of their full functionality, all staff who are part of the mail process should be trained on the system.

Setting Up Your Web-based E-mail Form

A web-based e-mail form is the most effective and efficient option for offices receiving e-mail. Nearly every House and Senate office uses web forms. Many have created their own, but House offices also have the option of using the Write Your Representative (WYR) service provided by House Information Resources (HIR). WYR allows constituents to fill out a message form that routes the message to the appropriate Member based on zip code information provided by the constituent.

Having an e-mail form (either WYR or one crafted by your office or vendor) on your website has many advantages. It ensures you get the information you need from constituents, and it helps automate data entry. In addition, the form can help filter out non-constituents if it's properly constructed. Your Systems Administrator can also craft filters and rules to keep non-constituent e-mail separate from constituent e-mail. If you don't devise a way to separate non-constituent e-mail, you have to sift through every message to determine which ones are from your constituents. Most Members choose to only respond to those they represent.

The web form can be accompanied by a pull-down menu of issues/topics and checkboxes that offer additional options such as "Add me to

MANAGEMENT FACT
All CMS/CSS packages can be setup to assign e-mail coming in through the web form directly to LCs, saving a step in the sorting process.

your e-newsletter list," or "Just wanted the Member to know my thoughts — no response necessary." Also, through your CMS/CSS, the constituent's communication can be automatically logged into their database record directly from the form.

Answering Via E-Mail

Most offices respond in kind to communications coming from their constituents. That is, if a constituent sends an e-mail, the office responds electronically. If the constituent sends a letter through the U.S. Postal Service, the office will print and send a paper response to that constituent. Wired constituents expect responses from Members of Congress to be fast and electronic. When offices respond to an e-mail with a printed letter, the Member will appear out-of-touch and unconcerned about the communications preferences of their constituents.

> **A Note About Public E-mail Addresses**
>
> Nearly every Member of Congress has abandoned their public e-mail address in favor of more efficient web forms. Why? Only a fraction of the hundreds and thousands of incoming messages were from constituents. Staff and interns spent hours daily manually reviewing messages, weeding out non-constituents and distributing the remaining e-mails to the appropriate legislative staff.
>
> If you choose to have a public e-mail account, you must set up proper rules and filters to help sort and manage the incoming volume and decrease the administrative burden on staff. ∎

People are constantly amazed when they discover that some Members of Congress refuse to send e-mail communications. Constituents use a high-tech, high-speed way to communicate with their representatives, but receive a low-tech, delayed, "snail mail" response. What constituents value most is a timely response to their immediate concerns. If they send you their thoughts at the speed of light, they expect the same in return.

Non-compliance with constituent expectations occurs for several reasons. Some offices lack the knowledge about their software's features. Others feel a paper reply on letterhead with the Member's signature seems more official. One common concern expressed by congressional offices is e-mail tampering. The fear of constituents altering and then forwarding e-mails has kept some congressional offices from responding to constituents in their preferred 21st century mode of communication, even though there has not been a documented case of this occurring in the millions of e-mails sent in response.

In fact, the consequences of congressional unresponsiveness may be worse than the chances of an altered e-mail causing damage. It's an opportunity-cost calculation: should your office be unresponsive to thousands of e-mailers because of apprehensiveness about what havoc one of your constituents might wreak?

If your office is going to respond to e-mail, you will need to meet constituent expectations for a speedy response as best you can. For more

Figure 14-2

Responding to E-mail With E-mail

Myth	Reality
"The text of our response will be altered if we respond with e-mail."	• Offices that respond to e-mail with e-mail have never reported that happening. • Your CMS/CSS system stores copies of all e-mail, providing a record of what your office has sent. • The constituent may forward the e-mail on to friends and family in a positive way, allowing you to reach more constituents. • If there are still concerns, affordable technologies are available to help track and "guarantee" that your e-mail is secure.
"E-mail will increase our workload."	• E-mail is actually more efficient. You can automate certain parts of the data entry, which will save time. You'll also save time folding letters and stuffing them into envelopes; not using paper and envelopes will also save money. • E-mail responses are not expected to be as long as postal letters, so the writing and review process could be easier.
"People like letters — they're more impressive."	• People who send e-mail are expressing their preference for an online reply. • Responding to e-mailers with a postal letter may make the Member appear out-of-touch.
"Constituents who write via e-mail are not as important as those who write via postal mail."	• E-mailers are some of your most important constituents. CMF research shows that people who are politically active online and those who have contacted their elected officials are far more influential in their communities than the general public. They're also far more likely to vote and participate in political campaigns.*
"We don't want to write shorter responses — constituents appreciate a good, quality response."	• A quality e-mail is not the same thing as a quality letter — it is a different medium with different expectations. E-mailers will generally place greater importance on the speed of the response than on its length and will view a long response as an unnecessary and difficult read.
"Answering e-mail with e-mail will encourage pen pals."	• E-mail does make it easier for pen pals to prolong the debate, but there are some easy techniques for managing their expectations. For example, making response policies clear on your website and in a "re-direct message" pointing back to the website if they would like to send in an additional message can reduce pen pals. • When sending an e-mail response you can link to your website, providing the constituent with access to much more information than can be included in a letter.

* Source: *Communicating with Congress: How the Internet Has Changed Citizen Engagement,* Congressional Management Foundation.

information about the myths and realities of responding to e-mail with e-mail, see Figure 14-2.

Create and Post Correspondence Policies

Taking the time to communicate your policies and your approach to constituent mail on your website benefits not only your constituents, but also your staff. Constituents will know what to expect, and staff will have a reference point as to the Member's vision and goals for constituent mail.

If your policy is not to respond to mail that originates outside your district/state, or to messages that contain profane language, then clarify that in your correspondence policies. If it is your goal to respond to every communication you receive, give constituents an idea of the volume of mail that the office receives and why it could take some time to receive a response. You should also explain to constituents that postal mail may be delayed by security screening procedures, and through which method(s) you prefer to receive communications.

MANAGEMENT FACT
Consumer studies show that people who send an e-mail to a business expect a reply within 12-24 hours.

Proactive Outreach Mail

Members who wish to send unsolicited mail have a variety of choices in targeting techniques and production methods. They may use postal patron newsletters, e-newsletters, town hall meeting invites, tele-town hall phone calls, questionnaires, or generic or personalized letters. A number of issues must be considered, however, in deciding whether to develop an outreach mail program.

The Outreach Mail Debate

Opponents of congressional outreach mail argue that unsolicited communications are an unfair advantage of incumbency. Some believe that it amounts to a taxpayer-funded subsidy for Members' re-election efforts. Critics point out that the levels of unsolicited mass mailings increase dramatically in election years and diminish in off years. They also argue that the content of outreach mail is focused primarily on the Member's accomplishments and only tangentially on policy issues — undermining the idea that this mail contributes to public discussion.

"Opponents argue that unsolicited mail is an unfair advantage of incumbency. Proponents argue that two-way communication is an essential part of democracy."

Proponents of outreach mail argue that two-way communication is an essential part of democracy and that the quality of representation is directly related to the contribution of the represented. Supporters maintain that questionnaires and town hall meeting notices encourage participation in the democratic process. Congressional outreach updates constituents on federal actions that affect them — in some cases news that the media doesn't detail due to time and space constraints. Moreover, proponents of outreach mail argue that constituents are entitled to know what a Member considers his or her priorities as well as his or her position on issues. If constituents disagree, it provides them an opportunity to tell the Member.

Many Members believe it is important to communicate, unfiltered by the media, their own message to constituents. One Chief of Staff recalled a conversation with the editor of a daily newspaper. When asked why the paper only printed bad news about his boss, the editor replied, "It is the Congressman's job to do the things he is paid to do, so that's not news." The readers, he said, do not want general government stories unless they contain some element of scandal or controversy.

Outreach mail programs have long been political issues because information about Members' mailing practices is readily available online. The National Taxpayers Union, for instance, publishes regular reports ranking Members from highest to lowest in terms of franked mail spending. If you decide to conduct an aggressive outreach mail program, you must be prepared to defend your position. Justifiably or not, it may become an issue.

Other Outreach Mail Issues

Members who believe that outreach efforts are a vital part of their representational functions need to decide how much of the office's resources to devote to this goal. Depending upon the method used, costs might include the Member's time, staff time, constituent list purchases, design and production, and franking. The office should have a written plan that relates each mailing to the office's strategic plan and justifies the dedication of resources.

The outreach mail plan should also clearly identify which staffers are to do what and by when. Whether your plan is very detailed or relatively simple, it should be carefully thought out. Guidelines for developing plans are in Chapter 11, "Strategic Planning in Your Office."

In developing and implementing an outreach program, your office will collect a treasure trove of information about your constituents. It is absolutely *illegal* to use any information from your office, including your database, for anything other than official business. *Once data is on your computer or becomes part of your office operations in any other way, you cannot lend it out, transfer it to your campaign, or use it for any other purposes.*

MANAGEMENT FACT
House and Senate rules prohibit unsolicited mass communications prior to any election, though House Members can send e-newsletters to those who have opted-in.

Finally, offices should educate themselves on the various House and Senate rules governing unsolicited mail, including e-mail. Violations of these rules can result in Ethics Committee investigations, financial penalties, and, of course, a boatload of bad press. Given the politicized nature of outreach mail, the Member who does not demand that staff be aware of and follow the rules — and the rules do change — does so at the peril of his or her reputation.

In election years, for example, Members of both the House and Senate enter into a blackout period (90 days for the House; 60 days for the Senate) before their primaries and the general election when they are prohibited from sending unsolicited mass mailings. House offices, however, are allowed to send e-newsletters to people who have opted-in for the service. Senators also face a ceiling each fiscal year on the amount they can spend on franking for mass mailings. The House Franking Commission (Democrats: 202-225-9337; Republicans: 202-226-0647) and the Committee on House Administration (Democrats: 202-225-2061; Republicans: 202-225-8281), and the Senate Ethics Committee (202-224-2981) and the Senate Committee on Rules and Administration (202-224-6352), provide detailed information and manuals on House and Senate mailing rules.

Conclusion

It's no exaggeration to say your success in Congress is greatly influenced by the decisions you make concerning constituent correspondence. It's likely to consume the largest percentage of office resources, and is a major link to your constituents. How you manage, prioritize, and above all, answer the mail is up to you, but these decisions will reverberate throughout your office and impact everything else you do. The dominance of e-mail has only increased the difficulty in being responsive, and social media communications tools present new and as yet unresolved issues of their own.

The CMF Mail System and other advice presented in this chapter can go a long way towards assisting offices in meeting these challenges and providing constituents with timely, accurate and informative responses. At the same time, offices will maximize their resources and be in a better position to address their many other responsibilities.

CHAPTER FOURTEEN

Chapter Summary
The DOs and DON'Ts of
Managing Constituent Communications

Do...

- **use a proactive strategy to reduce the volume of incoming constituent mail.** Keep constituents informed through a comprehensive and user-friendly website and regular e-mail and social media updates.

- **assess the priority of mail in your office.** It is counterproductive to assign mail a high priority and then fail to devote the resources to answer it appropriately.

- **adopt the CMF Mail System,** which enables an office to answer 85% of its mail with pre-approved form letters in about one week.

- **recognize that timeliness is of the utmost importance to constituents.** A prompt one-page response is more desirable than a longer, more detailed response received several weeks later.

- **treat mail backlogs as an office problem, not an individual staffer's problem.** It is the Member's reputation at stake, not the staff's.

- **adhere to a consistent and timely process for the logging and coding of constituent interactions.** Such a scheme will enable you to better track and respond to the needs of constituents.

- **answer e-mail with e-mail.** It can make the difference between meeting constituent expectations and appearing out-of-touch.

Don't...

- **ignore the differences between e-mailers and postal mailers.** E-mailers expect a faster reply and shorter responses than postal mailers.

- **discount the concerns of e-mailers.** Most of them are just as committed to their issues as traditional postal writers.

- **view mail as simply something to react to.** If you do, you will become a content provider instead of legislating, conducting outreach and district/state projects, and meeting the larger needs of constituents.

- **fail to establish clear mail policies.** Consider the desired turnaround; the quality of replies; which mail to answer; and the degree of Member involvement.

- **allow the Member to slow the mail approval process.** When the Member regularly functions as a mail logjam, ask him to rethink the priority of speedy mail turnaround, or come up with a strategy to approve mail more quickly.

- **violate House and Senate rules governing mass communications and e-mail** — both solicited and unsolicited — which can result in Ethics Committee investigations, financial penalties, and harmful press coverage.

CHAPTER FIFTEEN

Strategic Scheduling

> *This Chapter Includes...*
>
> ☆ How to develop and implement a strategic schedule
> ☆ Ideas for proactive scheduling in the district/state
> ☆ Managing the Member's DC schedule
> ☆ Suggestions for addressing common scheduling problems

A Member's time will face almost limitless demands. The grueling campaign schedule can quickly become a distant, vaguely pleasurable memory when compared to a schedule in office. The campaign schedule, while inhumane in the extreme, had two benefits probably not appreciated at the time. It was compressed into a relatively short, endurable timeframe, and the candidate had a great deal of control over what was done and when it was done. By contrast, unless a Member loses or retires, there is now no end in sight. And he has lost control over a large portion of his time: up to 70 percent of the time will now be spent dancing to someone else's tune. As a result, a Member might find that his schedule controls him, when he wants to be in control of his schedule.

It is possible to avoid this unhappy state of affairs. One can rise above the day-to-day minutiae commonly included in the term "scheduling" by instead practicing *strategic scheduling*. This means creating a focused framework for the scheduling process that reflects an office's strategic plan. This will ensure that strategic goals drive the schedule. A strategic scheduling process will preserve your office's sanity, which is especially needed by freshmen in the tough first term.

There will always be challenges in scheduling. But the office can reduce these challenges if a Member commits to a strategic scheduling method early in the term and sets up a process and framework to support it. And while it is easier to adopt a strategic scheduling framework when the Member has a clean slate, it is certainly possible for veteran offices to modify their scheduling practices if they wish to do so.

Strategic Scheduling Defined

Think of your time in office as a trip. Not a short jaunt, but a major cross-country trip. Going, say, from Washington, DC to Fresno, CA. And you are not going on the road alone. This is a bus trip, and you are the driver. Unfortunately, the tour company did not plan the trip well. Neither did they advertise it accurately, so the passengers on the bus all have their own ideas about both where they want to go and how to get there.

To complicate matters, you don't have all the maps you need. Some of your passengers know the best way through Kansas (you sure don't) and two of them (but you don't know which two) are the only ones who know how to cross the Rockies. If you let them have their way, you'll drive through all contiguous 48 states, stop at every tourist attraction within 40 miles of the highway, and ultimately visit everyone's second cousin twice removed. You might, eventually, get to Fresno, but how likely is that? And at what cost to you and the bus?

Remember, you're driving, and you are the one who wants to get to Fresno. How are you going to do this?

What does this parable teach about your office? If you're following our advice so far, you will soon have your goals in place (i.e., Fresno). But the people on the bus with you are all those folks — constituents, interest groups, local government officials, colleagues, committee chairs, lobbyists, staff, spouses and families — who have ideas about how you should spend your time. Some of them have the keys to your success (i.e., the map for Kansas). One or more may have make-or-break status (i.e., the path through the Rockies). You have to keep them happy, and you need them with you. But you can't lose sight of Fresno.

You are going to develop a system for getting their input, weighing it against your goals, taking advantage of opportunities where they exist and creating them where they don't. You are going to have to develop a strategic itinerary, which is a lot like strategic scheduling.

So what is strategic scheduling? Simply put, it is knowing where you want to go (even approximately), and using your time wisely to get there. If your budget is your strategic plan put to numbers, then your schedule is your strategic plan set forth in dates, times and locations.

Strategic scheduling is *proactive*. You don't just respond to requests: you decide where you need to go, who you need to see, and who needs to see you. It is *goal oriented*: you don't spend a minute more than necessary on those activities that aren't going to help you reach your goals. It is *creative*: your district/state trips aren't an endless stream of disconnected events that you attend at the request of others, but are a seamless expression of your strategic plan. It is *inclusive*: the schedule is created not by you alone, nor by your Scheduler, but by a group that works to ensure that everyone's views are heard, that needs are balanced, and that all bases are covered.

Six Steps to Developing and Implementing a Strategic Schedule

Step 1: Define office goals.

The foundation of strategic scheduling is a focus on, and adherence to, goal achievement. The importance of setting goals and various methods for developing them are discussed thoroughly in Chapter 11. Very little in the strategic scheduling model will work if there is not a clear sense of the office's priorities for the term.

Step 2: Evaluate the impact of office goals on scheduling.

An office's strategic plan will be translated into action through the schedule. Thus, the planning team should evaluate the impact that each of the goals will have on scheduling. This evaluation can provide answers to key scheduling questions, such as:

- How much time will be spent in the district or state?
- What specific times will be spent in the district or state?
- What type of events will the office create?
- What type of requests will get priority?
- What level of attention will be given to certain groups?
- What activities are "musts" either weekly, monthly, or yearly?

Some goals are stated explicitly in scheduling terms. A goal like "Increase favorability ratings in East Riverside by 20 percent" has obvious implications for the district schedule. The Member will probably be in East Riverside quite a bit, in addition to spending time playing a visible role on issues of importance to East Riversidians.

Other goals will need a little more translation. The impact on the schedule of a goal like "Introduce and obtain passage of Amusement Park Deregulation Act" is less clear. It may require time for hearings, time spent touring amusement parks or time working on behalf of causes benefiting children to soften the Member's image and deflect charges of endangering children for profit.

Step 3: Communicate goals to staff.

It sounds obvious, but it is not always clear. The office's goals cannot be translated into action unless staff understands them. How the Member's schedule is put together is critical to achieving his or her goals, and communicating these goals to staff will be critical in how the schedule is put together. CMF recommends that staff be involved with developing the office goals, but if they are not, the goals should be presented to staff in detail. Staff need to understand not only what the Member's goals are, but how the office intends to achieve them. This can be done through face-to-face meetings or written plans or memos. A common understanding and shared sense of mission will allow staff to work together in building the schedule and will vastly reduce internal staff conflict over scheduling matters.

Step 4: Assemble the scheduling team.

A good strategic scheduling system is inclusive, and a key element of that system is the scheduling team. The team should be comprised of those people who have input into the Member's schedule, for whatever reason: they have specialized knowledge or key insights (Communications Director, Field Rep); they have functional responsibility (Scheduler); or maybe just because they have creative minds.

Teams will vary across offices in size and composition. Senate offices tend to have larger teams, simply because they have greater functional and geographical specialization, and one or two staff are not going to have the whole picture or the understanding necessary to develop a good schedule.

Offices that do not use a scheduling team often divide the Member's available time and parcel it out to different staff members to schedule individually. The District/State Director is responsible for the weekend in the hometown, a Field Rep for a day in a far-reaching county and the Scheduler gets two hours on Friday afternoon for office visitors, etc. This approach inevitably results in a choppy schedule that lacks focus and cohesion, and does not create collaborative support for the office's goals.

> *"Offices that do not use a scheduling team often divide the Member's available time among different staff members to schedule individually, resulting in a choppy schedule that lacks focus and cohesion."*

CMF strongly recommends the team approach, but not that all scheduling decisions be made by committee. The scheduling team will have input into the schedule — making suggestions for activities, working as a group to create events and keeping each other apprised of events on the horizon that will require the Member's (and their) attention. Decisions on routine scheduling matters will be made by the Scheduler, with appropriate (and agreed upon) input from the Member and/or Chief of Staff.

According to CMF's research, the majority of House and Senate offices use a scheduling team, customized to their office's needs and personnel.

Offices have an endless variety of team configurations to choose from. In fact, House and Senate offices that responded to a recent CMF survey reported more than 15 different staffing configurations. There is no one correct structure or team composition. Regardless of configuration, the key is to define and agree on the roles of each person involved. Some possible team members, and suggested roles, are offered here:

Member. The Member must decide what level of involvement he or she wishes to have in setting the schedule. Weigh the time the Member will spend tinkering with the schedule against other pressing political and legislative demands. Ideally, the Member should develop enough trust in staff to allow them to make most scheduling decisions. Giving staff this responsibility is much easier when there are clear strategic goals to work toward.

Member's Family. The family might want a voice in setting the schedule and the team must accommodate their input. In some cases, a spouse might have knowledge of the district and its key issues that is unmatched by staff. In other cases, a spouse may want input on only a limited scope of decisions, or may only require early notification, not input into decision-making. (See page 259 for suggestions on how to determine the family's involvement and reduce conflict with staff.)

Scheduler. The Scheduler is ultimately responsible for the schedule. He or she must supply information about events as needed, provide a contact person for each scheduled event, develop the final schedule, respond to requests, and communicate with staff.

The amount of decision-making authority granted to Schedulers varies widely, depending upon their level of experience and the level of trust and comfort in their relations with the Member. Some Schedulers serve as the final arbiter on all matters of scheduling, while others readily defer critical scheduling decisions to others. Ultimately, a single individual should have the authority to add and remove events from the schedule. The Scheduler is uniquely situated to weigh all of the competing options and priorities. (See page 261 for a discussion of this role.)

District/State Director. The District/State Director is often considered the Member's overall "point person" in the district or state. As such, he or she should obviously be involved in shaping the district/state schedule, but might also have key information that would be helpful in developing the DC schedule. The DD/SD's familiarity with various constituent groups and key contacts can help a Scheduler decide which of the competing groups should be placed on the Member's schedule and which could be seen by staff.

Field Representative. Field Representatives are often the first to know about an issue or organization that deserves the Member's time. They should have input into the scheduling process, either directly or through the District/State Director. For offices in which Field Representatives cover specific regions, it may be best to alternate their participation on the scheduling team, so over time the entire district/state is taken into account.

Communications Director/Press Secretary. Press staff are usually a vital component of the scheduling team. If media coverage is desired, it is always easier to build that in when an event is being formed than to try, perhaps unsuccessfully, to graft it on at the end. The Communications Director/Press Secretary is the most reliable assessor of what the media will cover and what type of coverage to expect.

Legislative Director. The LD usually has input into the DC schedule, as he or she knows where the Member needs to spend time to achieve the office's legislative goals, but the LD could also be helpful in crafting the district/state schedule by connecting the Member's legislative priorities to outreach and events.

Chief of Staff. As the staff person with the "big picture" perspective, the Chief of Staff can ensure that the schedule is a model of balanced, focused, seamless continuity.

Others not on the "team." On an as-needed basis, some offices rely on input from political consultants, local government leaders, interest group leaders, and/or trusted advisors from the community. These folks are not a part of the regular decision-making team, but their suggestions are routinely solicited. It is not necessary or advisable to include these advisors in every meeting for several reasons: first, there are ethical limitations; second, they will have divided loyalties and their own agendas; and finally, because you don't want them to usurp the role of the staff.

Step 5: Develop scheduling criteria.

Once the team is in place, the office needs to determine how that team is going to make decisions and how they are going to identify and create opportunities to advance the Member's agenda and strategic goals. The best way to create this framework is to use the office's strategic plan and the Member's personal preferences to develop criteria that will be used both to create events and, more importantly, to respond to scheduling requests. Offices that use a clear set of scheduling criteria make faster, better, and more consistent decisions, with fewer conflicts.

CHAPTER FIFTEEN   Strategic Scheduling

Criteria are critical to an office's success in their "reactive" strategic scheduling. More than with proactive scheduling, it is easy to get distracted from the strategic goals when you are responding to invitations. It is tempting for many scheduling teams to oil the squeakiest wheel; for the Member to accept interesting, exciting or fun invitations that do not advance goals; or to attend others' events rather than dedicate the time and resources to create your own. Having a framework in place will not remove these problems, but it should significantly alleviate them. For example, it allows staff to make preliminary judgments and immediately classify individual requests as they come in to the office as a "yes," a "no" or a "maybe."

"Offices that use a clear set of scheduling criteria make faster, better, and more consistent decisions, with fewer conflicts."

Following is a list of questions an office can use to help determine what sort of criteria would be suitable. Using the answers to these questions as a starting point, an office can develop criteria for scheduling that reflect the strategic plan. It can then use these criteria to proactively identify and schedule promising opportunities, or to react to invitations already received.

- What are the office's short- and long-term goals? Where and how does the Member need to spend time to achieve them? What outreach strategies has the office developed to meet these goals in the district/state?
- With what individuals or groups could the office work closely to pursue outreach strategies and advance goals? How can the office best work with these individuals and groups?
- What are the regions of the district or state to which the Member must devote significant time? What kinds of events are appropriate for and work well in these areas?
- How important is media coverage? How likely is the office to get any media coverage and will it be positive?
- What is the Member's personal style? Is the Member better with scripted events or informal gatherings? With large or small groups?
- What personal preferences or activities of the Member must be considered (e.g., hates going to bed late, dislikes flying more than once a day, insists on jogging daily)?
- Are there certain times that should be blocked out strictly for the Member's family (e.g., late Saturday evenings or Sundays)?

It is, of course, imperative that the Scheduler have the ability to communicate "no" in a way that does not alienate constituents. It is important to be selective in scheduling, but the office obviously cannot afford to have constituents feel they have been treated carelessly. The Scheduler does not expect to be loved — part of the job is telling constituents something they do not want to hear — but the way in which the message is communicated can be the difference between disappointed understanding and outright anger on the other end of the phone.

Step 6: Conduct a strategic review.

Strategic scheduling works because it keeps your eyes on the prize. To maximize its benefit, an office must regularly evaluate three things: first, that the office really did keep its focus; second, that keeping the focus got the office where you thought it would; and third, that the original destination is still the desired destination.

> *"By evaluating where and how the Member spent his or her time, the office can tell whether scheduling decisions support the Member's goals."*

By evaluating where and how the Member spent his or her time, the office can tell whether scheduling decisions support the Member's goals. This "scheduling audit" will help keep the office on track and ensure that problems in the scheduling process are corrected before they have a chance to fester and grow.

1. **Compile and analyze a comprehensive report of district/state visits broken down into several categories:** subject (education, labor, foreign affairs, etc.); type of group (business organization, civic club, individual constituent, etc.); type of event (press conference, town meeting, etc.); locale (city, county, etc.); or any other breakdown that might be useful. This step is easy to complete if you have developed a good coding system for your computer's scheduling program.
2. **Compare this tally against the office's strategic plan.** Determine whether the allocation of the Member's time was consistent with the office's goals and outreach strategies. You should be able to analyze trends and discuss progress — or lack of progress — towards the stated goals.
3. **Decide whether changes are needed in the scheduling process to ensure that staff time is allocated more strategically.** An office might change the composition of the scheduling team, revise the scheduling criteria or target certain groups or areas in the coming year.

District/State Trips

An office will quickly find that proactive scheduling is both more important and more achievable in the district/state than in DC. In Washington, a solid

CHAPTER FIFTEEN   Strategic Scheduling

percentage of the Member's time (70 percent or more) will be occupied by "must-dos" — votes, committee mark-ups, caucus meetings, staff meetings, etc. In the district or state, on the other hand, the office will have much more opportunity to schedule proactive events. The goal for trips back home must therefore be as proactive as possible. Doing so requires that the office:

- **Develop a long-range scheduling plan** — for either the first session or the entire upcoming term. (A draft should be ready by the end of January each year.)
- **Create events** that either carry out a particular theme, target a specific constituency, or take the Member to a certain geographic region.
- **Accept selected invitations** to build the remainder of the schedule around, generally one or two for which significant advance notice is needed.
- **Review pending requests**, especially those with flexible dates, and accept those that suit the Member's strategic plan and travel pattern (e.g., civic groups that have placed an open invitation to meet with them). This file will probably wear thin with review. It's best to group requests by city or county to make it easier to fit them into the travel plan when needed.

The specific events in which the Member participates range in complexity from an individual appointment to creating a high-visibility public forum with guest experts, media coverage, and a large audience. Some types of proactive scheduling to consider include:

- **Individual appointments.** Plenty of people would like to spend some individual quality time with the Member and one of the simplest ways to accommodate that need is by scheduling regular office hours in the district/state office. It is convenient for the Member and for staff, and if done strategically, can ensure that the Member is meeting with the right people and gleaning the information needed for legislative activity or projects. However, individual appointments can become time-consuming and usually provide little visibility in the community at large.
- **Community or open office hours.** These events differ from individual appointments in that the Member usually travels to a public place to meet with constituents, rather than host scheduled appointments in the office. A similar option employed by a few Members is to operate or lease a "mobile office" that also allows the Member and staff to travel to constituents in various parts of the district or state. When considering these approaches, one difference is that mobile offices have additional maintenance and operational costs that must be factored into an office's decision-making.

When run effectively, these types of office hours can be an effective use of the Member's time because he or she can greet, chat and take photos with constituents, who get the opportunity to seek assistance and get one-on-one face time with the Member, even if it is limited. For House and Senate offices, these events not only increase visibility and encourage a proactive mindset, they also enable the Member to serve remote areas and reach constituents who may be unable to travel.

- **In-person town hall meetings.** The most traditional form of Member–constituent interaction is in-person town halls. Though some may question their effectiveness, many Representatives and Senators conduct these types of meetings one to six times a year. Town halls can accommodate a large number of people and usually result in media coverage, though at times the Member's message may be secondary to the strong opinions of a few attendees. Still, in-person town meetings provide an open, direct and unfiltered dialogue between citizens and their elected officials.
- **Tele-town hall meetings.** An innovative way that offices have reached out to constituents is through town hall-style meetings conducted over the telephone. Tele-town halls invite constituents, through automated calls, to participate in a live conference call with the Member at a set date and time. During these large-scale interactions, thousands of constituents may be on the line with the Member and can ask questions on a particular topic or a wide range of issues, depending on how the event is structured.

    These calls allow the Member to reach a large number of constituents in a relatively short timeframe (the calls usually last 30–60 minutes); they require less logistical prep than in-person meetings; and they allow the Member to conduct outreach in their states and districts while in DC. Citizens participate from their homes, usually resulting in a greater number of people on the call than could likely attend an in-person event. A criticism of these calls is that they can be seen as too much of a contrived political event, so staff should be careful with their moderation of the questions asked.
- **Online town hall meetings.** Similar in concept to tele-town halls, these sessions use Web-based software that allows constituents to interact with Members from the convenience of their home or workplace. Using a computer, constituents are able to see and hear the Member respond in real-time to questions they submit online.

    CMF, which produced this book, conducted research on the effectiveness of these events and found distinct benefits to engaging with constituents in this way. First, constituents like the sessions and find them to be valuable uses of their time (95 percent of CMF's participants said they

> *"Offices can serve more constituents by engaging in non-traditional events such as community office hours, tele-town halls, and online town halls."*

would like to participate in similar events in the future). Second, offices can reach a large number of constituents, as well as a more diverse and representative sample of the opinions in their states and districts. Finally, if conducted using best practices, online town halls can be a valuable tool to hear from constituents, have them learn from the Member and each other, and further engage them in the democratic process.
- **Site visits.** Sometimes whom the Member sees is not as important as where the Member is seen. Visiting certain sites (factories, child care centers, schools, transportation hubs, wildlife preserves, etc.) can help gain information and support needed to reach a goal. And sometimes information or support is not needed — simply being seen taking an interest in a particular area is sufficient.
- **Task forces/advisory boards.** More often than not, the Member's goals will not be achieved by the office alone, but by working in concert with a range of other interested parties. Offices that make effective use of task forces and advisory boards identify and draw upon the strengths and expertise offered by third parties. These participants are usually eager to offer assistance, ideas and solutions, especially when it relates to a priority issue of theirs. Taking time to form and work with task forces or advisory boards might make some goals more achievable. Even if it does not, it certainly gives the Member visibility and leadership on an issue, which can sometimes be almost as beneficial as actually achieving the goal itself.
- **Roundtables, conferences, field hearings.** These top-of-the-line events are complex to plan and execute and often involve many people outside the office (and thus outside its control) but offer high visibility. Visits by Cabinet secretaries, field hearings arranged through the Member's committees, informational or problem-solving workshops, etc., could spotlight an issue, highlight a problem or explain recent legislative changes. Focusing on a specific need and incorporating the expertise of others can make these events a highly effective means to promoting and achieving the Member's goals.
- **Press/visibility.** Obviously, the Member needs not only to do good, but to be seen doing good. District/state staff and media-savvy press staff will constantly be looking for good "photo opportunities." It may sometimes serve the Member's goals to appear at press visibility events created by others, but the office is likely to find the need to create its own events as well. Consider televised town meetings, site visits, individual chats with reporters and photos of meetings with award-winning constituents, along with the more common stand-up press conferences. Keep in mind that if events are viewed as all style and no substance, it could backfire and cause negative publicity for the Member.

For proactive scheduling to succeed, proper communication and coordination among staff and other key players are essential. In this regard they should:

- Hold weekly scheduling meetings.
- Seek input from appropriate staff and other advisors.
- Maintain regular communication with upcoming meeting/event hosts.
- Keep good records of conversations, decisions, and confirmations.
- Apprise all staff of the complete schedule at all times.

While our goal thus far has been to get the Member and the office to focus on "the big picture," district/state trips also involve a great deal of important logistical planning, coordination and follow-up, perhaps more so than DC events. It's often not enough to be proactive just in selecting the right events in the right places at the right times. The Member and staff also need to anticipate what will make the event a success. These needs might be content-driven, such as preparing briefing memos, speeches or talking points. Other needs might be logistical, such as determining which staff will travel with the Member, arranging lodging and driving directions and making sure related materials (i.e., plaques to be awarded) arrive on time. Still others involve taking steps to multiply an event's impact, such as ensuring that the Communications Director, who's undoubtedly been involved much of the way, has all the information needed to properly attend to press matters.

Follow-up is also important. After the event or the weekend, talk to staff who attended. If possible, seek the views of friends in attendance for candid assessments of what worked and what didn't. Only by knowing what went right and wrong can the office improve future trips. Distributing an evaluation form (see Figure 15-1) to constituents at district/state events is another valuable way of getting good feedback (as is telling constituents that you value their input).

The Weeks in Washington

Scheduling a Member's time in Washington presents a far different set of challenges than planning district/state trips. While there may be fewer logistical concerns, the vagaries of the floor schedule means less control over a Member's schedule.

Maintaining control over a Member's DC schedule requires three key elements: the creation of a schedule for a typical legislative week; weekly scheduling meetings; and the availability of schedule information for staff.

CHAPTER FIFTEEN Strategic Scheduling

Figure 15-1

Model Speech/Event Evaluation Form

As your Member of Congress, it is important to me to provide you with the best representation that I can. This survey will allow me to understand your needs better and to improve my ability to meet your expectations.

Please complete and return this form to me at the address listed below.

Event & date _____

Your name _____

Address _____

City, state & zip _____

E-mail address _____

Would you like to sign up for my e-mail newsletter?   ❏ Yes   ❏ No   ❏ Want more information

1. Did I address the subject(s) you expected or hoped to hear about?
   Yes _____ No _____
   If not, what subject(s) did you want to hear about:

2. Please rate the length of my speech.

   Too long   <   1   2   3   4   5   >   Too short

3. Please rate the level of detail in my speech.

   Too much detail   <   1   2   3   4   5   >   Not enough detail

4. Please rate the amount of time devoted to questions-and-answers.

   Too much time   <   1   2   3   4   5   >   Not enough time

5. How many times have you heard me speak in the past year?

6. What was your main reason for attending this event?

   Please return to:
   (Member's Name)
   (Member's Address)

   Thank you!

A Typical Schedule

Most weeks in Washington, while chaotic, are somewhat uniform. Certain things happen fairly regularly:

- In the Senate, you can count on hearings in the morning from Tuesday through Thursday, although many committees hold hearings in the afternoon.
- In the House, there has been a reasonably predictable Tuesday through Thursday schedule, with any votes Fridays or early evening Mondays scheduled and published in advance.
- In both chambers, you can count on regularly-scheduled party caucus or conference meetings.
- You can also be assured of late nights, lots of votes and, in some cases, even weekend sessions as recess weeks draw near.

With this as your framework, the office can create a schedule that sets blocks of time for predictable activities that require the Member's time daily or weekly — press availability, office visits, committee hearings, staff meetings, meals and exercise, evening activities, and even floor time (one-minute or special order speeches in the House, Morning Business in the Senate). Members of the majority party may also have commitments to be the presiding officer in the chamber for a couple hours per week.

Using this schedule as a template, the Scheduler will plug in obligations as information becomes available. He will get hearing notices, either directly from the committee or through the legislative staff. He will consult with the LA, LD or Chief of Staff to determine which committee activities the Member will likely want — or need — to attend. Using the office criteria as his guide, and getting input from other staff, the Scheduler will respond to requests from constituent groups and lobbyists for appointments, fitting them into the schedule in designated time blocks.

Each meeting or hearing will be coded to reflect the relative importance placed on each, especially if there are multiple events at the same time, which there often are. Some the Member will attend; some might be "drop-bys" with staff acting as backup; and some may go on the schedule as "FYIs," which the Member needs to know are happening, but probably will not attend.

The Scheduler will also notify appropriate staff of each commitment relative to their areas of responsibility, so they can provide the Member with any information needed before the meeting.

Of course, this sounds like an orderly and predictable routine — so what's all the fuss about? Well, often as not, events will occur that could not have been anticipated. No one knows (or if they do, they're not telling) what is going to happen tomorrow. Events have a way of taking shape just outside your peripheral vision. Next thing you know, they dart out in the road smack dab in front of you.

It is these events — those which are not part of a typical week's schedule — that are the true test of your strategic scheduling method. Press conferences on breaking news, participation in floor debates, shifts in committee schedules that bring the Member's amendments up two weeks early, responding to calls from party leadership for floor speeches on their issue-of-the-week — these are the events that will throw your schedule out the window. They will also offer a scheduling team the opportunity to shine. The scheduling team will need to respond quickly, yet nonetheless strategically to these unanticipated events.

"A great Scheduler will have the creativity and flexibility to get the schedule back on track."

While votes are expected during a typical week, *when* they actually occur can cause the Member to miss appointments and create a domino effect on the rest of the day. In these moments, a great Scheduler will have the creativity and flexibility to get the schedule back on track by coming up with alternative arrangements for meetings or by reshuffling the calendar.

Weekly Scheduling Meetings

Washington staff should meet weekly to discuss the upcoming week or weeks. In many offices this meeting takes place on Friday, after the Member is headed home, or first thing Monday, before the Member's return. This meeting should focus on key strategic questions including: What is our top priority for the week? What is on the schedule this week that directly relates to meeting our goals? What is likely to go wrong and what are our contingency plans? For more assistance, see Chapter Four's "Conducting Effective Meetings."

At this meeting the team should discuss those activities that are not routine. Sometimes, you will know in advance what will be on the floor next week or when your amendment will come up (more likely in the Senate than the House), or what the Administration will be doing that you will be involved in (one way or another). Giving these activities special attention in the weekly scheduling meeting will help them go more smoothly.

Often, however, staff will need to decide whether the Member should participate in events for which you've had no advanced notice whatsoever. Indeed the frequency of such events convinces some offices that setting goals, planning, and holding weekly meetings is futile. On the contrary, *it is precisely because of this unpredictability that these planning activities are valuable.* If the office has goals, staff will be better able to sort out which late-breaking activities merit your attention and which do not. Because you have a plan, you can determine which activities will likely accomplish something, and which will simply get the office off course. And because the staff has weekly meetings, they are more likely to have a shared understanding of what is truly important and what is secondary, making the inevitable schedule shuffling smoother and less time-consuming.

This meeting must be efficiently run — tightly focused, with an agenda and time limits for discussion items. As the congressional schedule heats up, some offices may find this weekly meeting schedule hard to adhere to, but every effort should be made to do so. It is precisely when things are flying fast and furious that you most need to keep your focus. If the meetings must be shortened, curtail their length and scope, but not their frequency. This short, structured, tightly focused meeting will do more to keep an office on track than any other method it could employ.

Availability of Schedule Information

An important key to effectively implementing strategic scheduling and minimizing breakdowns in communication is providing all staff in all offices with access to the Member's schedule. CMF has found much higher levels of staff cooperation and coordination in offices where all staff have access and are expected to review the daily and weekly schedule.

Most House and Senate offices use Outlook or the office's constituent database to schedule — the easiest ways to facilitate this practice because they store the current schedule in one easily accessible place. In an environment where schedules are constantly changing, an online schedule will:

- Save time on the part of the Scheduler;
- Provide Washington and district/state staff with access to the latest information; and
- Store, retrieve and organize data, allowing the office to assess progress towards its strategic goals.

For example, it is possible for the office to tally the locations and topics of meetings to determine if the Member's time is being spent wisely. This type of reporting is more difficult and complex to do if an office is using multiple programs or less collaborative methods. For these reasons, offices should consider streamlining their scheduling processes — or at least ensure they are coding information consistently for the strategic review recommended earlier. The benefits to the entire staff of doing so usually far outweigh the advantages to keeping an outdated or cumbersome system in place.

Addressing Common Problems

Even if an office is using a strategic approach, scheduling presents a number of difficulties. Some of these are unavoidable, and not the least of these is an erratic congressional calendar. Below are a number of common scheduling problems that offices face. The key to successful scheduling is identifying those problems that are avoidable and learning to cope with those that are not. Some suggestions for doing so are offered below.

Problem: Excessive travel time in the district/state due to a large or oddly-shaped district/state, unpredictable traffic, pressing commitments at opposite ends of the district/state or lack of commercial transportation between main cities.

The most the office can hope for is to make extra travel time semi-productive. Make sure the Member has plenty of reading material — for starters, information that will be useful on the trip. In addition to a briefing book, staff can compile other information of interest about the communities being visited — pending grant or casework requests, recent correspondence from VIPs, and clips from the local paper. This is also a good time to go through all the pesky items from the bottom of the Member's inbox. Of course, staff will need to develop mechanisms to ensure that the Member's travel briefcase does not become the "black hole" into which all important information vanishes.

Consider also the use of cell phones, mobile and handheld devices, laptops and digital voice recorders to help put that time to good use. Additionally, if there are long distances to cover, seriously consider using a driver. Balance your office's desire not to look "imperial" against the Member's need to prepare, mentally and physically, for the next event. The Member can work while the driver worries about traffic, and they can trade places just before the next stop if necessary.

The Member might also consider using travel time for personal business, such as listening to audiobooks, calling the family or writing thank you notes. These activities are hard enough to fit into the congressional schedule, and sometimes the Member will need a break from the stress to be a normal person. Frankly, catching up on sleep is a very good use of travel time.

Problem: Overscheduling.

Though there are other causes, overscheduling is largely a problem of being unable to say "no." If both the Member and the Scheduler have difficulty turning down requests — for fear of alienating current or potential support, or for other reasons — then overscheduling is inevitable. The Member must learn to tell requestors, "I'll check on it and get back to you," then pass the request on to the Scheduler, who becomes the "fall guy" if the invitation is declined. Veteran Schedulers compare their jobs to that of the Roman messenger. They cannot expect to be liked all the time. Schedulers must learn to say "no" diplomatically and be the ones to take the heat because of it. It's part of the job.

The Member will derail this process if he or she aids and abets those groups who will try anything to get around the Scheduler to secure the Member's participation at an event. And the Member certainly cannot get in the habit of accepting invitations and neglecting to inform the staff.

One option used by offices to reduce overscheduling in DC is to host constituent breakfasts. Very common in the Senate and increasing in popularity in the House, these one-hour meetings are an effective use of the Member's time because they offer an opportunity to greet, chat, and take pictures with constituents who might not otherwise fit into the schedule. For the same reasons, hosting open community or mobile office hours is an option to reduce overscheduling in the district/state.

Problem: Missing worthy events in the district/state because of an erratic congressional schedule or because many groups want the Member on a weekday.

Your office can't control the congressional schedule. The Member's schedule should anticipate the possibility of the House or Senate remaining in session later than planned on Thursdays and Fridays. Staff must make it clear to local organizations that want to see the Member on Friday that he or she might have to cancel at the last minute. In general, staff should attempt to restrict Friday events to those that can be canceled or postponed.

In addition, be creative about responding to requests that conflict with the congressional schedule. A family or staff member or a trusted local official can be a good surrogate to offer or have on call should the Member have to cancel on a moment's notice. Other alternatives include sending video greetings, teleconferencing and video conferencing.

Problem: Member unwilling to commit or slow to make decisions.

Getting Members to respond promptly to invitations can be a real challenge for the typical Scheduler. If the problem is slowness on the Member's part, the Chief of Staff, District/State Director, or Scheduler can point out the negative consequences of delaying a decision. Waiting to commit until merely days before events will reduce your opportunities to play a key role in good events. Also, the quality of staff briefing materials will decline in proportion to the

CHAPTER FIFTEEN   Strategic Scheduling

limited prep time. Opportunities missed due to late responses, or the anger of groups or individuals desiring the Member's presence are some of the consequences the office will face.

On the other hand, it may be equally damaging to respond to outside pressures and accept invitations prematurely. This can result in last-minute cancellations, angering the inviting group and annoying staff.

The office must strike a balance. For every request, there's an appropriate time for the definitive response from your office. It varies according to the type of event and according to the schedule. Good communication between the office and the requestor, as well as the combined political judgment of the Member and staff, will help a Scheduler develop a sense of proper timing for each unique set of circumstances.

Problem: Member overinvolvement in the scheduling "minutiae."

Members often learn that they are overinvolved in scheduling decisions only when their staff tells them they are and that they need to butt out. If the office or the Member suspects the Member is spending too much time on scheduling decisions, we recommend you work towards a *management-by-exception* arrangement. That is, once the Member is comfortable with the scheduling system and staff, the Member should give them the authority to make all routine scheduling decisions. The Member then gets involved in scheduling only when staff are unsure of the proper decision. Initially, staff could refer about one-third of the decisions to the Member. But over time, the office should become so confident with this arrangement that the Member makes fewer than one-tenth of the decisions. The Member's involvement is the *exception,* rather than the rule.

Problem: Scheduler provides inaccurate information.

Schedulers hate to send bosses to events ill-prepared, to say nothing of how much their bosses hate it when they do. This happens either because the Scheduler didn't ask enough of the right questions or because the requestor didn't describe the event thoroughly enough. Amazingly, the latter is sometimes deliberate. One Scheduler sent his boss to what was billed as an "informal meeting" with "a few members" of a local organization. The Member was on the opposite side of the group's main concern. When the Member arrived, more than 100 people (plus press) were present. During what became a "protest rally," the group unfurled a banner with a statement that would commit the Member to vote with them on that issue, and demanded he sign it. The Scheduler commented, "It's surprising how many groups have tried this approach. I've become very wary of groups that won't specify the number of people attending."

Figure 15-2

Sample Event Scheduling Form

BACKGROUND INFORMATION

Name/description of event: _____

Event sponsor: _____

Event date: _____ Event time: _____

Event location: _____

Sponsor contact name: _____

Sponsor contact phone, fax and/or e-mail: _____

Description of requested Member participation
(if speech, give length and topic; if activity, give details): _____
_____

Other VIPs attending: _____

Requested RSVP deadline: _____

Other info: _____
_____

ACTION TAKEN

Confirmed _____ Regretted _____ Date: _____

If Confirmed
Lodging (if needed): _____
_____

Driving directions: _____
_____

EMERGENCY CONTACTS

BEFORE EVENT DATE

Name: _____

Phone, fax and/or e-mail: _____

ON EVENT DATE

Name: _____

Cell phone, fax and/or e-mail: _____

Advance prep. needed (i.e., background briefing, talking
points, speech, press release): _____

Assigned to: _____

Date due: _____

Additional materials to bring
(i.e., award to be presented, generic outreach materials): _____
_____

Staff attending: _____

Other info: _____
_____

It is a Scheduler's job to ask questions and get details (see Figure 15-2). If certain information hasn't been divulged, he or she should call others who'll be attending to get the necessary answers, and follow up with a letter or e-mail outlining his or her understanding of the event.

Problem: Scheduler does not obtain complete information.
Many groups want the Member to do "visual" things, but neglect to tell the office beforehand. Members get asked to toss the baseball on opening day, ride an elephant in a parade, even serve as a dunk-tank victim for charity.

If anything goes wrong, it's usually the Scheduler who's accountable. Therefore, a Scheduler should do what good journalists do: get more information than necessary and edit out the nonessential details. A new Scheduler should develop a checklist of questions to which he or she can refer during conversations with requestors. These questions should try to gather the most specific and detailed information possible to prevent surprises.

Problem: Scheduler difficulty judging which events will be most worthwhile, inability to work with other staff in a team environment, inadequate coordination between Washington and district/state staffs.
These are actually problems with judgment. If your office has done a good job defining its goals and priorities, it is simply a matter of time and education for the Scheduler to learn to accurately assess the worthiness of invitations. He or she will become educated through working on a team with other staff and listening to their perspectives. A wise Scheduler will: keep abreast of both district/state and DC happenings, even if he or she is not responsible for both schedules; talk frequently with district/state staff, particularly those in the field, in addition to reading the daily newspaper clips; learn legislative procedure to assess the floor schedule; and develop good contacts on committees and with outside organizations. A Scheduler who has developed his or her judgment in this fashion will have little difficulty working in a team environment, and will seek the advice and input of staff when necessary.

Problem: Member's family demands on time or problems arising from spousal input.
Many Members are hesitant to address these thorny issues. Conflicts between staff and family, particularly between Schedulers and spouses, are bad news for everyone involved. And, unless the family never wants to see the Member and doesn't care in the least how he spends his time, *this conflict is inevitable*.

If the Member fears to tread here, the office is likely to experience increasingly dissatisfied Schedulers, resulting in more frequent turnover, and frustrated Chiefs of Staff as well. The Member is not likely to go through a series of spouses, of course, but the family will be unhappy unless these issues are dealt with.

The key to a cooperative and happy relationship between a Scheduler and a spouse is the negotiation of clear limits and responsibilities for both. The input a spouse will have in the Member's schedule, the guidelines for notifying the spouse about the schedule, and the amount of sacrosanct "family time" are among the issues to be addressed. Use the tips in the next section to resolve them now.

"The key to a cooperative and happy relationship between a Scheduler and a spouse is the negotiation of clear limits and responsibilities for both."

Scheduling Issues Faced by Members

Especially for the Member: Family

Problems between the Member's spouse/family and staff are most likely to become apparent around the schedule. This is understandable: both sides are in competition for a precious resource — the Member's time. To staff, the more time you spend on business the better. Your spouse and/or family, for their part, want only some reasonable facsimile of a normal family life.

Minimizing this conflict is only possible if you deal with it. Addressing the following issues up-front will create a framework for family/staff interaction that reduces conflict and tension.

1. **Clarify the roles and outline procedures for family input.** If the family's role is left vague, confusion and frustration will ensue. The types of questions to address are: Does the family get veto authority over scheduling decisions, or only the opportunity to raise concerns? Should the family review all invitations at the front end of the process or be consulted only on specific matters? Family input into the process is often more crucial to district/state scheduling as this cuts into the most precious family time — weekends and congressional recesses.
2. **Foster a comfortable relationship between the Scheduler and the family.** The Scheduler should communicate with the family often. The Scheduler, not the Member, Chief of Staff, or District/State Director, knows the schedule best and is in the best position to provide accurate information. At a minimum, the family should receive the schedule as

soon as it's available with enough time for staff to answer their questions or address their concerns.
3. **Block out important dates and family events.** Some Schedulers mark all family birthday and anniversary dates in the Member's calendar each year, just as any other event would be noted. All scheduling requests are then discussed in the context of those family occasions. Schedulers should also ask the family to notify the office of other events as soon as possible, such as vacations, parent–teacher conferences, etc.
4. **Establish clear limits on the spouse's claim to the Scheduler's services.** Inappropriate and unethical family demands on staff are most likely to come to the Scheduler, who must be supported in attempts to deflect them. At the same time, some Schedulers make inappropriate offers of assistance to spouses — because they view their jobs as "making life easier for the Member."

How To Pick the Right Scheduler

The Scheduler is not only critical to the functioning of the scheduling team; he or she will be critical to the Member's general health and well-being. The Member is going to need to trust this person immeasurably, so it's critical to hire or train the right person for the job.

So what do you look for in a Scheduler? In many cases, the same thing you look for in other staff — intelligence, political sensibilities, commitment. You want someone with a keenly honed ethical sense, someone who can tell if you're being invited to partake in an allowable event, and perhaps what the public and press might say about it. Additionally, scheduling requires incredible organization and a true love for managing details. "Big picture" thinkers and non-task-oriented people fail in this job.

It is also important to assess just how much decision-making authority you will be comfortable parting with. Realistically, it only makes sense to hire (and pay for) an experienced, politically savvy, top-notch Scheduler if you are able to stand not seeing every invitation and deciding which seat you want on the plane. Otherwise, it doesn't make sense.

In addition to scheduling duties, the Scheduler position in your office might have additional job responsibilities. In many House offices, the Scheduler serves as the Executive Assistant or Office Manager, and would thus need to have the skills or aptitude to carry out those duties as well.

Finally, the most important factors are personality and temperament. You want someone you can get along with, but someone who is strong, creative, and flexible enough to keep the Member and the schedule on track. This type of person, no matter how bright, enthusiastic, and hard-working, must be able to tolerate the parameters of working as a congressional scheduler.

Who Does District/State Scheduling?

Having stated the importance of a "single point person" for scheduling, that role may be filled by two people with separate responsibilities — one for DC and one for the district/state. Almost all Senate offices have two Schedulers, while House offices are split more evenly. Offices should consider a number of factors when deciding where to base the district/state Scheduler, such as how often the Member goes home. As Figure 15-3 shows, 83% of Representatives and 65% of Senators spend 30 or more weekends in the district or state each year. If the Member is home every weekend and every recess week, this makes a bigger scheduling workload than a once a month trip, and would argue for a separate district/state-based Scheduler.

Another factor to consider is the distance of the district or state from Washington. If it is three time zones away, making last minute schedule changes from DC is going to be a challenge, so a district/state-based Scheduler would work better. Finally, what are constituents used to? Having someone available locally can be seen as advantageous, but so can getting to deal directly with Washington. Do not unwittingly deprive constituents of something they perceive as having value.

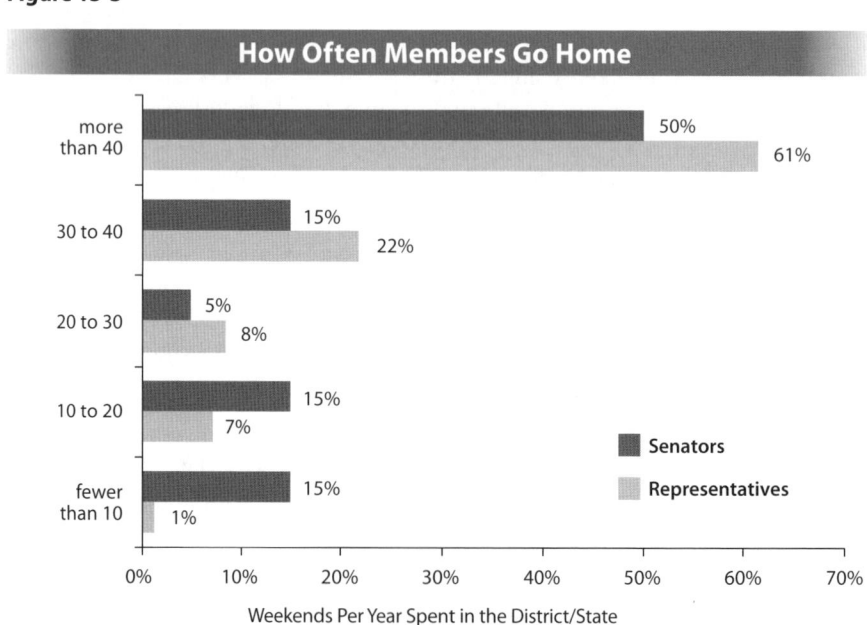

Figure 15-3

How Often Members Go Home

Weekends Per Year	Senators	Representatives
more than 40	50%	61%
30 to 40	15%	22%
20 to 30	5%	8%
10 to 20	15%	7%
fewer than 10	15%	1%

Weekends Per Year Spent in the District/State

Source: *Keeping It Local: A Guide for Managing Congressional District & State Offices,* Congressional Management Foundation.

Other advantages and disadvantages to both locations should be considered when making this decision. Having district/state scheduling done in DC provides the Scheduler and Member with immediate access to each other. It can lessen confusion and tension between Washington and district/state staff, and can simply be more efficient.

On the other hand, having scheduling done out of the district/state demonstrates roots in the community. It allows the Scheduler to visit event sites to assess their appropriateness. The Scheduler can form better relationships with constituents because he or she can meet with people instead of just talking to them on the phone. Additionally, the district/state-based Scheduler will have a much better understanding of the local geography and travel time between communities, and appear more accessible to constituents than would a DC-based counterpart. However, the district/state-based Scheduler might feel isolated from the decision-making center, and communication breakdowns are more likely on scheduling matters between the offices.

Keep in mind that, for House offices, the Scheduler position tends to include other duties. In DC, the Scheduler may also serve as the Office Manager or Executive Assistant. If this is the case, they may not have the capacity to schedule for the district as well and a separate position should be filled. In the district/state office, this person may also serve as the District/State Director, Constituent Services Rep/Caseworker or Field Rep.

Members should exercise great care in hiring and in deciding which office — Washington or district/state — to locate the person responsible for district/state scheduling. All too frequently, the decision about where to base the district/state Scheduler is made after-the-fact, and is based on personnel. If the Washington Scheduler is from the district/state and knows it well, he is more likely to be assigned district/state scheduling. Conversely, if the DD/SD has a staff person with whom she is really comfortable, then scheduling back home is more likely to be district- or state-based. An office's staffing situation may mesh perfectly with an objective assessment of its needs. But an office is better served in the long run if this decision is based on objective factors first, and then staff hired that can work within the configuration chosen.

Conclusion

An effective schedule will simultaneously achieve the Member's strategic goals, provide variety, satisfy constituent demands, accentuate the Member's strengths, protect the Member's personal and family needs, and effectively utilize travel time. Amazingly, this is not asking the impossible. A strategic scheduling system will do an excellent job of balancing these diverse demands.

A strategic scheduling system will help the Member use time to the best advantage because it is goal-focused. It will provide variety and accentuate the Member's strengths because it is proactive and creative. It will not drag the Member to an endless series of other people's events — the Member will participate in events that the office created to help achieve strategic goals. This satisfies multiple demands because it is an inclusive process — everyone has a place at the table and a voice in the decision-making.

The Member's commitment is critical to the success of this system. The Member must remain focused on goals and priorities — or at least allow the staff to keep him or her focused. The Member must let staff make decisions freely within the established framework. The scheduling team must be able to work together as a well-oiled, high-performance machine.

Like any good office system, the scheduling system can and must evolve. Revisions might occur because of changes in staff or priorities, or because the office wants to experiment with something new.

No scheduling system will ever be perfect, largely because of the environment within which congressional offices operate. But the goal should not be perfection — it should be effectiveness. The effectiveness of a scheduling system will be evidenced by a Member who is busy yet unhurried, highly visible but not without privacy, focused yet able to accommodate a wide range of constituencies.

CHAPTER FIFTEEN   Strategic Scheduling

Figure 15-4

Sample Event Preparation Request Form

(Given to Staffer by Scheduler, copy to Legislative Director or Chief of Staff)

TO: Staffer

FROM: Scheduler

If you need additional assistance,
let the Scheduler know as soon as possible!

Date: _____

Name/description of event: _____

Event sponsor: _____

Other VIPs attending event: _____

Event date: _____   Event time: _____

Event Location: _____

Other info: _____
_____
_____
_____

Description of requested Member participation at event: _____
_____

Type of advance preparation needed (i.e., background briefing,
talking points, speech, award presentation, press release): _____
_____
_____

Topics: _____

Time Limits: _____

Other info: _____
_____

Date due: _____

Submitted to: _____

Chapter Summary
The DOs and DON'Ts of
Strategic Scheduling

Do...

- **follow the six steps for developing and implementing a strategic schedule:**
  1. define office goals.
  2. evaluate the impact of office goals on scheduling.
  3. communicate goals to staff.
  4. assemble the scheduling team.
  5. develop scheduling criteria.
  6. conduct a strategic review.
- **determine roles and responsibilities for the Scheduler(s)** and any other staff who are part of the scheduling team.
- **forecast a long-range scheduling plan** for either the first session or the entire upcoming term.
- **serve more constituents by conducting a variety of proactive events in the district/state,** such as: individual appointments; community or open office hours; site visits; online, in-person, or tele-town halls; advisory boards; and field hearings.
- **consider the Member's travel schedule, the distance from DC to the district/state, and any additional job duties,** before hiring and deciding where to locate the person responsible for district/state scheduling.

Don't...

- **hire an experienced, top-notch scheduler** if the Member is still going to see every invitation and decide all details.
- **rely on reactive scheduling, where the office simply responds to invitations or requests.** Instead, actively seek and creative opportunities to achieve goals.
- **neglect to get feedback from event attendees.** Only by knowing what went right and wrong can the office improve future scheduling trips.
- **overschedule.** Schedulers must learn to say "no" diplomatically and take the heat because of it.
- **ignore the Member's needs for "down time" or reading time.** While Member's schedules are necessarily busy, they do not have to always keep pace with a hectic campaign-like schedule.
- **wait too long to respond to invitations** which angers those who invited you, nor reply too quickly, which might result in last-minute cancellations.
- **ignore or avoid conflict between the Member's family and staff.** Build a cooperative relationship by setting up ground rules for the family's involvement in scheduling and interaction with staff.

CHAPTER SIXTEEN

Managing Ethics

This Chapter Includes...

- ☆ Coping with the changed ethics environment
- ☆ Guidelines for managing ethics in congressional offices
- ☆ A nine-step process for conducting political/ethical analyses

This chapter does *not* discuss the rules of the House or the Senate, or how to interpret them. It is essential that you carefully study those rules, meet with the ethics committee staff to verify your understanding of them, send your staff to mandatory training, and ensure that you and your staff are in compliance. We assume that you behave in an ethical manner, that you will continue to do so, and that you wish to be perceived as behaving ethically.

Instead, we propose that ethics can, and should, be managed, just like any other important aspect of your office. This chapter outlines why you should manage ethics in your office and how to do so.

The Changed Ethics Environment

Having run against the "culture of corruption" in Washington, the House and Senate leadership in the newly elected 110th Congress moved quickly to pass legislation to more closely police their own conduct and that of lobbyists doing business on Capitol Hill. In the first few months of the session in 2007, both chambers approved rules further limiting the acceptance of gifts and travel, mandating ethics training for all staff, and imposing new disclosures on negotiations for future employment. That environment and ethics regime will be the starting point for the 112th Congress in 2011.

The lobbyist community is plagued by the specter of Jack Abramoff, convicted of crimes related to trading favors for policy considerations. Individual lobbyists — not just their organizations — are required to make detailed, quarterly reports on their contacts with the Hill.

Regardless of whether you believe the rules go too far or not far enough, this rising level of scrutiny and expectation does suggest that the dangers of getting into ethical hot water are increasing. For this reason, congressional offices need to acknowledge this reality and take an active approach to managing ethical decision-making.

The House and Senate rules give individual Members a certain degree of latitude and require them to use their best judgment. For example, it is well within the rules for a Member to contact an executive agency on behalf of a constituent. Staff members do this type of "casework" all the time. But how does assisting a constituent who is a contributor differ ethically from assisting one who is not? Does this automatically create an "appearance of impropriety" that should preclude a Member's intervention?

Because these gray area issues are the most troublesome and the most common issues facing congressional offices, this chapter focuses on how to manage them. More specifically, this chapter operates from the assumption that you and your staff will face ethical questions almost daily and that everyone must be capable of weighing ethical issues in order to manage ethics in your office with the same care you manage your legislative agenda, district/state schedule, outreach mail, or local press strategy.

The key to operating in today's environment is recognizing that the public increasingly sees itself as the arbiter of ethics matters when it comes to Members of Congress and their staff. And the public now has unprecedented access to information that was either unavailable or difficult to obtain even a decade ago. Many financial disclosures are available online, and watchdog groups and reporters are making sure the data is easily accessible. Add to

CHAPTER SIXTEEN   Managing Ethics

this mix a highly competitive media industry pressed by the 24-hour news cycle, talk radio shows, the proliferation of blogs, and the instantaneous and viral spreading of information through text messaging, video clips, and social networking sites, and you have an environment where a story can quickly be taken out of your hands.

What starts today as a question about your campaign finances is tomorrow a lengthy story detailing your personal, campaign, and official financial practices. Within a week, you could face an endless flood of negative publicity in which your side of the story is a mere trickle. It is far easier today for unsubstantiated allegations of ethical improprieties of public officials to enter the public domain rapidly and become a topic of national discussion. Therefore, the House Committee on Standards of Official Conduct, the Senate Select Committee on Ethics, and the Office of Congressional Ethics are not the driving force in the public debate on ethics in Congress. The courtroom or the ethics committee hearing rooms are no longer the venues for the Member to justify his or her actions — talk radio shows and Internet news sites are.

> *"The courtroom or the ethics committee hearing rooms are no longer the venues for the Member to justify his or her actions — talk radio shows and Internet news sites are."*

This increased public interest can be ascribed to a number of factors, including:

- The public is increasingly interested in judging its public officials by their "character." Ethically questionable or unacceptable behavior in today's political environment calls into question an officeholder's or a candidate's moral fitness to hold public office.
- This public interest in the "character" of politicians has encouraged candidates for office — challengers as well as incumbents — to raise ethical questions more readily, because playing the ethics card has become such a politically effective tactic.
- The public has decreasing faith in Congress' ability to police itself.
- The spate of ethics stories over the past two decades has heightened the public's sensitivity to ethics matters, increased its cynicism towards elected officials, and expanded its appetite for public scandals.

A common defense against charges of ethical wrongdoing traditionally was, "but I broke no law, violated no rule." This claim is not only ineffective, but non-responsive. The Member is not accused of breaking the law or violating a rule, but of behaving unethically. The working definition of ethics that prevailed in Congress for many years — anything that doesn't violate a House or Senate rule or break a federal criminal statute is ethical — is no longer acceptable in today's environment. The public now wants — if not demands — that its public officials be "innocent," not just "not guilty."

Unfortunately, the rising public standard for the ethical behavior of politicians is not precise. But it doesn't really matter. Your burden today, whether you like it or not, is to ensure that your behavior cannot be reasonably construed as improper. The very fact that questions about the appearance of a particular action are reported means that you have failed the public's "smell test." You are guilty of the "appearance of impropriety" and will have to suffer the consequences.

Coping with the Changed Environment

Recognizing that a different environment exists is the first step in effectively coping and adapting to the new standards. The next step is developing a method of managing ethics preemptively to minimize the risk of having to confront an unintended ethical crisis.

Managing ethics is critical because the political consequences of making ethical mistakes in the present environment are so severe. They are also much greater than the consequences of failing to effectively manage other areas of your office operations because, once damaged, your reputation cannot easily be fixed. Unable to get your constituents a timely response to their inquiries? You can fix that. Make a budget miscalculation that means your office has a budget shortfall? There is a fix. Cross your committee chairman on his pet project? It will take effort, but that can probably be fixed as well. But one ethical miscalculation, one lapse, one oversight by you or your staff, and you will pay a hefty price — possibly your seat in Congress.

As one Member told us, "My reputation, my image, is all I have. It is my 'product,' so to speak. What I have to sell. I have built it up with years of careful, thoughtful actions, and of course we spend hundreds of thousands of dollars to 'sell' it to my constituents every two years. I cannot afford to allow a miscalculation on my part or a mistake by a staff member to destroy it."

Most offices spend a substantial amount of effort developing and implementing checks against other lapses that carry far less severe consequences. A typical office, for example, will devote several hours each week to double-checking responses to constituent letters or e-mail. Typographical errors or misstatements of the Member's position are certainly embarrassing, but are unlikely to lead to public exposure, a loss of public confidence, or potential electoral defeat.

As with errors in constituent correspondence, the likelihood of an unintended ethics breach can be either high or low. An office that never proofreads letters

MANAGEMENT FACT
House and Senate employees in the Washington and district/state offices must participate in mandatory ethics instruction within 60 days of being hired. House staff must continue this training every year and certain senior staff must take an additional course. Offices are obligated to certify that all staff are in compliance.

runs a high risk of typographical errors. Similarly, an office that does not give adequate attention to managing ethics runs a high risk of an ethical lapse. Because Members can do little to control the cost of an unintended ethical lapse, they should make a concerted effort to minimize the risk of such an occurrence. Efforts to reduce the likelihood of ethical breaches should be given at least as much attention as those made to reduce the likelihood of low-cost errors such as typographical mistakes.

The following discussion provides guidelines that you should consider to reduce the risk of ethical breaches in your office. Incorporating the suggested methods into your office's operations will provide a workable framework for managing ethics in your office.

Guidelines for Managing Ethics in Congressional Offices

Recognize that there is a difference between not violating rules and being ethical. The House and Senate ethics rules are purposely drafted to give Members a good deal of latitude. Too often these rules are mistakenly viewed as a "fence" — any behavior that does not breach the fence is ethical, while anything beyond is forbidden. A better metaphor is to think of the rules as the eroding edge of a cliff you never want to approach. Going over the edge of the cliff is clearly disastrous, but walking near the edge is also dangerous and unwise. House and Senate rules are not the exclusive guidelines by which Members must conduct themselves. Members are ultimately responsible to their constituents, the public, and to the institution itself.

Most importantly, Members are responsible for guarding the "public trust," an oft-cited (but not thoroughly discussed) principle that holding public office requires officials to protect the public's trust in the integrity of the officeholder and governmental institutions as a whole. Our system of representative government is based upon this principle.

> **Recommendation:** The best way to preserve the "public trust" and steer clear of ethical controversy is for Members and staff to know what the rules are and to **examine every ethics rule with an eye to understanding its underlying principle**. These principles are basic and fundamental. The most common principles on which the House and Senate ethics rules are based are:
> - Represent all constituents equally. Show no special favor for political, financial, or personal reasons.
> - Do not use your public position for private gain.

- Do not use public funds or facilities for private or political purposes.
- Do not use your position to exert undue influence.
- Avoid actions that create an appearance of impropriety.

If you begin discussing ethical matters by identifying the underlying principles, you are more likely to arrive at a course of action which will keep you out of trouble and comply with good ethical judgment.

Recommendation: Use the ethics committee as a resource, *before* you get in trouble. Both the House and Senate committees have staff who will talk through an ethical matter with you or your staffs on a confidential basis. They will not only cite the relevant rules and laws, but also will help you undertake an ethical analysis that identifies the principles underlying the rules. Further, the committees will give written opinions in advance in appropriate situations.

Don't assume that smart, honest people will always make correct ethical judgments. Most ethical judgments rest on an individual's ability to weigh competing values. For example, casework requires balancing concerns for constituent needs with the need to respect the integrity of an agency's administrative process. Honest, well-intentioned Constituent Services Reps will occasionally disagree on how to balance these competing concerns. One staffer may place a much higher value on meeting a constituent's individual need, while another believes that maintaining the integrity of the process is of paramount concern.

Additionally, decisions with ethical consequences will be made daily by your staff, and very often without your input. As discussed earlier, because the cost of an unintended ethical lapse is so high, it is not acceptable for different staff in your office to handle similar ethical questions differently. Staff actions reflect on the Member and should consistently represent his or her ethical precepts, not the staff member's.

Recommendation: Develop clear written policies for how staff are to handle common ethical issues. The process of creating these policies should begin soon after you are sworn in and they will require constant updating.

At a minimum, your written policies should contain specific guidelines for dealing with the situations described on the next page. These four areas are identified by senior staff as those most routinely confronted by offices and those with competing claims that are most difficult to resolve. Additionally, the policy should contain a broad statement of the Member's general ethical philosophy and values.

Recognize that the Member sets the ethical tone in the office. The way the Member balances competing ethical (and political) concerns will tend to set the pattern of behavior for the rest of the staff. If the Member and Chief of Staff choose to "cut corners" when they find themselves between a political rock and an ethical hard place, they must expect that staff will see that behavior as condoning the violation or stretching of the rules.

Recommendation: Consciously set a high ethical tone that conveys that the end does not justify the means. This can be accomplished most effectively by communicating to your staff directly about difficult ethical situations you face and how you intend to resolve them. There is enormous impact in telling staff that you are not willing to take an action that is politically advantageous in the short run but ethically questionable. There is no clearer way to convey your ethical standards.

The Top Four Areas of Ethical Risk

Chiefs of Staff have identified the following areas as the trickiest places to negotiate. They should be addressed in your written office policy:

1 Balancing congressional work with campaign or political work. Congress is a political environment and the political and official interests of an office will overlap. How much these activities can overlap before your behavior is deemed unethical is a gray area that you need to carefully manage.

2 Meals and travel. It may appear that the rules give you all the protection you need by spelling out exactly what you can accept and from whom. But the more you read, the more confused you may get by when a cheeseburger is forbidden but a steak dinner isn't, by when you may accept an out-of-town trip for two nights but not for one, or when you must decline altogether. Meals, receptions, and travel have long been considered staples of political life, but these old standbys offer plenty of opportunities for missteps.

3 Handling family members and campaign contributors. This area probably has the greatest potential for the "appearance of impropriety." Any action involving the Member's family or campaign contributors, particularly those who gave a significant amount, is inherently questionable. Both the Member and staff must be careful that their actions are not seen as providing special access or preferential treatment. Some offices attempt to shield policy and casework staff from knowing who the Member's contributors are, believing that ignorance is the best defense. Others want staff to be familiar with these names so staff can be doubly sure that their actions raise no questions of impropriety.

4 Constituent services. Assisting constituents with problems they are having with federal agencies is a routine part of your duties. How far you can go on their behalf before you begin to exercise "undue influence" is a gray area. ■

Recognize the reluctance of staff to raise issues and question decisions on ethical grounds. This is unquestionably the most difficult, but probably the most crucial, factor in effectively managing ethics in your office. Congressional staff, on the whole, tend to be young and inexperienced. They are not likely to comfortably question the Member on any grounds, much less on such a sensitive ground as ethical judgment. And Members are frequently uncomfortable or even offended when their decisions are questioned by staff.

Recommendation: Create policies and practices that give staff license to raise ethical questions with other staff, with the Chief of Staff, and with the Member. Offices should establish the practice of routinely and openly airing ethical questions or concerns — among staff, between the staff and the Chief of Staff, and between the staff and the Member. Each office is required to designate an Ethics Certification Officer to report on compliance with mandatory training requirements. Offices also should establish whether that staffer will be the only designated contact with the ethics panel or whether all staff or a certain group of staff can contact the committee.

Ethics issues should also be routinely addressed in office-wide meetings, both in Washington and in the district or state. These meetings must provide not only a mechanism or framework for raising ethical issues, but also a way of demonstrating that the office is willing to discuss these issues and reward staff for raising them. Such mechanisms might include:

- Having the Chief of Staff keep a list of difficult ethical issues staff have raised and discussing a few of these issues at staff meetings every few months so that other staff have the benefit of conducting ethical analyses.
- The Chief of Staff and other management routinely asking staff if decisions they are recommending present any ethical concerns that need to be addressed.
- Office policy informing staff that it is their collective responsibility to ensure that the office does not overlook ethical issues, and that it is their duty to raise any ethical concerns they have with the decisions of other staff, the Chief of Staff, or the Member.
- Circulating or e-mailing articles relating to ethics for staff review and routinely selecting a few for discussion in staff meetings.
- Including an "ethical considerations" component in staff decision memos.
- Having the Chief of Staff or Member not answer every ethics inquiry from staff, but occasionally asking a few staff to hash it out and submit a recommendation on how to handle the matter.

This process of questioning decisions also provides the Member with checks in the process to ensure he or she is not overlooking ethical considerations. Members need to be protected not only from staff errors in judgment, but from

---

MANAGEMENT FACT

Invitations for privately sponsored trips must be pre-approved by the ethics committees. House Members and staff must submit travel requests no less than 14 days in advance and must file a Post-Travel Disclosure form with the Clerk of the House 15 days after their return. Senators and their staff have 30 days both for pre-clearance and to file a Disclosure of Travel Expenses form with the Office of Public Records.

their own as well. You should not have to bear the entire weight of analyzing the ethical dimensions of all of your daily decisions.

Recognize that good ethics frequently conflict with the politically expedient and balancing the two is a complex, sometimes time-consuming, process. One main reason offices find themselves in a quandary over ethical matters is simply that there is frequently a high-voltage tension between the politically expedient and the ethical.

For example, the rules say your congressional staff can't assist your re-election efforts during business hours, but they can help out on their own time. Certainly politically savvy and talented staff would be a great help to the campaign, and you get the benefit of not having to pay them out of campaign funds. But how might it look to the voters, or the local newspaper, having publicly funded staffers stuffing your fundraising envelopes, delivering campaign signs or driving voters to the polls on Election Day? Are these actions a violation of the rules? No. Can they be viewed as unethical or become the basis of a critical news story? Of course.

> **Recommendation: Offices should teach and model analytic processes that incorporate ethical considerations into the normal decision-making process.** Congressional staff and Members are far more experienced and skilled at conducting political analyses than ethical analyses. They need coaching to ensure that ethical concerns are properly considered in policy and political decisions. The nine-step process outlined below provides an analytic model offices can use for incorporating ethical considerations into the political analysis process. After presenting the model, we then apply it to a hypothetical scenario for illustration.

A Nine-Step Process for Conducting Political/Ethical Analyses

1. What are the relevant House or Senate rules that are applicable to this issue?
2. What are the ethical principles underlying these rules?
3. What is the politically advantageous course of action?
4. From an ethical perspective, what is the correct course of action?
5. What is the source of tension inherent in this situation?
6. What is the full range of options available to you?
7. What are the likely consequences of these options?
8. Which of these options could not be effectively defended if they became public? (Discard those options.)

9. Of the remaining options, which best balances your political and ethical interests?

We will now apply this analytic model to a somewhat common office issue in which political and ethical interests conflict:

Hypothetical Scenario. You are facing a tough reelection battle against a well-financed opponent. Because you have worked diligently on the issues of concern to the oil and gas industry in your state, your fundraiser suggests an event targeting this industry and asks you to supply a list of the top 50 lobbyists you have worked with on these issues. You have such a list on your office computer.

1. **What are the relevant House or Senate rules that are applicable to this situation?** Many, if not most, situations you will face do not have clear, well-defined, applicable rules. In this case, however, there are. Conclusion? *You are prohibited from giving your fundraiser the list.*

2. **What are the ethical principles underlying these rules?** You can probably get around the rule by following its *letter*, but violating its *spirit*. To ensure that you don't, you should identify the principle underlying the rule. In this case, it is: *You should not use official funds or resources for political or personal use.* The list in question was gathered by you or by staff on official time, in the performance of your official duties. It is kept on your office computer, which was purchased with and is maintained by official funds.

    You could probably get around the *letter* of this rule easily enough — by writing the list out by hand. Would this action violate the *spirit* of the rule? Most people would agree that it would.

3. **What is the politically advantageous course of action?** Clear in this case. You have the list. Your fundraiser wants the list, and having it would be of clear political benefit to you.

4. **From an ethical perspective, what is the correct course of action?** In this case, it is particularly unpalatable from a political perspective. You should not give your fundraiser the list, nor *any* information that you or your staff have obtained in the course of performing your official duties.

5. **What is the source of tension inherent in this situation?** In this case, it is clearly the conflict between the *political interests* of the office (providing a useful fundraising list) and the *written ethics requirements* (you cannot use a list from your computer for political purposes). But that is not the only possible conflict. In other situations you might see:
    - The political interests conflict with a broad ethical principle even though no rules have been violated (i.e., the action is within the rules but doesn't seem ethical).

CHAPTER SIXTEEN Managing Ethics

- The action violates no written rules and seems to violate no ethical principle, and yet is liable to raise "appearance" questions.

6. **What is the full range of options available to you?** This is the most important, and most creative, step in the process. Before you get locked into a good ethics vs. good politics trade-off, you should try to generate a full range of options. You should focus on trying to identify options that satisfy both the political and ethical interests. This process encourages creativity by forcing you to consider a fuller range of options than those which are immediately apparent. We present seven options for the fundraising list scenario under #8 below.

7. **What are the likely consequences of these options?** Also discussed under #8 below.

8. **Which of these options could not be effectively defended if they became public?** Remember here that you must analyze these options as though you expect your actions to become public, no matter how unlikely you think that is. The common refrain of, "How would anyone find out? We're the only ones who know," makes the dangerous assumptions that "we" will always be "we" and that staff never discuss office matters with anyone outside the office. But staff leave offices, sometimes under less-than-ideal circumstances, and staff exchange stories with friends.

   In this case, Options A and G below are the "good politics" and "good ethics" extremes, respectively. Other possible options are listed as Options B–F. Each option is followed by its possible consequences (from #7 above), and then by a determination of its defensibility.

Option A: Give the fundraiser the list from the computer.
- Possible censure, reprimand, expulsion.
- Indefensible.

Option B: Give the fundraiser a list taken "indirectly" from the computer.
- Ugly news story, possible ethics committee inquiry.
- Difficult to defend.

Option C: Develop your own list from memory, during non-office hours.
- Still a possible ugly news story, because you would be suspected of supplying the list from your computer and would have to prove the opposite. Plus you might not produce as good a list, and thus not have as effective a fundraising event.
- Defensible inside-the-beltway; how would it play at home?

Option D: Invite all energy lobbyists and hope your friends will come.
- Not as personalized, well-targeted fundraising effort, possibly reducing attendance. Or, possibly better attendance, since invitation list is larger.

- Again, defensible in Washington. How will your constituents view it?

Option E: Have one of the lobbyists in the industry produce the list for your fundraiser.
- Probably a good list, maybe even as good as your own.
- Is asking a lobbyist for this type of assistance going to create the appearance that you now owe him a favor?

Option F: Change the focus of the fundraiser and simply invite "all the usual suspects."
- Much harder to plan and pull off; very labor intensive effort for a possibly reduced result.
- Easily defensible. Hard to imagine this could make much of a story.

Option G: Don't hold *any* fundraisers with lobbyists — they just create an appearance of selling access to the Member.
- Leaves major funding sources untapped. Possible positive press from the "good government" types.
- Ethically defensible but probably not politically pragmatic.

9. **Discard all ethically indefensible options and choose among those remaining.** In this case, Options A and B are out. You can choose from Options C through G depending on your analysis of the other relevant factors — political, district needs and sensibilities, etc.

Conclusion

The ethical environment that exists today significantly increases the likelihood that ethically questionable practices will be made visible to an unforgiving public. This environment necessitates that congressional offices carefully *manage* ethics rather than trusting the judgment of a few individuals at the top to make wise choices.

Behaving ethically in Congress requires much more than simply abiding by the rules. It is a complex undertaking that frequently requires balancing specific political needs with general ethical principles. It demands development of a system within your office for flagging potential problems, vetting them before they become an issue, and executing a well thought out plan to avoid them.

While it's still essential for all staff to be familiar with the written rules, so that potential violations can be avoided, that is no longer enough. A model of ethical behavior, and a system within your office to manage that behavior, must be followed to live up to the public's higher standards. We believe that developing and following such a system will not only minimize costly ethical blunders by you and your staff but will promote the public's confidence in you and your office.

Chapter Summary
The DOs and DON'Ts of Managing Ethics

Do...

- **understand that some actions that fall into the "gray area" of ethics** — the gap between being in technical compliance with the rules and meeting the public's and media's expectations for public officials.

- **reduce the likelihood of ethical breaches** by developing clear written policies on how staff should handle common ethical issues.

- **recognize that the Member sets the ethical tone in the office.** The way the Member balances competing ethical and political concerns will set an example for the staff's behavior.

- **examine every ethics rule with an eye to understanding its underlying principle.** Knowing these basic, fundamental principles will help you navigate situations as they arise.

- **be aware that the four areas where you may be at greatest risk of a breach of ethics are:**
  1. balancing congressional and campaign work.
  2. meals and travel.
  3. handling family members and campaign contributors.
  4. the extent to which you can assist constituents with problems they are having with federal agencies.

Don't...

- **ignore new and higher standards for ethical behavior.** If you are guilty of only the "appearance of impropriety," there can be an outcry from the public and media.

- **assume that smart, honest people will always make correct ethical judgments.** Most ethical judgments rest on an individual's ability to weigh competing values.

- **forget to check with the ethics committees early and often with any questions.** Committee staff can discuss the relevant rules, laws and underlying ethical principles with you on a confidential basis.

Index

Index

A

Abramoff, Jack, 268
Accounting software, 85, 180
Accounting systems, 188–90
Action plans, 170–72
Active Directory, Microsoft, 83
Administrative Director, 32, 36, 69
Adolphus, King Gustavus, 153
Advisory boards, 249
Agriculture, Nutrition and Forestry Committee (Senate), 22
Agriculture Committee (House), 21
Airline Congressional Desks, 34
Alternate Computing Facility (ACF), 89
American Enterprise Institute, 14
Americans with Disabilities Act, 107
Appropriations Committee
    House, 21, 24
    Senate, 21, 22, 24
Archivist (Senate), 96
Armed Services Committee
    House, 21
    Senate, 21, 22
Audits, 190

B

Background checks, 79
Banking, Housing, and Urban Affairs Committee (Senate), 22
BlackBerrys, 84, 89
Blue Dog Democrats, 120
Bonuses, 207, 208
Browsers, Web, 84
Budget Committee
    House, 20, 21
    Senate, 22
Budgeting, 8, 27–45
    allocations, 28, 35–40
    contingencies and, 38
    development of, 33–42
    expense information in, 33–35
    goals and, 32, 41, 180–81, 183–87
    importance of, 180–83
    media scrutiny of expenditures, 182–83
    Member's role in, 32–33
    month-by-month, 41–42
    non-priority spending, 182
    overspending, 28, 182
    principles for, 28–31
    by Representatives, 28–30, 35–38, 42–43, 180
    revising budget, 183–87
    rule changes and, 185–86
    by Senators, 28–29, 30–31, 38–40, 42–44, 180
    software for, 85, 180
    worksheet for, 39, 40

C

Campaign contributors, ethics and, 273
Capitol Police. *See* U.S. Capitol Police (USCP)
CAPS (Congressional Accounting and Personnel System), 85, 180
Casework, 67, 106
Casework Supervisor, 36
Cell phones, 193, 255
Centralized management structure, 49–51, 54
Chairs, committee, 21–22
Chief Administrative Officer, Office of the (House), 34, 92. *See also* House Information Resources (HIR)
    Administrative Counsel, 107
    House Compensation Study, 37
    Office Services, 83, 111, 112, 192
Chief Counsel for Employment (Senate), 63, 73, 200, 201

Chief of Staff
  compensation for, 36
  hiring, 69–70
  responsibilities of, 32, 49, 51, 68, 69–70, 73, 142–43, 244
Civility in Congress, 123–24
Clerk of House, 274
CMF. *See* Congressional Management Foundation
CMS/CSS software, 81, 84, 87, 93, 224
  maintenance of, 192
  providers for, 83
  selection of, 232
  training on, 97
Combined Airlines Ticket Offices (CATO), 34
Commerce, Science, and Transportation Committee (Senate), 22
Committee assignments, 17–26
  evaluating potential, 23–24
  importance of, 7–8, 18
  process for obtaining, 18–22
  steps in, 19
Committee on Committees, 19
Committees. *See also* Committee assignments; specific committees
  categories of, 20–21, 22
  chairs of, 21–22
  House, 19, 20, 21
  party ratios on, 18–19
  ranking members of, 22
  Senate, 19, 20–21, 22
  sizes of, 19
Communicating with Congress: How Capitol Hill is Coping with the Surge in Citizen Advocacy, 91
Communicating with Congress: How the Internet Has Changed Citizen Engagement, 91
Communicating with Congress: Recommendations for Improving the Democratic Dialogue, 91
Communicating with Congress Project, 91, 215, 216
Communications Director, 36, 69, 244
Communication with constituents, 215–38. *See also* E-mail; Mail
  backup copy of, 222
  cost-savings considerations for, 192–93
  Mail System (CMF), 221–31
  plan for, 217–18
  policies for mail, 220–21, 235
  priorities in handling, 218–19
  promptness in, 221
  telephone calls, 66, 218
  town hall meetings, 248–49
  volume of, 216–18
Communication with staff, 55–60. *See also* Meetings, staff
  design of system for, 58–60
  enforcement of policies, 60
  feedback as, 147, 149
  of goals, 242
  input from staff, 147
  methods of, 56–58
  objectives of, 57
  planning and, 173–75
  sharing information with, 147
  staff meetings, 59
  written policy about, 60
Compensation. *See* Salaries
Compliance, Office of (OOC), 73, 200
Computers, 82. *See also* Technology, office
Conference calls, 193
Congress. *See also* House of Representatives; Senate
  culture of, 117–25
Congressional Accountability Act (CAA) of 1995, 73, 77, 197, 200
Congressional Accounting and Personnel System (CAPS), 85, 180
Congressional Black Caucus, 120
Congressional Ethics, Office of, 269
Congressional Management Foundation (CMF), 232. *See also* Mail System (CMF)
  Gold Mouse Project, 89, 91, 217
  Partnership For A More Perfect Union, 81, 91, 216
  resources from, 35, 91
  services from, 164, 232
  training by, 14, 232
Congressional Member Organizations (CMO's), 119
Congressional Research Service (CRS), 14, 119, 226

Index

Congressional Services Representatives, 108. *See also* General Services Administration (GSA)
Constituents. *See also* Communication with constituents
  accessibility of offices to, 104–105
  expectations of, 105
  services for, 105, 273
Constituent Services Representatives, 36, 68, 69
Constituent Services Systems (CSS). *See* CMS/CSS software
Constituent Services Systems (CSS) funds, 30
Core staff, 12–13
  compensation for, 36
  functions for, 66–70
  goals and, 70–71
  hiring, 9, 64–70
  House, 68
  Senate, 69
Correspondence Management Systems (CMS). *See* CMS/CSS software
Cost of living adjustments (COLA), 186
Counsel, 36
Covey, Stephen, 4, 5, 27
Culture of Congress, 117–25
  civility in, 123–24
  new members and, 122–23
  partisanship and, 123–24
  party ratios and, 120–21
  scheduling, 119
Culture of office. *See* Organizational culture
Customer Support Analyst (CSA), 83, 86, 92

D

Data Entry Clerk, 36
Demo Center (Senate), 93
Democratic Party
  House Committee restrictions, 20, 21
  Senate committee restrictions, 21
  Steering and Coordination Committee (Senate), 19
  Steering and Policy Committee (House), 19
Deputy Chief of Staff, 36

Digital signatures, 221
Digital voice recorders, 255
Dingell, Rep. John, 130
Director of Special Projects/Grants, 36
Disbursing Office (Senate), 28, 31, 42, 182, 183, 188, 189, 190
Disclosure of Travel Expenses form, 274
District, travel to
  budgeting for, 37, 40, 43, 185
  cost-saving advice for, 193
  frequency of, 262
  scheduling during visit, 246–50
  time use during, 255
District Director
  compensation for, 36
  responsibilities of, 32, 51–52, 68, 142
  on scheduling team, 243–44
District offices
  accessibility to constituents of, 104–105
  cost of, 43
  equipment for, 83, 96, 111–12, 113
  in federal buildings, 108–109
  furniture for, 111–12, 113
  importance of, 102–103
  lease for, 107
  location of, 106–109
  maintenance of, 107
  mobile, 109, 247
  number of, 43, 103–105
  office hours, 247
  opening first office, 110–11
  parking availability at, 107
  part-time, 104
  in predecessor's offices, 108
  in private buildings, 109, 194
  relocation of, 194
  rent for, 37, 107
  resources available for, 103
  safety of, 107
  scheduling by, 246–50, 262–63
  setting up, 9, 101–14
  shared space with state/local officials, 194
  size of, 107
  staff for, 36, 97, 105, 106, 107
  telecommunications for, 37
  utilities for, 37
  visibility of, 103, 106
Domenici, Sen. Pete, 130
Dreier, Rep. David, 131

E

Eckart, Rep. Dennis, 122
Economic Allocation Fund, 30, 86
Education and Labor Committee (House), 21
Education and Training, Office of (Senate), 97, 188
E-mail
   answering, 96, 192, 217, 233–35
   Mail System (CMF) and, 224, 232–35
   management of, 84, 90, 232–35
   newsletters, 217
   policies for, 220–21
   postal mail compared, 217
   priorities for, 218–19
   public address, 233
   software for, 84
   unsolicited, 236
   volume of, 216
   Web-based e-mail form, 232–33
   workshops and consultations, 232
Emanuel, Rep. Rahm, 131
Emergency Management, Office of (House), 95
Emergency preparedness, 95
Employee Assistance, Office of (House), 211, 212
Employee Assistance Program (Senate), 211, 212
Employee background checks, 79
Employee benefits, 29
Energy and Natural Resources Committee (Senate), 22
Energy & Commerce Committee (House), 21, 24
Environment and Public Works Committee (Senate), 22
Equipment. *See* Technology, office
Ethics, 267–79
   analysis process for, 275–78
   environment for, 268–70
   mail and, 237
   media scrutiny of, 269
   risk areas, 273
   rules violations compared, 271–72
   of staff, 272, 274–75
   staff training for, 270
   technology use and, 95

Ethics Certification Officer, 274
Ethics Committee
   House, 20, 21, 104, 183, 269
   Senate, 22, 31, 183, 237, 269
Evaluations, staff
   conducting, 203–207
   money discussion during, 207
   preparation for, 203
   self-evaluations, 203
Exchange, Microsoft, 84
Executive Assistant, 36
Expenses, office, 33–35

F

Family of Member, 7
   ethical concerns and, 273
   scheduling input from, 243, 259–61
Feingold, Sen. Russ, 133
Field Representative, 36, 68, 69, 244
File servers, 82
Finance Committee (Senate), 21, 22, 24
Finance Office (House), 28, 42, 182, 183, 188, 189, 190
Financial management. *See also* Budgeting
   accounting system, 85, 188–90
   auditing, 190
   cost-saving advice, 191–94
   monthly financial review, 190–91
   payment processing, 188–89
   policies for, written, 187
   procedures for, 187–91
   reconciliation, 189–90
   record keeping, 188
   team for, 32–33
Financial Management Information System (FMIS), 85, 180
Financial Services Committee (House), 21
FinMart, 85, 180, 188
FirstCall Customer Service Center (House), 72
Foreign Affairs Committee (House), 21
Foreign Relations Committee (Senate), 21, 22
Franking, 37, 43
Franking Commission (House), 237
Functional structure, 52–53, 54
Furniture, office, 30, 111–13

G

General Services Administration (GSA), 111, 112
   Congressional Services Representatives, 108
   furniture restoration by, 112
   lease rate set by, 31, 109
Gifts, 273
Goals
   budgeting and, 32, 41, 180–81, 183–87
   communication of, to staff, 242
   core staff and, 70–71
   decisions and, 10–11
   development of, 10–11, 166–67
   evaluation of, 167–69
   importance of, 145–46
   performance, 199–201
   scheduling and, 241–42
   technology and, 87
Gold Mouse Awards, 91
Gold Mouse Project (CMF), 89, 91, 217

H

Handheld devices, 84, 89, 255
Harvard's Institute of Politics, 14
Health, Education, Labor and Pensions Committee (Senate), 22
Heritage Foundation, 14
The Hill, 123
Hiring staff, 9, 63–80
   comparing candidates, 77–78
   core staff, 64–70
   goals and, 70–71
   interviews in, 73, 76–77, 78
   job analyses and, 75–76
   job functions and, 66–70
   process for, 73–79
   recruiting, 72
   reference checking, 78–79
   staff involvement in, 78
   tests in, 77
History and Preservation, Office of (House), 96
Homeland Security and Governmental Affairs Committee (Senate), 22
Homeland Security Committee (House), 21
Home State Furniture and Furnishings allowance, 30
House Administration Committee, 20, 21
   advice from, 28, 72, 92, 111, 112, 164, 183, 237
   audit by, 190
   MRA calculations by, 30
   remote access rules, 96
   technology use rules, 95
   telecommuting rules, 96
House Chiefs of Staff Association, 14
House Compensation Study, 37
House Democratic Steering and Policy Committee, 19
House Employment Counsel, Office of, 63, 73, 200, 201
House Information Resources (HIR), 83
   advice from, 37
   equipment standards of, 86
   services provided by, 35, 94
   Technical Support Representatives, 83, 86, 92
   Write Your Representative (WYR), 232
HouseNet, 83, 85
House of Representatives
   Clerk of, 274
   Combined Airlines Ticket Office, 34
   committees of, 19, 20, 21. *See also* specific committees
   Finance Office, 28, 42, 182, 183, 188, 189, 190
   FirstCall Customer Service Center, 72
   Franking Commission, 237
   funds authorization year for, 29
   House Employment Counsel, Office of, 63, 73, 200, 201
   Learning Center, 97, 188
   Office of Chief Administrative Officer (CAO), 37, 92, 107
   Office of Emergency Management (OEM), 95
   Office of Employee Assistance, 211, 212
   Office of History and Preservation, 96
   Office Services, 83, 111, 112, 192
   schedule for, 252
House Republican Steering Committee, 19

I

Important tasks, 5, 6
Indian Affairs Committee (Senate), 22

Information technology (IT). *See*
    Technology, office
In-person town hall meetings, 248
Institute of Politics, 14
Intelligence Committee
    House, 20, 21
    Senate, 22
Interviews, job, 73, 76–77, 78
Intranets, 84–85
iPhones, 84

J

Joint Economic Committee, 21, 22
Joint Library Committee, 21, 22
Joint Printing Committee, 21, 22
Joint Taxation Committee, 21, 22
Judiciary Committee
    House, 21
    Senate, 22

K

Keeping It Local: A Guide for Managing Congressional District/State Offices, 101, 163
Kucinich, Rep. Dennis, 134

L

Landrieu, Sen. Mary, 132
Lantos, Rep. Tom, 133
Leadership in office, 141–56
    delegation of duties, 12–13
    Member's role, 142–43
    organizational culture and, 143–49
    over-managing, 153–54
    priority setting and, 152–53
    style of, 149–51
Learning Center (House), 97, 188
Legislative Assistant, 36, 68, 69
Legislative Correspondent, 36, 69
Legislative Director, 36, 142, 244
Legislative Information System (LIS), 85, 226
Legislative insiders, 130–31, 138
LegiStorm, 35
Library of Congress, 119
    Legislative Information System (LIS), 85, 226
Lugar, Sen. Richard, 133

M

Mail. *See also* E-mail; Mail System (CMF)
    answering, 66, 192, 217, 220–21, 231
    budgeting for, 37, 43
    digital system for, 221
    e-mail compared, 217
    ethical considerations, 237
    format standards for, 220–21
    Member involvement in answering, 220
    outreach, 192–93, 218, 235–37
    policies for, 220–21
    priorities of, 218–19
    signature on, 221
    unsolicited outreach, 236
    volume of, 216
Mail Manager, 222, 223, 226, 228
Mailroom Supervisor, 36
Mail System (CMF), 221–31
    backlog alert, 230
    coding, 228–29
    date stamping mail, 224–25
    e-mail and, 224, 232–35
    fast track, 226
    flow chart, 227
    logging mail, 225–26, 229
    Member hoarding mail, 230–31
    opening mail, 224–25
    original draft track, 226
    process for, 223–28
    sorting mail, 224–25
    updating form letters, 231
    VIPs and, 231
Maintenance providers, 83
Management of office, 197–214. *See also* Performance management system
    delegating, 12–13
    motivating staff, 209–10
    responsibility for, 142–43
    structures for, 8–9, 48–54
Media
    ethics, scrutiny of, 269
    expenditures, scrutiny of, 182–83
    relationship with, 67
    visibility and, 249
Meetings, staff, 59
    planning, 164, 173–75
    scheduling, 253–54
    staff evaluation, 206
Member Binder, 56

Index

Members' Congressional Handbook, 28, 183, 187, 189
Members of Congress
 budgeting decisions by, 32–33
 leadership of, 142–43
 mail answered by, 220
 personal responsibility for finances, 28, 182
 roles for, 127–40
 scheduling involvement by, 243, 257
 travel frequency, 262
Members' Representational Allowance (MRA), 29–30, 86, 109
Microsoft software
 Active Directory, 83
 Exchange, 84
 Outlook, 84, 254
Mission. *See* Goals
Mission statement, 163–66
Mobile offices, 109, 247

N

National Taxpayers Union (NTU), 37, 236
Natural Resources Committee (House), 21
Networks, 82
New Democrat Coalition, 120
Newsletters, 192, 217, 237
Nussle, Rep. Jim, 134

O

Occupational Safety and Health Act, 107
Office Coordinators, 83, 92
Office Emergency Coordinator (OEC), 95
Office Manager, 32, 36, 69
Office of Chief Administrative Office (House), 37, 92, 107
Office of Compliance (OOC), 73, 200
Office of Congressional Ethics, 269
Office of Education and Training (Senate), 97, 188
Office of Emergency Management (House), 95
Office of Employee Assistance (House), 211, 212
Office of History and Preservation (House), 96
Office of House Employment Counsel, 63, 73, 200, 201
Office of Police Operations, Security and Emergency Preparedness (Senate), 95
Office of Public Records, 274
Offices. *See also* District offices; Representative's offices; Senator's offices; Staff, office; State offices; Technology, office; Washington office
 communication within, 8–9, 55–60
 culture of, 143–49
 expenses of, 33–35
 management of, 8–9, 48–54, 197–214
 mobile, 109, 247
 moving, 67
Office Services (House), 83, 111, 112, 192
Office supplies, 31, 38, 192
Office Support Services (Senate), 35
Officially related expenses, 31
Official Personnel and Office Expense Account, Senator's, 30, 40, 43, 86, 191
Ombudsmen, 132, 138
O'Neill, Speaker Tip, 101
Online town hall meetings, 248–249
Online Town Hall Meetings: Exploring Democracy in the 21st Century, 91
Organizational culture, 143–49
 defining, 143–44
 positive culture, 145–48
 staff appreciation and, 146–48
 unproductive, 148–49
 values and, 145–46
Organizational meetings, 14
Orientation meetings, 13–14
Outlook, Microsoft, 84, 254
Outsiders, 133–35, 138
Oversight and Government Reform Committee (House), 21

P

Partisanship, 123–24
Partnership For A More Perfect Union (CMF), 81, 91, 216
Party committees, 19
Party insiders, 131, 138
Party ratios, 120–21
Paul, Rep. Ron, 134
Payment processing, 188–89
PeopleSoft, 85, 180

Performance Improvement Plan (PIP), 205–207, 211
Performance management system
  coaching in, 202
  elements of, 198
  evaluating systems, 212–13
  feedback in, 201, 202
  implementing, 199–208
  monetary awards, 207, 208
  monitoring staff in, 201–203
  non-monetary awards, 208
  performance goals in, 199–201
  reasons for, 198–99
  rewarding high performers, 208
  staff evaluations, 203–207
  training in, 201–202
Personnel. *See* Staff, office
Placement Office (Senate), 72
Planning, 159–78
  action plan development, 170–72
  benefits of, 160–62
  evaluating goals, 167–69
  goal development, 166–67
  implementing plan, 172–76
  length of plan, 162–63
  measuring performance, 176
  mission statement and, 163–66
  process for, 162–76
  session for, 164
Police. *See* U.S. Capitol Police
Police Operations, Security and Emergency Preparedness, Office of (Senate), 95
Postal mail. *See* Mail
Post-Travel Disclosure form, 274
Press. *See* Media
Press Secretary
  compensation for, 36
  responsibilities of, 69
  on scheduling team, 244
Printers, 83–84
Printing expenses, 31, 38, 192
Progressive Caucus, 120
Publications, 193
Public Records, Office of, 274

R

Ranking members, committee, 22
Receptionist, 36

Reconciliation, 189–90
Record keeping, 188
Reid, Senator Harry, 72
Remote access, 89, 96
Remote Data Replication (RDR), 89
Report of the Secretary of the Senate, 34, 188
Representatives. *See* Members of Congress
Representatives, House of. *See* House of Representatives
Representative's offices. *See also* District offices; Staff, office; Washington office
  allotment for, 29–30, 180
  budgeting for, 28–30, 35–38, 42–43
  budgeting software for, 85, 180
  budget worksheet, 39
  communication with staff in, 58
  management structures for, 48–54
  scheduling by, 246–50
  staff for, 67, 68, 69, 105
  technology for, 82–85, 111–13, 191–92
Republican Party
  Committee on Committees (Senate), 19
  House committee restrictions, 20, 21
  Senate committee restrictions, 21, 22
  Steering Committee (House), 19
Republican Study Committee, 120
Role in office. *See* Leadership in office
Roles in Congress, 127–40
  changing, 139
  importance of, 128–29
  major, 135–36
  minor, 135–36
  selecting, 136–39
  types of, 128, 129–35
Rules and Administration Committee (Senate), 22
  advice from, 28, 92, 164, 183, 237
  audits by, 190
  remote access rules, 96
  technology use rules, 95
  telecommuting rules, 96
Rules Committee (House), 20, 21

S

Salaries
  allocation for, 35–37, 40
  average, 36
  bonuses for, 207, 208

Index

cost of living adjustments to, 186
  raises in, 207, 208
Sanders, Sen. Bernard, 134
Scheduler
  characteristics of, 261
  compensation for, 36
  judgment of, 259
  relationship with family, 260–61
  responsibilities of, 68, 69, 250, 252, 256, 259, 263
  on scheduling team, 243
Scheduling, 67, 239–66
  accurate information in, 259
  Congressional schedule and, 119, 256
  criteria for, 244–46
  development of schedule, 241–46
  in district, 246–50, 262–63
  evaluation of, 246
  Event Preparation Request Form, sample, 265
  Event Scheduling Form, sample, 258
  family conflicts and, 259–61
  flexibility in, 119
  goals and, 241–42
  long-range plan for, 247
  Member over-involvement in, 257
  overscheduling, 255–56
  problems with, 255–60
  promptness in commitments and, 256–57
  software for, 84
  Speech/Event Evaluation Form, sample, 251
  in state, 246–50, 262–63
  strategic, 239, 240–41
  team for, 242–44
  travel time and, 255
  in Washington, 250–54
  weekly meetings about, 253–54
Schumer, Sen. Charles, 18
Science and Technology Committee (House), 21
Secretary of the Senate's Report, 34, 188
Select Energy Independence and Global Warming Committee (House), 21
Select Ethics Committee (Senate), 22, 31, 183, 237, 269
Select Intelligence Committee
  House, 20, 21
  Senate, 22

Senate. *See also* Sergeant at Arms (SAA)
  Archivist, 96
  Chief Counsel for Employment, 63, 73, 200, 201
  Combined Airlines Ticket Office, 34
  committees of, 19, 20–21, 22. *See also* specific committees
  Disbursing Office, 28, 31, 42, 182, 183, 188, 189, 190
  Employee Assistance Program, 211, 212
  funds authorization year for, 29
  Office of Education and Training, 97, 188
  Office of Police Operations, Security and Emergency Preparedness (POSEP), 95
  Placement Office, 72
  schedule for, 252
  Technology Catalog, 93
Senate Democratic Steering and Coordination Committee, 19
Senate Handbook, 28
Senate Manual, 28, 183, 187, 189
Senate Republican Committee on Committees, 19
Senators. *See* Members of Congress
Senator's Account, 30, 40, 43, 86, 191
Senator's Allowance, 30–31
Senator's offices. *See also* Staff, office; State offices; Washington office
  allotment for, 30–31, 180
  budgeting for, 28–29, 30–31, 38–40, 42–44
  budgeting software for, 85, 180
  budget worksheet, 40
  communication with staff in, 58
  management structures for, 48–54
  moving, 67
  scheduling by, 246–50
  services for, 31
  staff for, 67, 69, 106
  technology for, 30, 43, 82–85, 96, 191–92
Senior Legislative Assistant, 36
Sergeant at Arms (SAA), 83, 107, 109
  Alternate Computing Facility (ACF), 89
  Customer Support Analysts (CSA), 83, 86, 92
  Demo Center, 93

equipment standards of, 86
Office Support Services, 35
Printing, Graphics and Direct Mail service, 228
services provided by, 31, 35, 94
State Office Liaison, 107, 108, 111, 112, 194
Servers, file, 82
The Seven Habits of Highly Effective People, 4
Shared employee, 189, 194
Site visits, 249
Small Business and Entrepreneurship Committee (Senate), 22
Small Business Committee (House), 21
Social media, 85, 96
Software. *See* specific types of software
Special Aging Committee (Senate), 22
Spouse of Member, 7, 243, 260–61
Staff, office. *See also* Communication with staff; Hiring staff; Performance management system; Salaries; specific job titles
    appreciation of, 146–48
    computers for, 82
    core, 9, 12–13, 64–70
    district office, 36, 97, 105, 106, 107
    employee benefits for, 29
    empowered, 147–48
    ethical judgments of, 270, 272, 274–75
    functions of, 66–70
    high performers, 209–10
    job descriptions for, 200
    motivating, 209–10
    number of, 67, 105, 107
    part-time, 193
    poor performers, 210–12
    professional development of, 147
    recruiting, 72
    self-evaluation by, 203
    shared, 189, 194
    state office, 36, 97, 106, 107
    training of, 97, 201–202
    transition period, during, 64–66
    trust relationship with, 202
    turnover rates for, 65–66, 147
Staff Assistant, 36, 68, 69
Standards of Official Conduct ("Ethics") Committee (House), 20, 21, 104, 183, 269

State, travel to
    budgeting for, 37, 40, 43, 185
    cost-saving advice for, 193
    frequency of, 262
    fund use during, 255
    scheduling during visit, 246–50
State Director
    compensation for, 36
    responsibilities of, 32, 51–52, 69, 142
    on scheduling team, 243–44
Statement of Disbursements of the House, 34, 188
State Office Liaison (SAA), 107, 108, 111, 112, 194
State offices
    accessibility to constituents of, 104–105
    equipment for, 84, 96, 111–13
    in federal buildings, 108–109
    furniture for, 111–13
    importance of, 102–103
    lease for, 107, 194
    location of, 106–109
    maintenance of, 107
    mobile, 109, 247
    number of, 103–105
    office hours, 247
    opening first office, 110–11
    parking availability at, 107
    in predecessor's offices, 108
    in private buildings, 109
    rent for, 31, 109
    resources available for, 103
    safety of, 107
    scheduling by, 246–50, 262–63
    setting up, 9, 101–14
    shared, 110
    size of, 107
    staff for, 36, 97, 106, 107
    visibility of, 103, 106
State Scheduler, 36
Statesmen, 132–33, 138
Steering committees, 19
Subscriptions, 193
Sunlight Foundation, 35
Supplies, office, 31, 38, 192
Systems Administrator
    compensation for, 36
    responsibilities of, 68, 69, 94, 95, 232
    training of, 97

Index

Systems Administrators' Associations, 92
Systems Consultants, 83

T

Task forces, 249
Technical Support Representative (TSR), 83, 86, 92
Technology, office, 9, 81–99
   budgeting for, 37, 43, 88
   compatibility of, 93
   Congressional system for, 82–85
   cost-saving advice for, 191–92
   for district offices, 96, 111–12, 113
   emergency procedures for, 95
   ethics and, 95
   file management, 95–96
   installation of, 93–94
   inventory of, 91–92
   maintenance of, 67, 94, 95
   policies for usage, 94–97
   portable, 84, 89, 255
   purchasing decision, 87–88, 90–94, 113, 191–92
   Representatives' offices, 82–85, 111–13, 191–92
   resources for, 91, 92
   security of, 90, 95
   Senators' offices, 30, 43, 82–85, 191–92
   for state offices, 96, 111–13
   training staff for, 97
   upgrading, 85–87, 95
Technology Catalog, 93
Telecommunications
   answering phones, 66, 218
   cell phones, 193, 255
   cost-saving ideas for, 193
   long-distance service, 31
Telecommuting, 89, 96
Teleconferences, 193
Tele-town hall meetings, 248
Town hall meetings, 248–49
Transition period, 3–16
   critical tasks during, 6–10
   guiding principles during, 10–13
   organizational meetings during, 14
   orientation meetings during, 13–14
   priority setting during, 4–6
   staff during, 64–66
Transition team, 12–13
Transportation & Infrastructure Committee (House), 21
Travel
   budgeting for, 37, 40, 43, 185
   cost-saving advice for, 193
   ethics and, 273
   frequency of, 262
   time use during, 255

U

Urgent tasks, 5, 6
U.S. Capitol Police (USCP), 79

V

Vasa, 153
Veterans' Affairs Committee
   House, 21
   Senate, 22
Video conferencing, 88, 193
Virtual Machine Infrastructure (VMI), 82
Virtual private networks (VPNs), 82, 89
Visitors, greeting, 66
Vouchers, 28, 188

W

Washington/District Parity Structure, 51–52, 54
Washington office, 29
   moving, 67
   scheduling by, 250–54
   staff for, 36
Washington Post, 123
Ways and Means Committee (House), 21, 24
Web browsers, 84
Web sites, 89, 96, 217
Webster, 85
Westerner Caucus, 120
Wolf, Rep. Frank, 132
Write Your Representative (WYR), 232

Authors
and
About CMF

Authors

Nicole Folk Cooper, CMF's Director of Marketing and Publications, supervised the revision and production of the 111th and 112th Congress editions of *Setting Course*, including the editing of all chapters. She also served as editor and project manager of *Keeping It Local: A Guide for Managing Congressional District & State Offices*; the *Congressional Intern Handbook: A Guide for Interns and Newcomers to Capitol Hill*; and *The Insider's Guide to Research on Capitol Hill*. During her tenure, Nicole has also co-authored or contributed to several CMF reports on technology and communications. She previously worked for a Member of Congress and for a CMS/CSS vendor to House and Senate offices.

Bradford Fitch, President and CEO of the Congressional Management Foundation, updated Ch. 16, Managing Ethics, and previously served as project manager of the 108th and 109th Congress editions of *Setting Course*. Brad organizes CMF's Member-Elect Staff Orientation, a workshop held every fall after the elections that helps new Members make a successful transition to Congress. He has also been active in CMF's *Communicating with Congress* Project, including co-authoring the report, *How Capitol Hill is Coping with the Surge in Citizen Advocacy*. Brad has taught journalism and public communications courses at American University, and is the author of *Media Relations Handbook for Agencies, Associations, Nonprofits and Congress* by TheCapitol.Net; "Best Practices in Online Advocacy for Associations, Nonprofits, and Corporations," a chapter in *Routledge Handbook of Political Management*; and articles on communications and advocacy. Brad worked in House and Senate offices for 13 years, serving as Press Secretary, Legislative Director, and Chief of Staff.

Kathy Goldschmidt, Deputy Director of CMF, wrote Ch. 6, Selecting and Utilizing Technology. She recently co-authored chapters in *Keeping It Local: A Guide for Managing Congressional District & State Offices* and co-authored *Online Town Hall Meetings: Exploring Democracy in the 21st Century*. Kathy has been involved with CMF's *Communicating with Congress* Project for more than five years, serving as co-author of *How the Internet Has Changed Citizen Engagement* and *How Capitol*

Hill is Coping with the Surge in Citizen Advocacy. A former Internet analyst and communications specialist for a consulting firm, Kathy has spoken extensively on congressional communications and legislative e-government. She also worked in a House office for two years.

Tim Hysom, CMF's Director of Communications and Technology Services, updated Ch. 6, Selecting and Utilizing Technology, and Ch. 14, Managing Constituent Communications. He serves as Director of CMF's *Partnership For A More Perfect Union*, which includes managing the *Gold Mouse Awards* and *Communicating with Congress* Projects. He also authored *Communicating with Congress: Recommendations for Improving the Democratic Dialogue*. Before joining CMF, Tim was a Legislative Assistant for a Member of Congress and also worked in a House district office.

Michael Patruznick, CMF's former Director of Research, co-authored Ch. 8, Understanding the Culture of Congress: An Insider's Guide, and Ch. 5, Hiring Your Core Staff. Michael worked in a House office for four years and as a congressional producer for C-SPAN.

Chester B. Rogers, Professor Emeritus of political science at Western Michigan University, wrote Ch. 1, Navigating the First 60 Days: November and December. Chet was a House AA for two years and has conducted extensive research on freshman Members and their transition to Congress.

Judith Schneider, Specialist on the Congress at the Congressional Research Service, wrote Ch. 2, Selecting Committee Assignments, co-authored Ch. 8, Understanding the Culture of Congress: An Insider's Guide, and contributed to Ch. 9, Defining Your Role in Congress. Judy is the author of over 100 papers on congressional operations and the co-author of the *Congressional Deskbook* by TheCapitol.Net, now in its fifth edition. She serves on the faculty of the Conference for New Members of Congress. Judy also received the Women in Government Relations Distinguished Member Award and was a Stennis Center Congressional Staff Fellow in the 108th Congress.

Craig Schultz, CMF's former Director of Research, wrote Ch. 3, Creating a First-Year Budget, and Ch. 12, Budgeting and Financial Management.

Laura D. Scott, Management Consultant with CMF and the University of Maryland, was the primary author of Ch. 15, Strategic Scheduling, and the co-author of Ch. 16, Managing Ethics. Laura continues to provide office consultation services to dozens of congressional offices. Previously she worked in a Senate office for eight years.

Richard Shapiro, former CMF Executive Director, wrote Ch. 4, Creating a Management Structure and a System for Communicating with the

Member; Ch. 7, Establishing District and State Offices; Ch. 9, Defining Your Role in Congress; Ch. 10, The Member's Role as Leader of the Office; Ch. 11, Strategic Planning in Your Office; and Ch. 13, A Process for Managing Staff. He co-authored Ch. 16, Managing Ethics; and contributed to several other chapters. Rick also authored the CMF publications: *Frontline Management: A Guide for Congressional District/State Offices*; *Working in Congress: The Staff Perspective*; *1990 U.S. House of Representatives Employment Practices: A Study of Staff Salary, Tenure and Demographics*. During his 18 years at CMF, Rick provided management services to more than 100 House and Senate offices. He also held senior staff positions in both the House and Senate.

About the Congressional Management Foundation

The Congressional Management Foundation (CMF) is a 501(c)(3) nonpartisan nonprofit dedicated to helping Congress and its Members meet the evolving needs and expectations of an engaged and informed 21st century citizenry.

CMF has pursued this mission for more than 30 years by working internally with Member, committee, leadership, and institutional offices in the House and Senate to identify and disseminate best management, communication, and citizen engagement practices through research, publication, training, consulting, and facilitation activities.

Management Books and Research Tailored for Congress

Only CMF produces publications adapted to the unique congressional environment. Our management handbooks and research reports for congressional staff include:

- *Setting Course: A Congressional Management Guide*
- *Keeping It Local: A Guide for Managing Congressional District & State Offices*
- *Congressional Intern Handbook: A Guide for Interns and Newcomers to Capitol Hill*
- *The Insider's Guide to Research on Capitol Hill*
- *111th Congress Gold Mouse Project*
- *Online Town Hall Meetings: Exploring Democracy in the 21st Century*
- *Communicating with Congress: Recommendations for Improving the Democratic Dialogue*
- *Communicating with Congress: How the Internet Has Changed Citizen Engagement*
- *Communicating with Congress: How Capitol Hill is Coping with the Surge in Citizen Advocacy*
- Studies on House and Senate office compensation and benefit practices
- A brief on managing the transition process for new committee chairs

Office Management Services

CMF provides a range of customized management services to congressional offices on a confidential basis, including:

- Office retreats that typically focus on strategic planning, office operations, team building, and DC–district/state office relations;
- Comprehensive assessments to examine office operations and personnel, identify office strengths and weaknesses, and develop strategies for improving performance; and
- Workshops to improve constituent correspondence management.

CMF also provides management services to House and Senate institutional offices, primarily through training, human resources, operational effectiveness, and strategic technology projects.

Staff Training

To meet the distinct needs of congressional offices, CMF provides free training workshops to top level congressional staff on topics including: strategic planning; performance reviews and staff development; employee engagement and retention; leadership and management skills; strategic communications, including constituent correspondence and websites; setting up your office and navigating the first 90 days (Member-elect staff orientation); utilizing staff and financial resources to provide outstanding constituent service; and improving internal office communications and DC–district/state office relations.

Under contract with the House of Representatives, CMF also conducts courses on writing constituent correspondence and orienting entry-level district office staff.

Partnership For A More Perfect Union

Launched in 2010, the *Partnership For A More Perfect Union* is a center within CMF that seeks to further our nation's progress toward "a more perfect union" by fostering the genuine and effective exchange of ideas between Members of Congress and citizens. The *Partnership* seeks to accomplish this mission by conducting research and education, promoting best practices, and creating innovative tools for everyone with a stake in our government. The *Partnership* disseminates best practices information through its website (www.pmpu.org), e-newsletters, webinars, videos, and training sessions. The *Partnership* is also the home of the *Gold Mouse Awards* that recognize the best websites on Capitol Hill.

For more information, contact CMF at 202-546-0100 or visit www.cmfweb.org.